Good luck to t

It From Scratch

The Urban Caveman Recipe Collection

Happy Cooking

Che

The Urban Caveman Recipe Collection

Paleo-inspired recipes for the 21st century

'Giving up doesn't mean going without...'

Eve Gilmore

Hammersmith Health Books
London, UK

First published in 2014 by Hammersmith Health Books – an imprint of
Hammersmith Books Limited
14 Greville Street, London EC1N 8SB, UK
www.hammersmithbooks.co.uk

The information contained in this book is for educational purposes only. It
is the result of the study and the experience of the author. Whilst the information and advice offered are believed to be true and accurate at the time
of going to press, neither the author nor the publisher can accept any legal
responsibility or liability for any errors or omissions that may have been
made or for any adverse effects which may occur as a result of following
the recommendations given herein. Always consult a qualified medical
practitioner if you have any concerns regarding your health.

British Library Cataloguing in Publication Data: A CIP record of this book is
available from the British Library.

Print ISBN 978-1-78161-045-9
Ebook ISBN 978-1-78161-046-6

Commissioning editor: Georgina Bentliff
Designed and typeset by: Julie Bennett, Bespoke Publishing Ltd
Cover design by: Julie Bennett, Bespoke Publishing Ltd
Index: Dr Laurence Errington
Production: Helen Whitehorn, Path Projects Ltd
Printed and bound by: TJ International Ltd

Contents

CONTENTS

CONTENTS

Conversion tables

Grams	Ounces	Grams	Ounces
10	½	20	¾
25	1	40	1½
50	2	60	2½
75	3	110	4
125	4½	150	5
175	6	200	7
225	8	250	9
275	10	350	12
450	1 lb (16 oz)	700	1½ lb
900	2 lb	1.3 kg	3 lb

Millilitres	Fluid ounces	Millilitres	Fluid ounces
55	2	75	3
150	5 (¼ pint)	275	10 (½ pint)
425	15 (¾ pint)	570	1 pint
725	1¼ pints	1 litre	1¾ pint
1.2 litres	2 pints	1.5 litres	2½ pints
2.25 litres	4 pints		

Oven temperatures

Centigrade	Fahrenheit	Gas Mark
140	275	1
150	300	2
170	325	3
180	350	4
190	375	5
200	400	6
220	425	7
230	450	8
240	475	9

Abbreviations

I have used the following abbreviations throughout all the recipes:

g – gram

oz – ounce

ml – millilitre

fl oz – fluid ounce

tsp – teaspoon

tbs - tablespoon

kg – kilogram

lb - pound

l – litre

pt - pint

dsp – dessert spoon

Acknowledgements

Warmest appreciation to my husband, Hugh, for his IT input and support, and for stepping up to do the ironing and for taking endless food photos. Thanks to Claire Gillman of The Writer's Workshop for her constructive criticism and advice, and to Georgina Bentliff of Hammersmith Books for taking a chance on a new writer. Much appreciation to Helen Clutton for her attention to detail and high boredom threshold in proofreading the recipes, and to Julie Bennett for her patience and creativity. Warmest thanks to my family and friends for eating their way through many experimental meals – often after having watched them go cold whilst they were photographed. Thanks also to my daughter Xanthe for her editorial skills and to my dear friends and colleagues, Julia Johnson and Muriel Hallatt, for their encouragement and feedback.

About the author

Eve Gilmore is a naturopath, clinical nutritionist and, homeopath who has been researching the links between diet, lifestyle and health for more than 20 years. She has discovered that most health problems today are the result of a combination of poor nutrition, toxicity and stress.

Eve runs a busy natural medicines practice in Essex, where she lives with her vet husband. Mother of four grown up children and an experienced writer and speaker on health, she also runs training courses for health professionals. Her first book, *Go Paleo – feeding the urban caveman* is a companion volume to her recipe book.

Introduction

From professional athletes to mothers with young children, Paleo-style (Stone Age) eating is catching on fast. Whether you want to improve your energy levels or are seeking relief from a health problem, the hunter-gatherer diet could provide you with maximum nutrition from foods that your caveman genes will love. The Stone Age diet is thought to represent the way we have eaten for millennia. It pre-dates agriculture and the domestication of animals, which were introduced comparatively recently and marked the explosion of grains, beans and dairy into the human diet – foods that are linked to digestive problems, fatigue, obesity, arthritis and autoimmune diseases.

A few hunter-gatherers still exist in remote parts of the world. Although their numbers are dwindling fast, they have been studied extensively over the last hundred years and have taught us a great deal about the relationship between diet and health. However, a genuine Paleo diet would have included many foods unavailable or repugnant to us today, such as brains, glands and insects, and the fruits were wild and not as sweet as they are today[1].

Until now, the modern version of the Paleo diet has been – well, a bit boring. After all, there is a limit to what you can do with meat, fish, eggs, veggies and fruit. Recognising that the world is vastly different from that of our Paleo ancestors, the Urban Caveman concept is certainly not about going without pies, puddings and pasta. It acknowledges that we are fundamentally cavemen living in an urban world and that it would be impossible authentically to recreate the Paleo diet today, were it even desirable.

The Urban Caveman diet is therefore not about turning the clock back to an imagined bucolic existence that personified pre-industrial living. It is about moving forward, beyond the foods of industrialisation towards a way of eating that is more aligned with our traditional diets. It is a positive way forward that embraces and celebrates the best of both worlds.

---

1 It is true that some modern hunter-gatherers do include dairy produce such as butter and raw milk, although dairy is not considered Paleo.

The diet was born from the recognition that a strict Paleo diet would be too restrictive for it to be sustainable as a lifestyle choice, and unappealing to anyone who loves food. So, rather than trying to replicate what we believe the ancestral diet to have been, Urban Caveman eating is a 21st century adaptation that will satisfy your palate and keep your Stone Age genes happy too.

Although there is evidence of their consumption during Paleo times, grains, legumes (that is, beans, peas, peanuts etc) and dairy were only eaten in minimal amounts, if at all. They were also wild and bore no resemblance to the hybrids we have available to us today. Not only is the modern diet very high in carbohydrates from grains, but it is low in saturated fat – the ingredient which tended to account for most of the calories in the ancestral diet. Often nutritionally disappointing and laced with chemicals, the modern diet can be a prescription for low energy, obesity and degenerative disease. Most of us know that already, but continue to eat it nevertheless because it tastes good and we naturally have little motivation for cutting out our favourite foods unless confronted by a major health problem.

The Urban Caveman diet bridges the gap between the Stone Age and modern diets. It delivers the health benefits of a Paleo-style diet but in an appetising and familiar form that is designed to satisfy the 'stodge factor' and predilection for comfort foods prevalent today. This recipe collection therefore shows you how to make grain-free, low-carb breads, creamy desserts and even mock cheeses whilst still being faithful to Paleo principles. Never before has it been so easy to eat healthily and never before has it been so delicious. This book takes Paleo eating to another level – replicating familiar foods like pizza and ice cream – so you *can* have your cake and eat it!

Food today is not just about sustenance. It is also a lifestyle choice, and how and why we eat says a lot about who we are. We eat for pleasure, for solace and for social reasons. Eating together is an integral part of important milestones in our lives - from baby showers to funerals. Food has to be a feast for the eye as well as the stomach. Almost every glossy supplement includes restaurant reviews and recipes, and much air time is dedicated to cookery programmes. The era of the celebrity chef has arrived and cookery has been elevated to an art form. There is no doubt that food nourishes us on many levels.

Whilst our Paleo ancestors undoubtedly ate and lived communally, food for them was largely functional. Although the diversity of foods was greater than it is today, geographical and seasonal availability determined what would have been a fairly monotonous menu at times, and scarcity was a regular threat. Today, for the first time in history, we are suffering from the opposite – overabundance – to which we have no genetic capacity to adapt.

How is the Urban Caveman diet different to the Paleo diet?

The recipes in this book are based on Paleo *principles* and reproduce modern dishes using alternatives to grains, milk, sugar and legumes. Dr Loren Cordain, the world's foremost researcher into Paleo eating, does not advocate a strict Paleo diet, permitting alcohol, butter and egg-white protein powder[2]. Recognising that most of us lead suburban lives and enjoy much of what modern living has to offer, the Urban Caveman diet won't appear very different from the sorts of meals you eat now.

Hunter-gatherers did not restrict themselves to muscle meat as it is lower in vitamins and fat compared to glands and offal. They would also have taken much of their meat uncooked, eating every part of the animal starting with the DHA-rich brain (DHA is an omega-3 fatty acid), and then working their way through, often discarding the muscle meat altogether. They would also have eaten anything they could catch, from horse, water buffalo, elephant, rhinoceros and monkey to grubs, slugs and insects[3]. The Urban Caveman diet, you'll be relieved to hear, does not include any of the aforementioned.

Much of the Stone Age diet was raw and, with the possible exception of perhaps Parma ham and sushi, a largely uncooked diet would not be suited to urbanites living in colder climates. Furthermore, the modern digestive system, often low in stomach acid and enzymes and ravaged by over-cooked, processed foods, might not be robust enough to digest uncooked, high-fibre foods. (Incidentally, modern raw diets are nothing like the Paleo version, eschewing animal produce whilst being predominantly nut and seed based.)

Our tastes have also been influenced by the availability of exotic foods and foreign travel. We now have restaurants on our doorstep serving food from around the world, which has further broadened our culinary choices. So, a Stone Age diet of mostly raw meat, fish, eggs, fruit and veg, with the occasional nut and seed thrown in, would be unlikely to have many takers today. Nevertheless, by excluding or reducing non-Paleo foods, carbs and polyunsaturated fats, the Urban Caveman diet remains faithful to the

2 Some Urban Caveman recipes suggest undenatured whey protein as an option (see 'Whey protein' on page 15).
3 Piggott S. *The Stone Age Hunters*. 1967. London: Thames and Hudson.

Paleo spirit, enabling you to enjoy the comforting foods of your childhood. And if you enjoy what you are eating you are likely to forget that you are 'on a diet' at all.

The Urban Caveman recipe collection is written by a UK-based nutritionist so leans towards traditional English and European cooking. Those comforting foods of your childhood – like Yorkshire pudding and apple pie – can be enjoyed once again, but as healthier and less fattening versions, which after all is the dream diet.

Unlike most Paleo recipe books, you won't find many recipes which call for nuts. Due to their seasonal availability, nuts and seeds were eaten only rarely, and archaeological evidence suggests that they weren't eaten by all hunter-gatherer communities anyway. More importantly, nuts and seeds contain enzyme inhibitors and other toxins which make them as difficult to digest and provocative to the immune system as grains, and would never have been eaten without pre-soaking. They are also high in polyunsaturated fat, and despite modern health propaganda extolling the virtues of polyunsaturates, these are not good news if you want to increase energy, lose weight or slow ageing.

Dr Weston Price was a dentist who studied 14 indigenous cultures in the 1930s and -40s. The diets of those modern hunter-gatherers, like the Stone Age diet of our ancestors, were high in saturated fat, with polyunsaturates making up only four per cent of the total calorific intake. In fact, it was about 10 times higher in fat, generally with very little carbohydrate. Our cells were designed to burn energy from fat, but the toll from years of eating sugar has altered our physiology with the result that many of us can no longer metabolise fat efficiently and tend to store it as excess weight. Furthermore, high-carbohydrate/low-fat diets can cause liver and gall bladder congestion, which is rife in the industrialised world, and which could make a high-fat diet difficult to tolerate. These are compelling reasons why the Paleo diet has had to be adapted to modern needs. Although our genes are still in the Stone Age, our bodies are living in the 21st century.

Modern hunter-gatherers do not suffer from weight problems or degenerative diseases – that is, unless they switch to the so-called 'civilised' diet which causes them the same problems as it does us. They are athletic and muscular, and enjoy better levels of stamina than we do. However, I believe Dr Loren Cordain to be wrong in advocating a high intake of protein. He suggests the optimal ratios between the food groups should be around:

- 50 per cent protein
- 15 per cent fat

- 35 per cent carbohydrate from green vegetables and fruits.

However, health researcher Barry Groves in *Trick or Treat* recommends a high-fat diet with ratios of:
- 65 per cent fat, saturated
- 25 per cent protein
- 10 per cent carbohydrate.

The higher-fat/lower-protein ratios concur with the findings of Dr Weston Price, but fly in the face of current health dogma. Research by Dr Ron Rosendale also supports the high-fat/low-carb approach, recommending fat intake to be between 50 and 70 per cent.

The reality is that there is no standard hunter-gatherer diet. What was eaten varied according to geographical location, climate and seasonal availability. What all traditional diets have in common is avoidance of grains and legumes combined with a high intake of animal fat.

Reducing dietary fat often leads to an increase in protein in an attempt to curb the carbs. This is a dangerous mistake as protein becomes toxic in the absence of fat. There is mounting evidence that high-protein diets are not good for us and may be stressful for the kidneys. In the BBC Horizon documentary *Eat, Fast and Live Longer* Michael Mosley highlighted research showing that if the protein intake is too high the body reverts to a destructive rather than regenerative mode, which can encourage the growth of cancer. Furthermore, sapped by years of trying to break down starches, our digestive systems tend to under-produce juices and enzymes for protein and fat digestion and so may need a gradual transition from high carb to high fat.

Providing you can metabolise it, fat helps you eat less and will keep you satisfied longer. You could try this for yourself by eating a carb-based breakfast of cereal and toast on one day, and having bacon and eggs cooked in butter or coconut oil the following day. You are likely to find that you won't be in need of a carb fix mid-morning on the bacon and eggs day, but suffer an attack of the munchies on the cereal and toast day.

The ideal fat:protein ratio will also vary according to your activity level. You may be surprised to learn that the body can make carbohydrate from fat and protein – so you don't actually need to eat it at all. Furthermore, not all carbohydrates are equal. Carbohydrates from vegetables are better metabolised than those from grains and legumes, which are quickly converted to sugar. In fact, wheat will cause your blood sugar to spike more quickly and to a higher level than if you had actually eaten sugar. This is one of the reasons for the 'post-prandial slump', when those who have feasted on sandwiches for lunch find it almost impossible to stay awake during the afternoon.

For anyone accustomed to ready meals and convenience foods, the Urban Caveman diet may seem a bit daunting at first because everything is made from fresh ingredients. Although it is theoretically possible to mass-produce convenience foods using only Paleo ingredients, a fundamental principle of any healthy diet would be the elimination of pre-packaged foods. Swapping convenience foods for meals made from fresh ingredients not only increases the nutritional value of your food, but reduces your sugar intake as well because sugar is often used as a cheap preservative. This is why it is added to most manufactured foods, including savouries like pizza and meats. However, with a little planning, weaning off ready meals doesn't usually present a problem. Doubling up on portion sizes when cooking enables you to freeze half, thus saving on cooking time and ensuring there is always a meal ready for when you are busy. Most of the recipes in this book are quick to make, the only exceptions being those for special occasions – much like any other cookery book – and you could find that trying new recipes and acquiring the cooking habit may even stimulate a renewed interest in food.

It's not just about what you don't eat. Try to obtain the best quality food possible. In our age of GM, irradiation and crop spraying, it can be quite a challenge to find un-adulterated, naturally produced organic food. This is explored in my companion book *Go Paleo? – feeding the Urban Caveman* which examines what is wrong with the modern diet and why fresh Paleo-friendly foods are so good for us. Once a vegetable or fruit has been picked, it starts losing vitamins and minerals – and if it wasn't organically grown, it may not have had many to start with. Furthermore, much of the so-called fresh produce in supermarkets will have been harvested too early and transported vast distances. Subjected to treatments like irradiation, gassing in the case of bananas, or partial freezing to delay ripening as a means of controlling supply, the supermarket definition of 'fresh produce' should not be taken literally and should probably be expanded to mean anything that doesn't come in a tin or packet! These practices have contributed to the decline in the nutritional content of modern foods over the last 50 years by an average of 80 per cent. Even organic produce is frequently unripe at the time of picking, which is why cannonball pears and green bananas are a common finding in the modern supermarket.

Growing your own would be the ideal option and most towns in the UK now have a waiting list for allotments, but if time is in short supply, you could buy from local producers, farm shops or independent butchers and greengrocers. Specialised organic co-operatives, of which Riverford Organic and Abel & Cole are the most well known, offer weekly deliveries of ethically sourced, organic foods. There is now a growing awareness that to save local communities, preserve the countryside and reduce air miles, services are best provided by small, independent local producers and in Britain there is now a government initiative called Go Local (www.yourgolocal.co.uk).

Tips on changing your diet

Rotational diets

Most of us eat the same foods every day, and this can sometimes lead to the development of allergies or intolerances. For example, if you decide to keep raw dairy in your diet you may wish to eat it no more than once every four days. If you wanted to vary the flours used in baking you could use coconut flour most of the time, but use chestnut flour and even gram flour (chickpea flour, heat-treated only) or buckwheat flour occasionally. Although these flours are not Paleo, they usually present no problems and are a much healthier alternative to wheat. It is necessary to cut the suspect food out altogether for a while – at least 18 months for wheat, and three months for dairy – before reintroducing them. Eating foods on an occasional basis would concur with Dr Cordain's advice to eat 80 per cent Paleo.

Withdrawal symptoms

If grains and dairy (or any other food) are problematic for you, you may at first experience withdrawal symptoms, which can make you feel a bit hung-over. This is a sign that some of the foods you were eating were having a drug-like effect. You may experience cravings as you come down from the opioid high provided by gluten (a protein found in some grains) and casein (a protein found in dairy). However, the withdrawal phase usually only lasts a few days and drinking lots of water, eating fat and resting can help.

If your diet has been high in carbs and low in protein, you may no longer be producing enough stomach acid to digest red meat, and this is a common problem today. Since low stomach acid can cause a burning sensation, it is often wrongly assumed to be a problem of over-acidity, but this, in fact, is rare. If you have been accustomed to a high-carbohydrate diet, it may be helpful when eating meat to take a stomach acid supplement or drink diluted lemon juice or apple cider vinegar with meals until your digestive system adjusts.

Perhaps you've been unconsciously relying on stimulants like sugar, tea or coffee for energy? They do a great job in camouflaging fatigue by provoking the release of stress hormones like adrenaline and cortisol. Unfortunately, stress hormones provide a temporary burst of energy by spiking the blood sugar, but this is swiftly followed by a dip which can cause agitation, light-headedness, hunger, sweet cravings, brain fog and the need for a 'pick-me-up'. If you are riding the see-saw of fluctuating blood sugar, the low-carb Paleo diet would be especially good at helping to stabilise your energy levels, although you may feel more tired at first whilst your liver gets used to the idea that it has to crank up glucose production again.

Eventually, a diet high in carbs and sugar can cause the body to become less responsive to insulin, the hormone essential for getting sugar into cells. (This is called 'insulin resistance'.) If your cells are not getting their glucose fix, your brain will think you need to eat and you will crave sweet foods – even if you are full of them. Dips in blood sugar and the consumption of opioid foods can lead to bingeing and food addiction. Unfortunately, this is not something that can easily be overcome by will power because if your brain thinks you are hungry it will override your most determined efforts not to overeat.

If you are overweight

Linked to insulin resistance, weight gain is a *symptom* of a deranged metabolism in which the ability to burn fat for energy has largely been lost. This is why many overweight people struggle to exercise and why exercise is ineffective at facilitating weight loss. Although the Paleo diet would be excellent for stabilising blood sugar, professional help may also be required to help reset the metabolism.

Note for athletes

Athletes and sportsmen/women have slightly different nutritional needs and require a higher intake of carbohydrate. This can be supplied by root vegetables, except potatoes which are not classified as Paleo as, like grains, they contain enzyme inhibitors. For more information the books *The Paleo Diet for Athletes* by Dr Loren Cordain, and *The Paleo Solution* by Robb Wolf are recommended.

Mental attitude

The best way to ensure the success of any diet is to approach it with enthusiasm and curiosity. Seeing it as the start of an exciting new phase in your life that will enhance your feelings of well-being, boost your energy, and expand rather than restrict your gastronomic repertoire can make all the difference. Even though you may be putting more time into food preparation, you might find you actually achieve more because you are focused and efficient. Once through the withdrawal phase, you may also notice that your mood is lighter, you are more motivated and you have increased energy for exercise. Having experienced the benefits of Paleo eating for yourself, you are unlikely to revert back to the old, 'heavy' foods that make up much of the modern diet.

If you look upon your new way of eating as a nurturing, indulgent experience and not as some form of deprivation, you are more likely to succeed. Any change in diet is bound to be difficult until you have got used to it. It can be a bit like breaking an old habit. At first, you have to put more thought into what you are going to eat, but before long you are likely to forget you ate any other way.

This recipe collection takes the 'diet' out of diet. It is an enjoyable and sustain-able way of eating and represents a healthy lifestyle choice. So, try to contain the first flush of enthusiasm and don't rush in without first having familiarised yourself with the new ingredients. Some will have to be sourced, and you will also need to ensure that you have some stand-bys in the freezer so you don't get caught out and end up reaching for a ready meal. All the ingredients are available online, and many can be found in your local health-food shop or supermarket.

Changing the way you eat can have a positive impact on other areas of your life, too. Rather than gulping down a TV dinner that you have put little time or love into preparing, why not make meals an occasion to be enjoyed with family and friends? I have entertained using Urban Caveman recipes and many guests were unaware – until it was pointed out – that they were grain- and dairy-free.

You will encounter your biggest challenges when travelling or eating out. This is because the restaurant and hotel industry haven't caught up... yet (although the world's first Paleo restaurant has opened in Berlin). With a little imagination and the substitution of a few key ingredients, most restaurants would have no trouble providing interesting Paleo-friendly alternatives. Until they do, it is prudent to take some supplies with you – even if you do end up eating them in your hotel room. Until restaurants catch on to the fact that they are losing business because of the not-insignificant numbers of people on elimination diets, eating out can sometimes boil down to a meal of meat or fish without any sauce, vegetables or salad without any dressing and foregoing dessert whilst you watch everyone else tucking in. That's why I think it's advisable to have a few treats on you when away from home. Vegetarians suffered the same fate in the 80s when they were usually offered a choice between omelette and lasagne – I know, because I was one of them. Now there is no shortage of imaginative vegetarian fare in modern restaurants, which is a pity since they are over 20 years too late.

Hard though it may be, try to avoid becoming evangelical about your new diet. Freed from the low energy and brain fog that afflict most of us to some degree, it can be difficult to resist the temptation to convert everybody to your new way of eating. Remember, not everyone wishes to change their diet and some may find it stressful to step outside the norm. Some have no interest in food or health, whilst others lead lives that are so pressurised they subsist on takeaways and would find it hard to do more than stagger from the freezer to the microwave.

So what about you? What have you got to lose – apart perhaps from a little weight and low energy? You have the power to rewrite your genetic heritage. You can make changes in your diet and lifestyle that will boost your vitality and increase your chances of enjoying a productive, healthy old age.

Kitchen equipment

It isn't necessary to buy a lot of expensive kitchen gadgets. Most urban caveman recipes can be made using equipment you are already likely to have.

Equipment that is good to have in your kitchen

Slow cooker – My slow cooker is in almost constant use during the winter months. I have the biggest one available and fill it with nourishing stews which can either feed the family for several days or I freeze half for those times when I don't have time to cook. Slow cooking was a method used by our Paleo forebears, and not only improves the texture of meats, but also draws the flavours out, as all the goodness of the ingredients is contained within the stock. Slow cooking requires much less fluid compared to casseroling in an oven. The great advantage of slow cooking is that a meal can be quickly prepared by throwing the ingredients in before going to work and letting it work its magic over six to eight hours. There is nothing better than being greeted by the aroma of a home-cooked meal when you open the front door at the end of a long day!

Bread maker – If bread is not an important part of your diet, you may find that you won't miss it, but if you love bread or need the convenience of taking sandwiches to work, then a bread maker becomes essential. Try to find one without a non-stick pan as non-stick coatings release toxins into the food. At the time of writing, the Cuisinart bread maker has a non-stick lining. Urban Caveman breads are quick and easy to prepare but take four hours in the machine. Most modern bread makers come with timer controls so you can set them to produce a hot loaf for when you get up in the morning – delicious!

Food processor – This is essential for the home cook as it can save a lot of time. I use mine for grating vegetables for coleslaws, juicing lemons, puréeing soups and making dressings. Some food processors also have an attachment for beating egg whites.

Electric stick blender – This is also an essential piece of kitchen equipment that I seem to use more than any other. It is great for puréeing smaller quantities – like a smoothie, for example – or for creaming part of a soup whilst it is in the cooking pot. I also use it to blend the ingredients for bread, cakes and biscuits.

Knives – It is important to have good quality sharp knives so that you can cut foods finely. Blunt knives can easily slip and cause serious injury. Knives should be sharpened before each use – not once they have become blunt. A good vegetable knife, a chopping knife, a carving knife and a bread knife are usually all that are needed. Choose knives that feel comfortable in your hand. The heavier the handle the more control the knife will give you.

Ice-cream maker – This is a bit of an indulgence. Ice cream can be made without an ice-cream maker but you have to remove it several times from the freezer and whisk it up in order to get it to the desired consistency. I have found the cheaper ice-cream makers that require pre-freezing of the bucket to be a bit hit and miss, so if you are thinking of investing in one it is probably preferable to splash out and get one that will freeze whilst mixing. Home-made ice cream is best eaten freshly made. It will often be too hard to use straight from the freezer and therefore require a little time to soften at room temperature. Urban Caveman ice cream is low carb and high in good fats.

Yoghurt maker – Yoghurt makers are inexpensive, and home-made coconut-cream yoghurt makes a delicious instant dessert. You can mash in seasonal fruits to vary the flavours, or use plain yoghurt in cooking. Alternatively, you can make yoghurt in a thermos flask.

Waffle iron – Obviously, a waffle iron is not essential and there are plenty of other desserts on the Urban Caveman diet. I find guests love seeing waffles warming at the table. They make an impressive dessert that requires very little preparation – simply make up your batter in advance, or even freeze it, have some Urban Caveman ice cream standing by, and top with fresh berry fruits.

Dehydrator – By no means essential, a dehydrator can be useful for making jerky and dehydrating fruits and vegetables for use in some recipes. Dehydration is similar to leaving foods out in the sun, but in countries where sunshine is scarce, it is more economic than leaving something on a low oven for many hours, unless you have an Aga or equivalent.

Heavy-bottomed cast-iron griddle pan – This is good for steaks and for searing meats prior to slow cooking – but again, by no means essential. The heavy base to the pan ensures heat is evenly dispersed and that high temperatures can be reached without damaging the pan itself.

Maslin pan – This is for the serious cook who wants to go the whole hog and prepare chutneys and pickles. Also used for jam making, the maslin pan enables you to cook evenly over several hours without burning. A maslin pan is worth considering if you are going to find it difficult to wean off commercially produced pickles and other relishes which are high in sugar and often contain genetically modified corn starch and other nasties.

Measuring spoons – Certain recipes rely upon precise measurements to get the consistency and flavours just right, so measuring spoons are well worth having.

What you don't want in your kitchen

Non-stick cookware – The coating on non-stick cookware releases chemicals, including fluoride, into the food. Stainless steel, ceramic and cast iron are healthier alternatives.

Aluminium foil – Nearly everyone today is contaminated by aluminium, which is a toxic metal associated with a range of health problems, including neurotoxic illness. Wrapping and heating food in aluminium foil is therefore best avoided, especially if the food is fatty, as fats tend to hold on to toxins rather like they do in the body. The **Roastcosy** is a reusable foil replacement for use when roasting joints of meat and is available to order online. When on a picnic wrap food in kitchen roll or greaseproof paper first.

Microwave oven – Microwaving not only alters the molecular structure of the food and emits harmful radiation into the surrounding atmosphere, but it also damages many of the nutrients. Food left too long in the microwave turns to a plastic consistency. Studies have shown immunological changes in the blood 15 minutes after eating microwaved food that are similar to those found in cancer patients.

Plastic food containers – Plastic is an oestrogenic substance which can disrupt hormones by occupying hormone receptors in the body and preventing the body's natural hormones from being effective. It often contains PVC and BPA, which are potent toxins. Store food instead in glass or stainless steel containers, or in bowls topped with clingfilm, but make sure the clingfilm does not come into contact with the food. Non-PVC clingfilm is slightly better, but food should first be wrapped in greaseproof paper to avoid contact with the plastic. Fatty foods are the most liable to become contaminated from contact.

Cooking oils and margarines – All vegetable oils – except for coconut and olive – are too unstable to withstand heating, which causes them to become rancid. Margarine was first developed as a plastic! It cannot be broken down in the body, where it clogs up cell membranes. Margarines are made from fats that have been heated and processed, and most contain 'trans fats', which are associated with disease.

Urban Caveman ingredients and replacements for common non-Paleo ingredients

Although it is easy to recreate many of your favourite foods on the Urban Caveman diet, you obviously have to replace some store-cupboard staples. I have listed these below. As general principles, note:

- Meats should be from grass-fed, free-range animals, ideally organic
- Fish should be wild or organic
- Butter should be from grass-fed cows, goats or sheep.

Dairy substitutes

It is up to you whether you want to eliminate dairy altogether and substitute with coconut milk and oil, or whether you are happy to include raw milk and butter in your diet. Goat's and sheep's milks are closer in mineral ratios to human milk compared with cow's milk.

Milk and cream

Tinned coconut milk comes in three concentrations: light, which is watery, normal or cream. The most important thing is to make sure it is unsweetened and does not contain additives. If you prefer to make your own coconut milk, this can easily be done by whizzing coconut *powder* (*not* flour) with hot water in a food processor, but make sure you buy powder that is free of sodium caseinate, which is derived from dairy. Although nut and seed milks are considered Paleo, the Urban Caveman diet keeps nuts to a minimum since, like grains, they contain enzyme inhibitors that make them difficult to digest. With the exception of macadamia nuts and hazelnuts, they also tend to be high in polyunsaturated fats which are best avoided by the weight conscious. If you are using nut milks, make sure they do not have added sugar.

Undenatured whey protein

Although Dr Loren Cordain is right in stating that whey protein is not Paleo, Mark Sissons, author of *Primal Blueprint* and the Paleo website *Mark's Daily Apple*, considers that the health benefits conferred by whey outweigh (pun intended) its non-Paleo

undeniable that our immune systems may not be as efficient as they
ⁿany of us suffering from allergies and chronic viral or yeast infec-
ᵤₒₙs, like herpes or athlete's foot. Added to smoothies and ice cream, whey can help
achieve a more authentic flavour whilst increasing the protein content. Since it is a
pre-digested protein it can also be a life saver for those with weak digestion. In the
same way that grass-fed raw butter is rarely problematic, even for those with dairy
allergies, undenatured whey protein is generally well tolerated[4], and Pink Sun supply
whey protein made from goat's and sheep's milk. Whey also contains proteins that
help the body detoxify (glutathione and N-Acetyl-Cysteine). Steer clear of cheap whey
proteins marketed for body builders as they are usually a by-product of the cheese
industry and are likely to have been heat treated. However, if you wish to avoid milk
products altogether, dried egg-white powder would be a great alternative.

Butter

Some hunter-gatherers do consume butter and milk, but it is obviously unpasteurised
and without any added colouring, 'natural' or otherwise. Butter is familiar to the body
because it is an animal fat. Dr Weston Price noted the health benefits of butter due to
its high content of fat-soluble vitamins and its beneficial effects on health, especially
when taken with DHA (docosohexaenoic acid), an omega-3 fat found in bone marrow
and oily fish and important for the brain and nervous system. Allergies to dairy are
usually provoked by lactose (milk sugar) or proteins (casein, in particular), but not
the fat itself. This is why butter is included on the Urban Caveman diet, but if you
prefer to avoid it altogether, coconut oil is recommended for cooking as vegetable oils
become rancid upon exposure to light and heat as low as body temperature. A tiny
fraction of milk proteins may leach into butter so if you are extremely sensitive, 'ghee',
otherwise known as clarified butter, would represent a safer option. You may find that
cutting out all dairy for about a year would enable you to reintroduce butters without
any trouble. There was a study carried out in 1987 which suggested high levels of
oxidised cholesterol were present in ghee. It appears that this was incorrect and that
the amount of oxidised cholesterol in ghee is just 1.3 per cent. The advantage of ghee
is that it has been heated to remove the proteins and is therefore often well tolerated in
those with intolerance to casein.

---

4 *Undenatured* means the whey has not been subjected to pasteurisation or other treatments that can damage,
or denature, the proteins. It is usually damaged proteins that provoke an immune response and this is why
allergies to dairy were virtually unknown before pasteurisation.

If you are sensitive to casein, you may be better having goat's or sheep's butter, although it may be necessary to avoid it initially. Goat's and sheep's milks contain a more digestible form of casein called 'A2'. Milk containing A2 casein is now available but since it is pasteurised the other proteins in the milk would also have been denatured so I would not recommend it.

Lactose is a sugar found in milk that needs to be broken down by the enzyme lactase before it can be absorbed via the small intestine. Five per cent of northern Europeans, 71 per cent of Sicilians and more than 90 per cent of Africans and Asians are deficient in this enzyme so drinking milk can result in fermentation in the large intestine causing bloating and discomfort. Since lactose is water- rather than fat-soluble, only a tiny amount finds its way into butter, but because goat's and sheep's milks are lower in lactose than cow's milk and it is completely absent from ghee, these butters generally represent a good alternative, and if you wanted to play safe you could take a lactase supplement when eating butter.

Cheeses

Urban Caveman soft cheeses are made by souring coconut milk or cream with vinegar or lemon juice. Hard cheeses are not fermented so are not really cheeses at all but a cheese flavour is achieved from a combination of nutritional yeast flakes, onion pow-der and tamari.

Flours

Urban Caveman baking is grain free, with organic coconut flour replacing wheat. To increase the protein content and decrease the carbohydrate content, egg-white protein is used as a flour. If you are sensitive to coconut, you could use chestnut flour and egg-white powder instead. Non-organic coconut flour may have been processed and damaged by heat treatments, so beware of some of the cheaper brands. When substi-tuting coconut flour in recipes, make sure you add more fat and fluid as coconut flour is very absorbent.

Coconut powder

You can make an instant coconut milk by blending coconut powder with hot water, but I sometimes use it as a flour in baking to reduce the heaviness. Coconut powder is 62 per cent fat so increases the fat content of the food whilst reducing the carbohydrate. Be sure to check the ingredients though, as some powdered coconut products contain sodium caseinate.

Egg-white protein powder

This is the only protein powder recommended by Dr Loren Cordain. It can be mixed with coconut flour in breads as it produces a better consistency than simply using coconut flour on its own.

Eggs

Eggs are an excellent food providing they have been produced by free-range hens whose eggs are high in omega-3 and saturated fat. In baking they are used as a leavener, to increase moisture and improve texture and as a binder. If you are sensitive to eggs, you could replace with any of the following:

- ⅓ cup apple purée with 1 tsp baking powder (gluten-free)
- ¼ cup coconut yoghurt
- 1 tbs ground flaxseed in 3 tbs water
- ½ banana, mashed
- commercial egg replacer, although these are not strictly Paleo as they contain potato starch. They often also contain tapioca which is not a grain but the root of the cassava plant.

Nuts

Very few Urban Caveman recipes call for nuts as, like grains, they contain enzyme inhibitors and are high in carbohydrate, and their fats tend to be polyunsaturated rather than saturated. Polyunsaturated fats include the omega-3s and -6s and it is predominantly the -6s that are found in most nuts and seeds. The hunter-gatherer diet was high in saturated (animal) fat, followed by omega-3 but with little omega-6. The modern diet tends to be too high in omega-6 and this fat can encourage weight gain and reduce energy.

Table 1: The carbohydrate and fat content of 1 oz (28.3 grams) of commonly eaten nuts and seeds

	Cal	Total carb	Fibre	Net carb	Sat fat	Mono fat	ω-3 fat	ω-6 fat
Almonds	161	6.1	3.4	2.7	1	8.6	0.2	3.4
Brazil nuts	184	3.4	2.1	1.3	4.2	6.9	0.05	5.8
Cashews	155	9.2	0.9	8.1	2.2	6.7	0.2	2.2
Chestnuts	60	12.8	2.3	10.5	0.1	0.2	0.03	0.22
Chia seeds	137	12.3	10.6	1.7	0.9	0.6	4.9	1.6
Coconut	185	6.6	4.6	2	16	0.8	0	0.2
Flaxseeds	150	8.1	7.6	0.5	1	2.1	6.3	1.7
Hazelnuts	176	4.7	2.7	2	1.3	12.8	0.24	2.2
Macadamia nuts	201	4	2.4	1.6	3.4	16.5	0.06	0.36
Peanuts	159	4.5	2.4	2.1	1.9	6.8	0	4.4
Pecans	193	3.9	2.7	1.2	1.7	11.4	0.28	5.8
Pine nuts	188	3.7	1	2.7	1.4	5.3	0.31	9.4
Pistachios	156	7.9	3.0	4.9	1.5	6.5	0.71	3.7
Pumpkin seeds	151	5	1.1	3.9	2.4	4	0.51	5.8
Sesame seeds	160	6.6	3.3	3.3	1.9	5.3	0.11	6
Sunflower seeds	164	5.6	2.4	3.2	1.2	5.2	0.21	6.5
Walnuts	183	3.8	1.9	1.9	1.7	2.5	2.5	10.7

Some of the carbohydrate found in nuts and seeds comes in the form of fibre. This is why the highest in fibre – chia, flax and coconut – are also amongst the lowest in net carbs. Leaving aside the fact that coconut is not really a nut, it is also the highest in saturated fat followed by brazil nuts. Seeds, brazils and pecans are the highest in polyunsaturated fat respectively, whilst coconut with 0.2, and macadamia with 0.36, are among the lowest. Flax, chia and walnuts are the highest in omega 3. Both omega-3 and omega-6 are polyunsaturates, so are best not being eaten in large quantities. Macadamia nuts and hazelnuts are relatively low in carbohydrate and most of their fat is monounsaturated.

Salt

Refined salt contains 97 per cent sodium chloride, fluoride, a few toxic chemicals, but no other minerals, so it is definitely not recommended. It can raise blood pressure, upset blood-sugar regulation and acidify and dehydrate the body as it draws on the body's water reserves. A ratio of 23:1 water to refined salt is required. Its molecular structure is damaged by the refining process, during which it is heated to 1,200 degrees F.

Unrefined salt is high in minerals, including potassium, which needs to be kept in balance with sodium. Until recently sea salt was considered a healthy alternative to table salt, but the dumping of pollutants like dioxins, PCBs and mercury into the oceans has changed this and, to make matters worse, 89 per cent of the world's sea salt is now refined, damaging its delicate crystalline structures and making it hard to absorb and metabolise.

Himalayan salt is unrefined and contains 84 minerals and trace elements in colloidal form, making them easy to absorb. Whilst refined salt can raise sodium levels in the body, Himalayan salt contains the right balance of potassium to sodium. Having been formed over 250 million years by tectonic pressure it has a perfect crystalline structure which confers many healthy properties. Uncontaminated but mineral dense, Himalayan salt is therefore the optimal salt to use for cooking, and adding a pinch to drinking water could be a healthy habit to develop as it also helps to alkalise the body.

Throughout the book, whenever I say 'salt' I mean unrefined Himalayan, with sea salt or Celtic salt the best alternatives if Himalayan is not available.

Pepper

Pepper contains an alkaloid called piperine which boosts nutrient uptake, including proteins. Pepper also has a stimulatory effect on digestive enzymes in the pancreas and reduces free-radical damage. Coarse-ground black pepper is therefore a great condiment to add to your meals.

Mayonnaise

Commercially produced mayonnaises usually contain preservatives, sugar, pasteur-ised dried egg and heat-treated vegetable oils, often including rape. Urban Caveman mayonnaise can be freshly made in the food processor using raw eggs, lemon juice, mustard and coconut and olive oils. It will last for weeks in the fridge, although it does need softening at room temperature before serving. Mayonnaise is a great way to eat raw eggs which are good for gut health and provide good fats including phosphatidyl choline, needed for brain and cell membrane health.

Vinegar

Vinegar is great for imparting flavour, and a dash of vinegar added to soups releases minerals from meat bones, making stocks and soups more nutritious. Although vinegar is not Paleo, if you choose your vinegar wisely it can be a healthy condiment. Avoid vinegars made from grains and those that are mass produced as they will not have undergone the fermentation process. Raw-apple cider vinegar has many healing properties and there are excellent vinegars made from grapes and even coconuts available nowadays.

Thickeners and binders

Kuzu

This is made from the starch of a Japanese root vegetable and can be used to thicken gravies and sauces. Kuzu gives sauces a glaze, making them very appetising. It has been shown to be good for the cardiovascular and hormonal systems, to relieve chronic migraines and to reduce stiffness in the neck and shoulders. Research at Harvard University has shown that kuzu can lessen the craving for alcohol and help reverse the effects of alcoholism. Its healing properties are likely to be linked to kuzu's isoflavones, plant sterols and glycosides.

Arrowroot

A cheaper alternative to kuzu, arrowroot is a great thickener for sauces but does not give a glaze. Made from the root of a starchy tropical fruit, arrowroot may not be suitable for everyone as it can have a constipating effect. (Read ingredients carefully too as some products entitled 'Arrowroot' are actually ground tapioca which comes from a different plant – the cassava plant.)

Gelatine

Gelatine helps stabilise blood sugar and is good for the bones. It is great for setting desserts and widely available from supermarkets, but check the ingredients and make sure you buy a gelatine that is unsulphured. Some makes have added sulphur dioxide. It is possible to buy pure gelatine and The Real Food Company (www.therealfood-company.org.uk) supplies online gelatine from free-range, organically reared pigs.

When used in baking, gelatine forms a sticky, stretchy gel similar to gluten. You would make it up by first soaking in water and then adding to the dough.

Xanthan gum

Xanthan gum is a high-fibre thickener that helps bind foods together and forms a sticky consistency similar to gluten. It is added commercially to mayonnaises, sauces and ice creams. Low in calories, it is often found in diet products. Xanthan gum is a polysaccharide (sugar) produced by the fermentation of sugar, usually from corn, by bacteria called *Xanthomonas campestris*. However, it is well tolerated even by those sensitive to corn, as the corn has been pre-digested by the bacteria and requires no further digestion. First discovered in the 1960s, xanthan gum is a low-carb food containing 32 per cent soluble fibre and as little as three per cent carbohydrate, with one tablespoon providing only 35 calories. Xanthan gum improves the texture of gluten-free breads and, like coconut flour, has the ability to absorb water. However, it will absorb water from the gut too, so be sure to drink plenty of water when eating bread made from xanthan gum.

If you prefer to avoid xanthan gum, there are other alternatives that work almost as well, which I will discuss next.

Psyllium fibre

Often taken to relieve constipation, psyllium fibre attracts water from the body, which softens the stool. In baking it makes a satisfactory gluten substitute as its hydrophilic (water-binding) quality helps to hold the dough together, preventing it from becoming dry and crumbly. Scientists in Kuwait were surprised to discover that the addition of five per cent psyllium caused bread to rise better and retain more moisture, and it also increased the overall volume. Psyllium mimicks gluten in that it forms a film-like structure.

Seeds

Chia or flax seeds form a gelatinous gloop when added to water and are often used in gluten-free baking for this reason. They can be ground and added dry to flour mixes, soaked overnight in cold water or stirred into boiling water and used immediately.

You simply substitute xanthan gum with the same weight of seeds and double the volume of water. For example, if a recipe calls for 50 grams xanthan gum you would add 100 millitres of water and 50 grams of seeds. Although a suitable substitute for gums in baking, chia seeds are high in phytic acid which can prevent minerals from being absorbed. Prior soaking helps to reduce phytic acid levels.

Gluten-free baking powder

This is available from supermarkets and health-food shops and works just as well. Some commercial brands are contaminated with gluten in the manufacturing processes.

Cream of tartar

Seven-thousand-year-old traces of calcium tartrate have been found in Middle Eastern pottery, so its use in cooking goes back a long way, but not as far back as Paleo. Best known for stabilising egg whites and for helping to cream mixtures, it is often added to meringues. Cream of tartar is half baking soda and half an acidic salt of potassium hydroxide and tartaric acid.

Flavourings

Meat cooked in a slow cooker often produces a tasty gravy without the need for added flavouring, apart from seasoning with salt and pepper. If cooking a roast dinner, vegetables such as onions, carrots, parsnips, garlic and celery can be placed under the meat and later puréed with the juices from the joint and the water from accompanying steamed vegetables to make a delicious and nutritious gravy.

However, there are occasions when gravies and soups benefit from a little extra flavouring. To add that little bit of zing, you could use a mixture of balsamic vinegar and tamari, or Coconut Aminos, which is a soy-sauce substitute.

Making your own stocks is quick and easy and they can be frozen ready for use. Once you have tasted a meal made with home-made stock you are unlikely to use anything else. During the winter, you can make a batch of stock each month and freeze in mug-sized portions. If you forget to defrost the stock in time, just stand the mug in hot water until it can be poured. Home-made stocks are packed full of goodness, including glucosamine and chondroitin, which are great for strengthening joints and bones.

Yeast extracts

Whilst excellent for flavouring gravies, yeast extracts are best avoided as they may contain MSG (mono-sodium-glutamate). MSG is a food additive that cannot be processed without vitamin B6. Yeast extracts from health-food shops may contain a small amount of glutamic acid, which is similar to MSG.

Soy-sauce substitutes

Made from the soya bean, soy sauce is not Paleo. For the problems associated with soy, please see my companion book, *Go Paleo?* Tamari, a soy-sauce-flavoured liquid made from fermented soy beans, would be acceptable in small amounts as the fermentation process overcomes many of the problems associated with soy.

However, it is now possible to obtain an alternative 'soy' sauce made from coconut, called 'Coconut Aminos', although it does need to be refrigerated after opening. Avoid Shoyu, which contains gluten, and all other soy sauces as most contain MSG and are unlikely to have been fermented.

Pasta and rice

'Noodles', 'fettucini' and 'rice' made from konjac (pronounced cognac) are a grain-free alternative to pasta. Konjac contains 'glucomannon', is high in fibre and provides only 10 calories per portion. Glucomannon helps blood sugar regulation and is thought to encourage weight loss. If weight is not an issue, or you are quite active, konjac will not fill you up, in which case kelp noodles would be a better option. Finely shredded cabbage cooked al dente and served with black pepper and raw butter is a great spaghetti substitute. You could also try sautéing courgette strips in butter or virgin olive oil with garlic and seasoning. Can also be mixed with pesto (see recipe on page 304). PaleoPasta.com, a US-based company, supplies ready-made Paleo pasta in a variety of flavours. Made from nuts, arrowroot and vegetables, they are not a low-carb food, but would be great for any pasta addicts missing the 'stodge factor'.

Some Asian food stores stock vermicelli made from sweet potatoes. Konjac rice is also available, but you could easily grind raw cauliflower in a food processor and cook it (see page 268). This makes a delicious rice substitute.

Fats

The Urban Caveman diet differs from most Paleo diets in that it is *low* in polyunsaturates but is high in saturates (see *Go Paleo? – Feeding the Urban Caveman* for a discussion about fats that explains why I recommend this). In summary, I believe this is closer to the original Paleo diet. Raw butter is a high-vitamin food and a saturated fat familiar to the body. Coconut oil contains fats similar to those found in human breast milk and has many health benefits.

Coconut butter

Not to be confused with coconut 'fat' or 'oil' (which terms are interchangeable), the butter also contains coconut meat and can therefore be used as a thickener in desserts. You need to place it in a bowl over a saucepan of simmering water and heat bain-marie style to melt it. I use it to stabilise coconut yoghurt (see page 39) as it gives them a thickness normally only found in Greek yoghurts.

Bread

The Urban Caveman recipe collection includes grain-free breads activated by yeast in the normal way. Lower in carbohydrate and higher in protein and fat than traditionally baked breads, they are also delicious.

Natural food colourings

Artificial food colourings are made from chemicals that cannot easily be broken down in the body and can have a stimulatory effect, causing hyperactivity in susceptible people, especially children. Healthy alternatives made from the original foods are available from health-food shops and online, although any food has the potential to cause problems in some individuals.

Horseradish powder, onion powder and garlic powder

These powders are available online and are great for adding instant flavour to dishes, including mock 'cheeses'.

Beans and legumes

Legumes, or 'pulses', are a cultivated food which requires prior soaking and cooking or sprouting to make it edible; they are not Paleo. Some are made into flours, like gram flour, which although not Paleo is higher in protein than other flours. Green beans belong to the same family and are often avoided by Paleo dieters but since the bean is immature and it is often the pod that is eaten, green beans do not have the same toxicity and digestive problems associated with legumes.

Cocoa and carob

Made from beans, cocoa and carob are not strictly Paleo. I have included a few recipes that use cocoa or carob, but you can omit them if you prefer. It may be preferable to use them heat treated rather than raw to help break down some of the starches which can make legumes difficult to digest in some people.

Sweeteners

Welcome to the contentious subject of sweeteners. 'Paleo' and 'sweet' are an oxymoron. Although some hunter-gatherers would theoretically have had occasional access to honey and maple syrup, they were not accustomed to sweetening their food. Over the last few decades, modern fruits have been bred to contain 40 per cent more fructose. Having been accustomed to an excessively sweet diet, foregoing the sweetness we love is not really an option for most people. Finding an acceptable sweetener that does not spike the blood sugar, clog up the liver or interfere with brain chemistry – as artificial sweeteners do – has become imperative. The quest for a healthy sweetener is the nutritional equivalent of the search for the Holy Grail, and below is detailed everything I have learned on the way. So let's now take a look at the 'natural' sweeteners on the market today.

Fructose

Since the introduction of high-fructose corn syrup (HFCS) in the 1970s, there has been an explosion in obesity and diabetes. The difference between sugar and fructose is that fructose is exclusively metabolised in the liver, where it is converted to fat, producing aldehyde as a toxic metabolite. To the liver, fructose is no different to alcohol. It is broken down by the same pathway and is responsible for the appearance of non-

26

alcoholic fatty liver disease in adolescents consuming soft drinks and other foods saturated with HFCS. Many people today have difficulty neutralising aldehydes, which can raise the blood pressure and cause brain fog, muscle aches and inflammation. In addition, fructose increases resistance to insulin and leptin, two hormones necessary for the regulation of weight and appetite, disruption of which can lead to obesity and diabetes. Fructose also interferes with the heart's uptake of the minerals magnesium, copper and chromium.

Fruit juice

Fructose is what makes fruits sweet, but it would be necessary to eat enormous amounts of fruit for the fructose to have an adverse effect in the body because fruit comes packed with fibre and it is fibre that puts the brakes on fructose uptake. Juicing is a modern process which removes the fibre and concentrates the fructose whilst eliminating the protective effects of eating the whole fruit.

Agave

Agave is produced in Southern Mexico from the core or 'pina' of the blue agave plant, which is a succulent of the aloe vera family. The sap is extracted and heated to release the carbohydrates, which are then refined into the liquid sweetener known as agave. Although low on the glycaemic index, agave may at first appear to fit the bill, but its low glycaemic rating is misleading as it is due to the fact that it doesn't activate insulin. Higher in fructose than HFCS and usually highly processed, agave is arguably the most damaging to health of all sugar substitutes. Up to 90 per cent fructose, it won't spike the blood sugar but it will raise triglyceride levels and encourage weight gain around the middle.

Many agaves on the market are genetically modified. Described by Dr Kohlstadt of the American College of Nutrition as '...highly processed fructose syrup with great marketing...', agave is in some ways worse than sugar.

Maple syrup

With a sucrose content of 87 per cent, maple syrup is sugar in all but name, but is high in minerals. Like sugar, maple syrup will stimulate an insulin response. As the hunter-gatherer diet did not include sweeteners, Dr Cordain does not consider maple syrup Paleo. Maple syrup in bread making would be fine as sugar is necessary to activate the yeasts and this would be counteracted by the bread's low-carbohydrate and high-fibre content. If using it, do so sparingly.

Coconut flower sugar

Made from the sap of coconut trees (which would normally be used by the tree to nourish the coconuts) the sap is extracted from the flowers by evaporation, which leaves behind a sugar residue. The clamour for a healthy alternative to sugar combined with optimism, greed and ignorance have paved the way for coconut sugar to capitalise on coconut's reputation as a health food. The potential profits to be made from a healthy sweetener have encouraged many producers to switch from coconut to coconut sugar production, reducing the availability of coconuts generally, but a tree that has been de-sapped cannot grow coconuts at the same time and those that revert back experience a 50 per cent drop in yield.

Coconut flower sugar is rapidly gaining in popularity due to the surge in interest in coconut as a health food, but it would be premature to assume that the health benefits of coconuts also apply to the sugar. In fact, only one study has been carried out on its glycaemic effects and that was by the not-impartial Philippine Department of Agriculture which, after studying its effect on 10 people, pronounced its glycaemic index to be 35, compared with refined sugar, which is 60 and unrefined, 64. Whatever its true glycaemic rating, between 70 and 80 per cent of coconut flower sugar is sucrose, making it almost as high in calories as sugar itself.

Coconut flower sugar does have some nutritional advantages over 'table sugar' (sucrose). It contains potassium, magnesium, zinc, iron and the B vitamins 1, 2, 3 and 6, together with polyphenols and antioxidants, 16 amino acids including glutamine, and some short-chain fatty acids – although at levels much lower than would be obtainable from food. It also contains the soluble fibre inulin, which has prebiotic effects favouring the growth of beneficial bacteria in the gut, increasing calcium absorption and slowing glucose uptake. However, inulin may be poorly tolerated by anyone with irritable bowel syndrome or inflammatory bowel disease.

Honey

For those hunter-gatherers brave enough to extract honeycomb from bees' nests, honey would have been an occasional treat. Whilst Manuka honey is undoubtedly good for the gut and immune system as it can boost the growth of beneficial gut bacteria, the high fructose content of honey renders it unsuitable for frequent use.

Molasses

Molasses is produced by heating and centrifuging sugar cane. It is unrefined sugar and high in calories, with around 332 calories per 100 grams. It can be a good source of minerals such as iron, but it is sugar nevertheless. Molasses comes in three forms: sulphured, unsulphured and blackstrap. Sulphured is to be avoided, with the blackstrap being the most nutritious.

Luo Han Guo

Nicknamed the longevity fruit, the Chinese herb Luo Han Guo – or 'monkfruit' – is named after the Luo Han monks who first cultivated it. It is a cousin of the cucumber and related to the gourd family and is made by drying and powdering the leaf. Its sweetness comes from mogrosides, which do not affect blood sugar or weight. Mogrosides are a bound sugar, 300 times sweeter than sucrose. It contains 2% of the calories of sucrose and is stable when heated. Mogrosides have antioxidant properties and prevent the spike in blood sugar by inhibiting absorption of maltose from the small intestine. Monkfruit is currently under investigation for potential medicinal properties which may include anti-tumour effects and the metabolism of stored body fat. It has traditionally been used in China to relieve digestive and respiratory problems. Only a tiny amount needs to be used – as little as a quarter of a teaspoon will sweeten 24 fairy cakes, although most people prefer to use more. Avoid brands that have artificial sweeteners added or which contain maltodextrin, which is made from corn.

Stevia

A South American herb, stevia has been used as a natural sweetener for 1,500 years. Available as a leaf or a powder, its sweetness comes from glycosides[5]. Like Luo Han Guo, it is 300 times sweeter than sugar, but unlike Luo Han Guo, alcohol (ethanol or methanol) is needed to extract the sweetest part of the leaf, known as 'Reb A' or 'rebiana'. Traces of ethanol or methanol may be left in the stevia which could upset some people. It is suitable in cooking, although, like Luo Han Guo, it does not caramelise and can be tricky to use if making meringues. Virtually calorie-free, pure Stevia does not upset blood sugar or contribute to weight gain. The flavour varies according to the brand, with some leaving a bitter aftertaste. Always check the ingredients as many commercially produced stevia also contain artificial sweeteners.

---

5 A glycoside is a molecule in which sugar is bound by a glycosidic bond to another substance, rendering the sugar inactive.

Xylitol

Less powdery and more like sugar in texture, xylitol is still a very sweet food and concerns about its effects on health have recently surfaced. Its ability to spike the blood sugar is 40 per cent that of table sugar. Xylitol is subject to hydrogenation, a process which is harmful to fats and which may or may not be harmful to carbohydrates. Nickel, which can be toxic at high levels, is used as a catalyst in the manufacturing process. Xylitol is either derived from corn, which is nearly always GM, or from tree bark. Xylitol can cause fermentation in the gut, worsen acid reflux and is thought to increase the incidence of fits in epileptics.

Erythritol

Erythritol is a polyol, or 'sugar alcohol', although it is neither sugar nor alcohol. Discovered in 1948 by the British chemist John Stenhouse, it is found in fruits and fermented foods, including mushrooms. However, today, it is usually commercially manufactured by fermenting glucose with yeast. It contains around 60 to 70 per cent of the calories of sugar. Its reputation as a low-calorie sweetener is due to the fact that 90 per cent is absorbed from the small intestine and then eliminated via the kidneys, so it does not technically enter the body. However, the remaining 10 per cent ends up in the colon where it can cause bloating and diarrhoea. Stomach rumbling and headaches have also been reported.

Palmyra Jaggery

Palmyra Jaggery has recently become available in the UK, and has 40 per cent the glycaemic index of sugar but is much sweeter, so less can be used. Made from the sap of the palmyra tree, this sweetener contains vitamins and minerals including B_{12}. In fact, it is the only known available plant form of B_{12}. (Other plants contain a reversed (analogue) form of B_{12} which blocks uptake of the vitamin from animal sources, which is the active form needed by humans. Long-term reliance on plant foods for B_{12} ultimately results in pernicious anaemia.) Palmyra Jaggery contains more iron than a steak, with 8.5 g per 100 g, 75 mg magnesium and 40.1 mg B_3. Used in Ayurvedic medicine for blood sugar imbalances, it can also break down the opiate-like dependence on addictive foods, including sugar, and can thereby help sweet cravings. For sleep problems, 1 tsp of Palmyra Jaggery before bedtime may help and it can also help calm an over-stimulated nervous system in the hyperactive. Palmyra Jaggery has a pleasant caramel flavour and it is light brown in colour, so may not be suitable for some recipes where colour is important. Make sure you get Palmyra Jaggery as other jaggeries (traditional uncentrifuged sugars) are not the same and may have been made from corn.

Sweeteners – conclusion

Sadly, there is no such thing as a Paleo sweetener, although as a dried plant Luo Han Guo appears to satisfy the need for sweetness without compromising health or contributing to weight gain. It is calorie free, may confer some health benefits and does not trigger uncontrollable eating in the way that sugar can. Since it is consumed in minute quantities it seems to be an acceptable sugar substitute. Palmyra Jaggery is a good substitute and helps reduce cravings. Stevia, like Luo, is 300 times sweeter than sugar so again only minimal amounts are needed. Check the ingredients as some brands add artificial sweeteners. Maple syrup, used sparingly, would be acceptable.

Below is a rough guide to sugar substitutes in the recipes; the amount of sweetness depends upon personal taste. It is certain mogrosides that are 300 times sweeter than sucrose; some parts of Luo Han Guo can be bitter. I say a rough guide as this is based on my experience of cooking with these different sweeteners.

Sugar	Luo Han Guo	Stevia	Palmyra Jaggery	Maple Syrup
1 tsp	¼ tsp	¼ tsp	½ tsp	1 dsp
1 dsp	½ tsp	½ tsp	1 tsp	1 tbs
1 tbs	1 tsp	1 tsp	1 ½ tsp	1 ½-2 tbs

A word about coconut

Although coconut oil is well tolerated by almost everyone, there have been some concerns raised about the sugar content of coconut products due to their natural sweetness. So, let's have a look at this in more detail. The total sugar content of coconut products is comparatively low, with unprocessed coconut water containing only 2.95 grams per 100 millilitres, coconut milk around 3.3 grams – although there is slight variation according to brand – and coconut cream containing the highest level of sugar at 7 grams per 100 millilitres. To put this into context, the lactose (sugar) content of cow's milk varies between 3.8 and 5.3 per cent. A study in 2010 at Monash University declared that the low fructose content of coconuts made them acceptable for those on a low polysaccharide, or low FODMAP[6], diet.

Of the sugars found in coconuts, only 15 per cent are fructose, with the remainder being comprised of 50 per cent glucose and 35 per cent sucrose.

Canned coconut products

Most of us obtain our coconut milk and cream from tins. However, tin cans may leach metals into their contents, and many also contain BPA (bisphenol-A), a type of plastic linked to hormonal and other problems. Urinary levels of BPA were found to diminish when canned foods and foods stored in plastic containers were eliminated from the diet. Celebes, a company which produces good-quality coconut products, removed BPA from its cans in 2008. Biona, who supply organic coconut products, have traces of BPA which they say is protective against other toxins in cans.

Guar gum is a naturally occurring gum which is added to some tinned coconut products to help stabilise them. Guar gum contains a sugar called galactomannon, which is a polysaccharide. Well tolerated by almost everyone, it can sometimes interfere with cheese and yoghurt making when using coconut milk.

---

6 The low FODMAP diet eliminates complex starches which are difficult to digest in people with some forms of irritable bowel disease. (FODMAP is an acronym for 'Fermentable Oligo-, Di-, and Mono-saccharides and Polyols'.)

If you prefer to avoid canned products altogether, you can easily make your own coconut creams and milks by dissolving coconut powder[7] (not flour) in hot water and blending in a food processor. The ratio of powder to water determines how creamy or milky the end product will be. For those of an adventurous character and with strong muscles and time on their hands, it is possible to make your own from fresh coconuts. However, it is first necessary to crack open the shell and this may involve hammers and chisels and is not advised if you have just cleaned your kitchen! Likewise, coconut water can be extracted from fresh, young, green coconuts, but this too is not an activity for the faint-hearted.

---

7 Coconut powder is available from Asian shops. It is important to check the ingredients as many contain sodium caseinate, a derivative of cow's milk.

Snacks

It is essential that you have some snacks standing by so that you don't get caught out and end up breaking your diet. Below are some suggestions of convenience foods that are healthy and delicious.

- Organic unsweetened fruits (berry fruits, apples)
- Urban Caveman cheese with bread, savoury crackers or celery, and served with pickles or chutney
- Urban Caveman cakes or biscuits
- Cold meats and fish, including jerkies (home-made as bought ones contain sugar)
- Smoothies
- Yoghurts (made from coconut cream).

RECIPES

The Urban Caveman Dairy

- *Creams and yoghurts*

- *Ice cream*

- *Sorbets*

- *'Cheeses'*

Creams and yoghurts

Urban Caveman coconut yoghurt

I have not found it necessary to use a sweetener to activate the yoghurt as coconut cream is naturally sweet.

Ingredients:
- 3 x 400 ml tins of coconut cream (not milk)
- Approx 1-2 tbs coconut butter (Artisana or Coconut Manna – not coconut oil) to thicken the yoghurt and to help prevent separation – or butter
- Yoghurt starter

Equipment:
- Yoghurt thermometer
- Yoghurt maker or thermos flask

Heat one tin of coconut cream and the coconut butter, or butter, in a saucepan until the fat dissolves.

Whisk in the remaining two tins of coconut cream and stir well.

Test the temperature. It should be no higher than 40 degrees. If too hot, allow to cool, and if too cold, warm to desired temperature before stirring in the yoghurt starter.

Transfer to yoghurt maker.

Leave for a minimum of 12 hours.

Use about 1 tbs of this yoghurt as the starter for the next batch. You can make up to six batches before using a new starter culture.

You can flavour the yoghurt by mashing in fresh fruit – but do this just before serving to preserve the nutrients.

Baobab yoghurt

Baobab powder is made from the baobab fruit, which is high in calcium, magnesium, potassium and antioxidants.

Ingredients:
- 1 portion of Urban Caveman coconut yoghurt
- 1-2 tsp baobab powder
- Pinch of sweetener of choice
- Optional: 1 heaped tsp egg-white powder or whey protein if you want to increase the protein content

Mix all ingredients together and serve.

Coconut kefir

Kefir (pronounced keefa) is derived from milk so is not Paleo. It is made from gelatinous grains (available online) which contain a beneficial bacteria/yeast mix and a milk protein called casein. It works in a similar way to yoghurt as the microbes ferment the milk, making a healthy probiotic drink. Since the organisms break down the casein, even those who are sensitive to dairy usually tolerate kefir well. Due to its immune-boosting properties and positive effect on bowel ecology, it is good for yeast problems. However, it is best taken slowly at first – just 1 tsp per day as it has mild antibiotic properties and may cause die-off of unwanted microbes which can make you feel unwell. Kefir is delicious chilled from the fridge and has a slightly tangy, fizzy taste.

Ingredients:
- 3 x 400 ml tin coconut milk (organic and without additives)
- 1 packet kefir starter grains

Equipment
- Yoghurt thermometer
- Yoghurt maker or thermos flask

Warm the milk to around 40°C.

Stir in the grains.

Transfer to yoghurt maker or warmed thermos flask and leave for 24–48 hours. The longer it is left, the sourer it becomes.

The kefir is ready once it has thickened.

You can take 6 tbs from the kefir and use as a starter for your next batch. It can be reused up to seven times.

Kefir will last for about a week in the fridge.

Soured cream

Ingredients:

- **200 ml/7 fl oz coconut yoghurt**
- **200 ml/7 fl oz coconut cream**
- **5 tsp lemon juice**
- **½ tsp salt**

Blend all ingredients together using an electric stick blender.

Cover and refrigerate until thickened.

Lasts for about five days in the fridge.

Instant single cream

Ingredients

- **1 x 400 ml tin coconut cream**
- **Dash vanilla extract**
- **1 egg yolk**
- ***Optional:* Pinch of sweetener of choice**
- ***Optional:* 1 dsp undenatured whey protein powder for flavour**

Whisk all the ingredients together and serve.

Cover and refrigerate.

Quick and easy whipped cream

Ingredients:

- 1 x 400 ml tin coconut cream, refrigerated overnight to thicken
- Equivalent of 1 tsp sugar using sweetener of choice
- ½ tsp vanilla extract or seeds from 1 vanilla pod
- Optional: ½ tsp cream of tartar (if your cream is too thin)

Carefully remove the cream from the can, leaving the coconut water behind. (This can be used in smoothies or custard or drunk neat.)

Sweeten and add the vanilla extract.

Using the egg-beater attachment on a food processor, whisk the cream until soft peaks are formed, adding cream of tartar if extra thickness is needed.

Double cream 1

Ingredients:

- 300 ml/10 ½ fl oz coconut cream
- 2 eggs, separated
- 50 g/2 oz butter, coconut fat or ghee
- Equivalent of 1 ½ tsp of sugar using sweetener of choice
- 1 tsp arrowroot
- Optional: 1 dsp undenatured whey protein powder

Heat three quarters of the coconut cream, the egg yolks and butter, coconut fat or ghee and ¼ tsp sweetener in a saucepan and stir the arrowroot into the remainder of the fat and coconut cream.

When almost boiling add the arrowroot mixture to the saucepan and stir until thickened.

If using whey, stir it into the fat/coconut cream mix when cooled.

Set aside to set.

Using the egg-beater attachment on the food processor, whisk the remainder of the sweetener into the egg whites until soft peaks are formed, rather like making meringue but don't overwhisk.

As the peaks form, *slowly* dribble the fat/coconut cream mix into the food processor until enough of the mix is in to make it thick and creamy.

Cover and refrigerate.

Double cream 2

Ingredients:

- 1 x 400 ml tin coconut cream, refrigerated overnight
- 1 dsp arrowroot
- Dash of sweetener of choice
- 50 g/2 oz raw butter, coconut fat or ghee
- ½ tsp vanilla extract or seeds from 1 vanilla pod
- Optional: 1 dsp undenatured whey protein powder

Remove the coconut cream from the top of the can and place it in the fridge.

Dissolve the arrowroot in the remaining coconut water.

Warm the arrowroot, sweetener and coconut water in a small saucepan and stir in the butter, coconut fat or ghee, and vanilla.

Once thickened, refrigerate.

Once cooled, whisk into the coconut cream adding whey if using.

Refrigerate before use.

Urban Caveman ice cream

All the ice creams described here are low carb. The addition of undenatured whey protein powder gives them a dairy-like flavour. If you prefer to avoid whey, you could use egg-white powder instead.

There are two methods of making ice cream: you can whisk all the ingredients together, chill and transfer to the ice-cream maker; or you can stir the egg yolks into the coconut milk and warm in a saucepan, stirring until thickened, then chill before adding the other ingredients.

Vanilla ice cream 1

Ingredients:
Serves 6
- 3 egg yolks
- 1 tbs undenatured whey protein powder or egg-white powder
- 1 x 400 ml tin coconut milk 'light', or dilute coconut milk 50/50 with water
- Equivalent of 1 tsp sugar using sweetener of choice, to taste
- ¼ tsp vanilla extract or seeds from 1 vanilla pod
- Optional: a little melted butter added to the mix makes the ice cream softer when coming out of the freezer

Equipment:
- Ice-cream maker

Beat all the ingredients together with a hand whisk and leave to chill in the fridge before transferring to the ice-cream maker.

Pour the mixture into the ice-cream maker and switch on.

Once ready, transfer to a chilled non-plastic container and eat or freeze.

Fresh fruit ice cream

Use the above recipe but replace the vanilla extract with fresh fruit of your choice, such as strawberries, raspberries, peaches, etc.

Baobab powder ice cream

Use the above recipe but replace vanilla essence with baobab powder.

Vanilla ice cream 2

Ingredients:

Serves 6

- 3 egg yolks
- 1 x 400 ml tin coconut cream
- 1 tsp vanilla extract or seeds from 1 vanilla pod
- 1 tsp maple syrup, or pure stevia (Luo Han Guo may curdle)
- 1 tbs undenatured whey protein powder or egg-white powder
- *Optional*: a little melted butter added to the mix makes the ice cream softer when coming out of the freezer

Beat egg yolks into one third of the coconut cream.

Add the vanilla seeds or extract and maple syrup to the remaining coconut cream.

Warm the egg yolk/coconut cream mixture, and butter if using, in a small saucepan, stirring until thickened like a custard.

Whisk into the vanilla mix and cool in a non-plastic container in the fridge.

Once cooled, whisk in the protein powder.

Pour mixture into ice-cream maker and switch on.

Once ready, transfer to chilled dish and eat or freeze.

Minted mockachoca ice cream

Ingredients:
Serves 6
- 3 egg yolks
- 1 x 400 ml tin coconut milk 'light' (or dilute coconut milk 50/50 with water)
- 2 tsp pure mint essential oil
- Pinch of sweetener of choice
- 1 tsp vanilla extract or seeds from 1 vanilla pod
- 1 dsp melted coconut oil or raw butter
- Grated mockachoca (see recipe, page 101)
- *Optional for protein and flavour:* 1 tbs undenatured whey protein powder *or* egg-white powder

Chill a glass container in the fridge.

Beat the eggs into the coconut milk and warm, stirring until thickened.

Add all the ingredients except the mockachoca and whisk together using an electric stick blender and chill in the fridge.

Whisk in whey protein if using.

Transfer the cooled mixture to the ice-cream maker and process.

Pour into the chilled container and stir in the grated mockachoca using a metal spoon, and either eat immediately or freeze.

White chocolate ice cream

Ingredients:
Serves 6
- 1 bar of home-made white chocolate (see recipe, page 103)
- 2 egg yolks
- Pinch of sweetener of choice
- 1 x 400 ml tin coconut milk 'light' (or dilute coconut milk 50/50 with water)

- **1 tsp vanilla extract or seeds from 1 vanilla pod**
- **Grated mockachoca (see recipe, page 101)**

Chill a glass container in the fridge.

Melt the white chocolate in a glass bowl over a saucepan of simmering water, stirring.

Whisk the white chocolate mixture into all the other ingredients, except for the grated mockachoca.

Transfer the chilled mix to the ice-cream maker and, once made, stir in the grated mockachoca with a metal spoon.

Pour into the chilled container and either eat immediately or freeze.

Sorbets

Sorbets can be easily made by using fresh fruit, a little lemon juice and sweetener of choice if required – but most fruits do not require sweetening.

All the sorbet recipes require an ice-cream maker.

Raspberry and redcurrant sorbet

Ingredients:
Serves 4
- **450 g/1 lb raspberries**
- **450 g/1 lb redcurrants**
- **Sweetener of choice to taste**

Crush and sieve the fruit, then stir in the sweetener. Pour into the ice-cream maker and churnto freeze. Either eat immediately or store in a sealed container in the freezer.

Fresh mango sorbet

Ingredients:
Serves 4
- **3 fresh mangos, peeled, stoned and chopped**
- **Sweetener of choice to taste (mango is sweet so doesn't really need sweetening)**
- **Juice of 2 lemons**

Chill a glass container in the fridge.

Place the mango flesh into food processor with sweetener and lemon juice.

Blend the fruit mix to a purée.

Transfer to the ice-cream maker and churn to freeze.

Either eat immediately or store in the freezer.

'Cheeses'

Urban Caveman 'cheeses' aren't fermented in the traditional way so are not technically cheese at all, but they make an acceptable substitute. The cheesy flavour is achieved by combining nutritional yeast flakes and onion powder. Nutritional yeast flakes are produced by an organism called *Saccromyces cereviscae* and are high in B vitamins and minerals, especially chromium. Make sure you use a naturally produced nutritional yeast, such as Engevita, as some brands contain MSG.

See the recipe for savoury crackers which are delicious with these cheeses (page 91).

Cream cheese

Ingredients:
Makes a small bowl
- 1½ x 400 ml tin coconut cream
- 1 tsp Himalayan salt
- 2 tbs apple cider vinegar
- 2 tbs freshly squeezed lemon juice

Special equipment:
- Cheesecloth
- Colander

Warm the coconut cream and simmer for a couple of minutes.

Allow it to cool (not cold, but warm), and stir in the salt, vinegar and lemon juice.

Line a sieve with cheesecloth and place it on top of a bowl.

Pour the mixture into the sieve and allow the 'whey' to drip into the bowl. You will be left with the curd 'cheese' in the sieve.

Place in a glass or stainless steel container, cover and refrigerate.

Cream cheese with chives

Make as above, but stir in chopped, fresh chives.

'Ricotta' cheese

Ingredients:
Makes a small bowl

- 50 g/2 oz nutritional yeast flakes
- 1 tbs coconut oil, melted
- 1 portion Urban Caveman cream cheese
- 3-4 crushed garlic cloves, or 1 tsp dried garlic powder
- ¾ tsp Himalayan salt
- ½ tsp dried oregano
- Pepper to taste

Dissolve the nutritional yeast flakes in the melted coconut oil.

Place all the ingredients in the food processor and blend together well.

Transfer to a glass or stainless steel container, cover and refrigerate.

'Mozzarella'

Makes about 500 g (enough to cover 1 pizza)

Ingredients:

- 1 x 400 ml tin coconut milk or cream
- 20 g/¾ oz nutritional yeast flakes
- 1 dsp coconut flour
- 2 tbs coconut oil or half coconut oil and half butter or ghee
- 1 dsp kuzu
- 4 tbs freshly squeezed lemon juice
- 1 heaped tbs onion powder
- 1 tsp Himalayan salt

Place all the ingredients in the food processor and purée until smooth.

Place in a saucepan and heat slowly, stirring until thickened.

Transfer to a greased dish and cover to prevent a skin from forming. Then refrigerate for about 12 hours. It is now ready for use.

If using on a pizza, pour over the pizza whilst still warm.

'Parmesan'

Makes about 250 g

Ingredients

- 50 ml/1 ¾ fl oz coconut oil
- 75 g/3 oz butter
- 50 g/2 oz nutritional yeast flakes
- 1 tbs onion powder
- 1 dsp coconut flour, sifted
- ¾ tsp xanthan gum
- 1 tsp Himalayan salt

- 1 tsp kuzu
- 2 tbs coconut cream or coconut yoghurt (see page 39)
- 1 dsp freshly squeezed lemon juice
- 1½ tsp tamari or coconut soy-sauce substitute

Melt the fat and allow it to cool in the fridge, but still be in a liquid state.

Blend the dry ingredients in the food processor.

Add the rest of the ingredients to the food processor and blend well, adding more oil if too dry.

Transfer to a saucepan and bring to the boil, stirring constantly. Simmer and stir until the kuzu becomes transparent.

Transfer to an airtight, non-plastic container and refrigerate until set. Stir occasionally whilst setting.

Grate when needed using a fine grater.

Cheddar-style hard cheese

Makes about 500 g

Ingredients:

- 200 ml/7 fl oz coconut oil
- 200 g/7 oz butter
- 50 g/2 oz nutritional yeast flakes
- 2 dsp onion powder
- ½ tsp xantham gum
- ⅓ tsp Himalayan salt
- 1 tsp kuzu
- 3 tbs coconut cream
- 1 tsp tamari or coconut soy-sauce substitute

Melt the fat and allow it to cool in the fridge, but still be in a liquid state.

Blend the dry ingredients in the food processor.

Add the coconut cream and tamari to the food processor and blend well.

Slowly dribble the cooled fat into the food processor as if you are making mayonnaise, to prevent curdling. It may curdle if the fat is too hot.

Transfer to a saucepan and bring to the boil, stirring constantly. Simmer and stir to allow the kuzu to glaze.

Transfer to an airtight glass or ceramic (not plastic) container and refrigerate until set. Stir occasionally whilst setting to prevent the fat from rising to the top.

This cheese can be sliced, grated or melted.

- **Bread**

The Urban Caveman Bakery

Bread

Urban Caveman bread is grain-free and higher in fibre, protein and fat, and lower in carbs, than traditional bread.

Yeast-free raw bread rolls

These are made in a dehydrator. Buckwheat technically isn't a grain, but a seed of the rhubarb family. However, it does have similar properties to grain so is not Paleo. This recipe ferments the seed, which reduces the anti-nutrient levels. When first going Paleo, buckwheat may help you wean yourself off grains.

Ingredients:
- 750 g/1 lb 9 oz unroasted organic buckwheat
- 200 g/7 oz caraway seeds
- 1 tsp Himalayan salt

Soak the buckwheat and seeds in water and place in a warm space, such as an airing cupboard, for 24 hours.

Drain off the water and rinse well, and cover with fresh water.

Leave in a warm cupboard for a further 24 hours.

Rinse and drain well and stir in the salt.

Process in the food processor until a dough is formed.

Shape into round balls and place in the dehydrator set to 100 for five hours, after which time turn and dehydrate for a further five hours. If you do not possess a dehydrator, warm on the lowest oven setting instead.

Recipes requiring a bread maker

Information and tips on making Urban Caveman bread with a bread maker

Gluten

Gluten provides the distinctive texture and structure of bread as it encapsulates carbon dioxide bubbles produced during the proving. Over the last 50 years the gluten content of wheat has increased by 50 per cent, and the lack of traditional preparation of the grain, such as fermentation, has contributed to an increase in gluten sensitivity which goes way beyond coeliac disease. When making gluten-free breads, substitutes have to be used, such as soda bicarbonate or xanthan gum, to give the dough elasticity. I have found that you need to add 10 grams of xanthan gum to every 100 grams of total flour weight, including the gum.

Flours

Coconut or nut flours can be used instead of grains, with chestnut flour being the most similar in consistency to wheat. However, nut flours are quite high in carbohydrate, and almond and hazelnut, which are often used, can be a little 'cakey'. Using egg-white powder as part of the flour mix reduces the carbohydrate content and improves the texture.

Coconut flour

Higher in protein and fibre and lower in carbohydrate compared with wheat flour, coconut flour makes an excellent alternative. It takes a little time to get used to baking with coconut flour – too much water and it can be too heavy and too little and it can be too crumbly. I have found it best to combine it with flour substitutes (see below).

Table 2: The nutritional values for 100 grams of three different flours

Flour	Carbohydrate	Fibre	Protein	Fat	Calories
Coconut	26 g	39 g	19 g	8.52 g	413
Chestnut	78 g	9.2 g	6.5 g	3.7 g	371
Wholewheat	73 g	12 g	14 g	2 g	339

Table 3: The average nutritional values for the basic Urban Caveman loaf compared with brown bread made with wholewheat flour

	Fat	Carbohydrate	Fibre	Protein
1 loaf basic Urban Caveman bread baked with coconut flour/coconut powder and egg-white powder	123.6 g	101.6 g	104 g	133.1 g
1 loaf brown bread baked with wholewheat flour	0.2–1 g	228 g	3.6 g	66 g

You can see from the above chart that Urban Caveman bread contains less than half the carbs, more than 100 times the fat, 26 times the fibre and more than double the protein, with the protein and fat content being almost equal. This means the Urban Caveman bread is not only a weight-watcher's dream but it also conforms closely to the ratios between the food groups of the hunter-gatherer diet.

Table 4: The approximate percentages of the major food groups in the basic Urban Caveman loaf compared with brown bread made with wholewheat flour

	Fat	Carbohydrate	Fibre	Protein
1 loaf of basic Urban Caveman bread baked with coconut flour/coconut powder and egg-white powder	37%	19%	17%	27%
1 loaf brown bread baked with wholewheat flour (figures are averages as brands and recipes differ)	15%	69%	1%	15%

Coconut flour contains more fibre than any of the grains. Altogether, 93 per cent is insoluble fibre, which means that it helps bulk the stool by attracting water into the bowel, but it is not itself absorbed. Therefore, it does not contribute to weight gain.

The drawback with using coconut flour is that it contains nothing to help it hold together and it also absorbs fluid. This can be overcome by using a gluten substitute like xanthan gum, or eggs, and increasing the oil and liquid content.

Xanthan gum

This helps bind the loaf together and increases elasticity.

Yeast

Yeast is a living organism that requires food (sugar), moisture and warmth to survive, which is why it remains dormant in the dried state. There is some controversy around the use of yeast for people with yeast overgrowth, as there may be cross-reactivity if you have antibodies to *Candida* or other yeasts.

Vitamin C

Used as a bread improver, vitamin C helps the yeast work faster, allowing quick rising. However, most vitamin C is synthetic and derived from corn syrup. Baobab powder is high in vitamin C and would be a suitable alternative.

Salt

Salt plays a vital part in bread making as it improves the flavour, helps regulate the action of the yeast and makes the loaf last longer.

Sweeteners

Luo Han Guo and stevia will not work in bread making. Maple syrup contains as much sucrose as sugar and Palmyra jaggery 4%, so both provide sugars for the yeast to work on. All breads require some kind of sweetening to kick-start the yeast, and to ensure a quick rise. Sugar substitutes will not work. Palmyra jaggery, coconut flower sugar, maple syrup and/or molasses do. However, too much sugar could stop the yeast from working, so it is important to reduce the sugar content when adding fruit to bread.

Liquid

Any liquid can be added to bread, such as coconut milk, juice, cold tea, beer or water. The important point is that the liquid needs to be at the correct temperature to activate the yeast, and this is why bread makers start by setting the room temperature to around body temperature (37°C) before the first knead. Therefore, the liquid should be room temperature. The yeast will die if the temperature is too high, and if the mix is too cold it will not be activated. The general rule for adding liquid to flour is that you add equal amounts of each, so a recipe that calls for 375 grams of flour would require 375 millilitres of fluid. However, I personally find this to be a little too much liquid.

Fat

Olive oil, butter, ghee or coconut oil can be used in the recipes, as they are all stable when heated. Coconut oil and butter need to be melted before adding to the mixture.

Measurements

It is essential to use accurate measurements when working with coconut flour. Measuring spoons and jugs are better than guesswork.

Bread makers

Try to find a bread maker that does not have a non-stick coating on its pan.

Don't use the gluten-free programme as the bread tends to benefit from longer kneading.

Bread makers knead the bread by rotating a small paddle at the base of the pan, but it can get stuck or leave a gaping hole in the bottom of the loaf. You may prefer to remove it after the machine has finished kneading the dough, just before the rise programme. This is around one to two hours into the programme.

The bread must be removed from the pan as soon as it is ready or it will steam, which can make it heavy.

Troubleshooting

Making bread without gluten is not without its challenges, and making bread without grains can pose additional problems. Too much liquid could make your bread soggy, whilst too little could make it crumbly. It may also be necessary to make minor adjustments to the recipes to suit your bread maker. Below are some tips that may help you with your bread making.

Tip 1: Always weigh ingredients accurately. Use measuring spoons and jugs.

Tip 2: Although I usually whisk water, eggs, vinegar, sweetener, salt and oil together, some manufacturers recommend placing the ingredients in the bread pan in the following order:
1. Water/egg mix

2. Salt
3. Oil
4. Flour and xanthan gum mix
5. Yeast.

Tip 3: Don't use the 'gluten-free' setting on the bread maker. This only bakes the bread for two hours and for best results a longer bake of four hours is preferable.

Tip 4: Stir in the flour. Gluten-free flour can stick around the edges of the pan, so using a plastic spatula you may need to scrape any stragglers from the edges of the pan about five to 10 minutes after kneading starts.

Tip 5: When using nuts and fruit, only a small amount can be added to a recipe because they can stop the bread from rising properly and interfere with the mixing. As they increase the sugar content, you need to reduce the amount of sweetener added to the mix. Fresh fruits are high in water compared to dried fruits and so you will also need to decrease the fluid content of your bread when using them. Make sure dried fruits are completely dry before adding to the dispenser. If they have the tiniest amount of liquid on them they may get stuck and will not be released into the dough.

Tip 6: Yeast – Always use 'Easy Bake' or 'Fast Action' dried yeast. If it is not 'Easy Bake' it will require fermentation. Never let the yeast come into contact with the liquid before kneading.

Tip 7: The possible causes of poor volume are:
• Not enough maple syrup or molasses to fully activate the yeasts.
• Not enough xanthan gum.
• Insufficient liquid.
• The liquid touched the yeast before kneading.
• Too much salt (which kills the yeast) – decrease by ¼ teaspoon.
• The yeast was too old.

It may also be helpful to add ¼ tsp vitamin C powder to enhance the action of the yeasts.

Tip 8: Possible causes if the loaf is too holey or full of air pockets:
- Too much yeast.
- Too much liquid – try reducing the water by 10–20 millilitres.
- Liquid or fat was too hot – it should be room temperature.
- Not enough salt so the yeast was overactive – increase the yeast by ¼ teaspoon next time.

Tip 9: Possible causes if the loaf rises too much:
- Too much yeast.
- Too much liquid – try reducing the water by 10–20 millilitres.
- Too much flour.

Tip 10: Possible causes if the loaf is sticky:
- Not enough, or old, yeast.
- Power-supply interruption.
- Left in bread maker too long.
- Not cooked for long enough – change setting to large loaf next time.
- Too much liquid.

Tip 11: Possible causes if there is excess flour around the sides and bottom of the loaf:
- Too much flour.
- Not enough liquid.

Tip 12: Possible causes if the loaf is lop-sided:
- Not enough liquid.
- Not enough flour.

Tip 13: Possible causes if the sides have collapsed and the bottom is damp:
- Loaf was left in the bread maker for too long.
- Power-supply interruption.

Tip 14: Possible causes if the blade stays in the loaf after baking:
- Dough is too stiff.
- Crust has built up under the blade.

Tip 15: Possible causes if the loaf collapses:
- Too much liquid – try reducing the water by 10 to 20 millilitres.
- Too much yeast – reduce by ¼ teaspoon.
- Not enough salt – increase by ¼ teaspoon.
- Lid opened during baking.

Tip 16: Possible cause if the loaf is dry and crumbly:
- Mixture was too dry.

Tip 17: Possible causes if the crust is too brown:
- Too much maple syrup.
- Crust setting was too high for that loaf – reduce setting from dark to medium crust next time.

Basic grain-free bread

Ingredients:
- **2 eggs**
- **325 ml/11 fl oz water**
- **1 tsp Himalayan salt**
- **1 tsp cider vinegar or lemon juice**
- **2 tbs butter, ghee or coconut oil, melted**
- **Equivalent of 1 tsp sugar using sweetener of choice (more if not using molasses**
- **1 dsp blackstrap molasses (optional)**
- **150 g/5 oz coconut flour**
- **110 g/4 oz coconut powder (dried coconut milk)**
- **50 g/2 oz xanthan gum**
- **110 g/4 oz egg-white powder**
- **1 dsp caraway seeds (optional)**
- **1 x sachet of Easy Bake dried yeast**

Using an electric stick blender, whisk together the eggs, water, salt, vinegar, cooled coconut oil, maple syrup and molasses and check the temperature, warming if necessary.

Pour into the bread pan.

Mix the coconut flour, coconut powder, xanthan gum and egg-white powder together and add to the pan. They will sit on the top of the liquid.

Sprinkle caraway seeds (optional) and finally the yeast on top.

Set the bread maker to Basic/Medium/Medium crust.

Remove from the machine as soon as the bread is ready and cool on a wire rack.

Bread rolls

Make as above, but add 1 tsp baking powder to the flour mix.

Set the bread maker to 'Dough only' (about 2½ hours).

Remove from the bread maker and form into rolls, and place on a greased baking tray.

Cover loosely with clingfilm and place in an airing cupboard or similar warm place for about 45 minutes until the rolls have doubled in size.

Remove the clingfilm and bake at 150°C/300°F/GM 2 for about half an hour.

Buckwheat loaf

This contains potato and buckwheat flour so is not really Paleo. Although buckwheat is a seed it behaves like a grain so the body responds to it as if it were. It is included here for those transitioning to a grain-free diet, but for anyone who has been off grains for a while it is likely to provoke a reaction. The addition of buckwheat and potato flour also makes this bread quite high in carbs so it is not recommended for anyone wishing to lose weight.

Ingredients:

- 2 eggs
- 370 ml/13 fl oz water
- 4 tbs melted butter, ghee or coconut oil, cooled to room temperature
- 1 tsp lemon juice or cider vinegar
- 1 tsp Himalayan salt
- Equivalent of 1 tsp sugar using sweetener of choice
- 250 g/9 oz coconut flour
- 20 g/¾ oz potato flour
- 75 g/3 oz buckwheat flour
- 70 g/2¾ oz xanthan gum
- 1 sachet Easy Bake dried yeast

Using an electric stick blender, whisk together the egg, water, fat, lemon juice or vinegar, salt and sweetener, and pour into the bread-maker pan.

Mix the flours together and then stir in the xanthan gum.

Add to the pan.

Sprinkle the yeast on top.

Set to basic/bake/medium or dark crust which takes about four hours.

When ready, cool on a wire rack but if you prefer a drier texture, pop in your oven on 180°C/350°F/GM 4 for 15 to 20 minutes before transferring to the wire rack.

White loaf

Ingredients:

- 2 eggs
- 275 ml/10 fl oz coconut milk 'light' warmed to 30–35°C
- 2 tbs butter, ghee or coconut oil, melted
- 1 tsp Himalayan salt
- 1 tsp vinegar or lemon juice
- Equivalent of 1 tsp sugar using sweetener of choice

- 150 g/5 oz coconut flour
- 110 g/4 oz coconut powder (dried coconut milk)
- 110 g/4 oz egg-white powder
- 50 g/2 oz xanthan gum
- 1 sachet Easy Bake yeast

Whisk the eggs, milk, fat, salt, vinegar and sweetener together and add to the bread-maker pan.

Combine the coconut flour, coconut powder, egg-white powder and xanthan gum and add to the pan.

Sprinkle the yeast over the top.

Set the machine to Basic/Bake/Medium/Medium Crust.

Remove from the machine as soon as it is ready and cool on a wire rack.

Focaccia bread

Ingredients:

- 2 eggs
- 325 ml/11 fl oz water, warmed to 25–30°C
- 5 tbs olive oil
- 1 tsp lemon juice or cider vinegar
- Equivalent of 1 tsp sugar using sweetener of choice
- 1½ tsp Himalayan salt plus 1 tsp Himalayan salt, coarse
- 150 g/5 oz coconut flour
- 110 g/4 oz coconut powder
- 110 g/4 oz egg-white powder
- 50 g/2 oz xanthan gum
- 1 sachet of Easy Bake yeast

Beat the eggs, water, 4 tbs of olive oil, lemon juice or vinegar, sweetener and salt and place in the bread-maker pan.

Mix the coconut flour, coconut powder, egg-white powder and xanthan gum together and add to the pan.

Sprinkle the yeast on top of the flour mix.

Set the bread maker to 'Dough'.

Oil a loaf tin.

Remove the dough from the bread maker after it has been kneaded for about 2½ hours.

Knead by hand with a little extra flour, and place in the oiled tin.

Spray dough with water, cover with oiled clingfilm and leave in an airing cupboard or other warm place to rise (about an hour).

Pre-heat your oven to 190°C/375°F/GM 5 if fan-assisted and 220°C/425°F/GM 7 if not.

Remove the risen dough from the clingfilm and make indents in the top into which you pour a little olive oil.

Sprinkle with coarse salt and mist with water.

Bake in the oven for about 50 minutes, but spray with water twice during cooking to keep the crust moist.

Cool on a wire rack but cover with a damp tea towel.

Eat whilst still warm.

Tomato and olive loaf

Ingredients:
- **6 sun-dried tomatoes**
- **2 eggs**
- **1 tsp lemon juice or cider vinegar**
- **Equivalent of 1 tsp sugar using sweetener of choice**
- **3 tbs olive oil**
- **1 tsp Himalayan salt**
- **325 ml/11 fl oz water**
- **110 g/4 oz coconut flour**
- **110 g/4 oz coconut powder**

- **110 g/4 oz egg-white powder**
- **50 g/2 oz xantham gum**
- **1 tsp garlic powder**
- **1 tbs dried onions, or chopped spring onion**
- **Black pepper to taste**
- **1½ tsp dried oregano**
- **1 sachet Easy Bake yeast**
- **¼ red pepper, finely chopped**
- **Approx 8 olives, chopped finely and dried on kitchen towel**

Soak the sun-dried tomatoes in hot water for 20 minutes, drain, chop and cool and pat dry.

Beat the eggs, lemon juice or vinegar, sweetener, olive oil and salt into water and pour into the bread-maker pan.

Mix the coconut flour, coconut powder, egg-white powder, xanthan gum, garlic powder, onion, black pepper and oregano together and place on top of the liquid.

Sprinkle the yeast on top.

Mix together the red pepper, tomatoes and olives and place in the raisin dispenser, squeezing out any moisture into a kitchen towel first (if the vegetables are too moist then they could get stuck in the dispenser). Don't overfill the dispenser.

Set the bread maker to Basic/Bake Raisin/Medium/Dark crust and bake for about 4 hours.

Cool on a wire rack, but if you prefer a drier texture, pop in the oven set at 180°C/350°F/ GM 4 for 15 to 20 minutes before transferring to the wire rack.

Carrot and herb bread

Ingredients:

- 2 eggs
- 1 tsp lemon juice or cider vinegar
- 1½ tsp Himalayan salt
- 60 ml/2½ fl oz melted ghee, butter or coconut oil
- 75 g/3 oz grated carrot
- Equivalent of 1 tsp sugar using sweetener of choice
- 325 ml/11 fl oz water warmed to 25–30°C
- 150 g/5 oz coconut flour
- 110 g/4 oz coconut powder
- 110 g/4 oz egg-white powder
- 1 tsp dried thyme
- *Optional*: ¼ tsp vitamin C powder or baobab powder
- 1 tsp mustard powder
- 1 tsp onion powder
- 50 g/2 oz xanthan gum
- 3 tbs black mustard seeds
- 1 sachet Easy Bake dried yeast

Beat the eggs, lemon juice or vinegar, salt, fat, grated carrot, sweetener and water and add to the bread-maker pan.

Then mix the coconut flour, coconut powder, egg-white powder, thyme, vitamin C, mustard powder, onion powder and xanthan gum together and add to the pan.

Sprinkle mustard seeds and yeast on the top.

Set the machine to Basic/Medium/Medium crust.

Remove from the pan as soon as bread is ready and cool on a wire rack.

Almond and apricot bread

Ingredients:

- 2 eggs
- 1 tsp cider vinegar or lemon juice
- 1 tsp Himalayan salt
- 2 tbs melted coconut oil, butter or ghee
- 1 tsp almond oil
- Equivalent of 1 tsp sugar using sweetener of choice
- 325 ml/11 fl oz unpasteurised apple juice, room temperature
- 150 g/5 oz coconut flour
- 110 g/4 oz coconut powder
- 110 g/4 oz egg-white powder
- 110 g/4 oz ground almonds
- ½ tsp baking powder, gluten free
- *Optional*: ¼ tsp vitamin C powder
- 50 g/2 oz xanthan gum
- 110 g/4 oz dried chopped apricots
- 1 sachet Easy Bake dried yeast

Beat the eggs, vinegar, salt, fat, almond oil and sweetener into the apple juice and pour into the bread-maker pan.

Mix the coconut flour, coconut powder, egg-white powder, ground almonds, baking powder, vitamin C and xanthan gum together and add to the pan.

Place the dried apricots in the raisin dispenser.

Sprinkle yeast over the top.

Set machine to Basic/Medium/Medium or Dark crust, selecting Bake Raisin under Options.

Remove from machine as soon as the bread is ready, transferring it to a wire rack to cool.

Quick and easy cheese and onion bread

Ingredients:

- 325 ml/ 11 fl oz coconut milk, room temperature
- 110 g/4 oz nutritional yeast flakes
- 2 eggs
- 1 dsp cider vinegar or lemon juice
- 1 tsp Himalayan salt
- 3 tbs ghee or butter, melted and cooled
- Equivalent of 1 tsp sugar using sweetener of choice
- 1 tbs Urban Caveman coconut yoghurt (see page 39)
- 150 g/5 oz coconut flour
- 110 g/4 oz coconut powder
- 110 g/4 oz egg-white powder
- 50 g/2 oz xanthan gum
- 1 tbs onion powder
- Black pepper
- *Optional*: ½ tsp vitamin C powder
- 1 tsp gluten-free baking powder
- 1 tbs sage, fresh, chopped
- 1 sachet Easy Bake yeast
- ¼–½ onion, finely chopped

Dissolve nutritional yeast flakes in coconut milk.

Beat the eggs, vinegar or lemon juice, salt, ghee or butter, sweetener, and yoghurt into the coconut milk and pour into bread-maker pan.

Mix the coconut flour, coconut powder, egg-white powder, xanthan gum, onion powder, pepper, vitamin C powder if using, baking powder and sage together, and place on top of the liquid.

Sprinkle yeast on top.

Set the bread maker to Basic/Bake Raisin/Medium/Medium crust programme and place the chopped onion in the dispenser. Don't overfill or it will not release into the dough.

Remove from the machine and set on a cooling rack as soon as it is ready. If you prefer a drier texture pop in the oven set at 180°C/350°F/GM 4 for 15 to 20 minutes.

Fruit tea bread

This is a moist bread, a bit like a malt loaf.

- 3 eggs
- 1 tsp apple cider vinegar
- 1 tsp Himalayan salt
- Equivalent of 1 tsp sugar using sweetener of choice
- 2 tbs melted coconut oil, butter or ghee, cooled
- 330 ml/12 fl oz unpasteurised apple juice warmed to 25–30°C
- 150 g/5 oz coconut flour
- 110 g/ 4 oz coconut powder
- 110 g/4 oz egg-white powder
- *Optional:* ¼ level tsp vitamin C powder
- 1 tsp ground cinnamon
- 1 dsp allspice
- 50 g/2 oz xanthan gum
- 1 tsp baking powder, gluten free
- 1 sachet Easy Bake dried yeast
- ¼ eating apple, chopped small
- 25 g/ 1 oz mixed vine fruit, or raisins or sultanas, dried on kitchen paper

Beat the eggs, vinegar, salt, sweetener and melted but cooled coconut oil into the apple juice and pour into the bread-maker pan. Check the temperature is around 25–30°C.

Mix the coconut flour, coconut powder and egg-white powder together and stir in the vitamin C if using, cinnamon, allspice, xanthum gum and baking powder and add to the bread-maker pan.

Sprinkle the yeast over the top.

Set the machine to Bake/Basic/Medium/Medium crust, selecting Bake Raisin under Options.

Dry the apple and fruit on kitchen paper, and place in the nut dispenser so it will be automatically added after the first knead.

Remove from the machine as soon as it is ready and cool on a wire rack.

Quick and easy pizza base

Ingredients
Makes one large pizza
- 250 ml/9 fl oz water
- 1 egg
- ¾ tsp Himalayan salt
- Equivalent of 1 tsp sugar using sweetener of choice
- 225 g/8 oz coconut flour
- 50 g/2 oz coconut powder
- 50 g/2 oz egg-white powder
- 1 tbs arrowroot
- 1 dsp xanthan gum
- 1 sachet Easy Bake yeast

Whisk the water, egg, salt and sweetener together and pour into the bread-maker pan.

Mix the coconut flour, coconut powder, egg-white powder, arrowroot and xanthan gum together.

Tip on top of the liquid mix in the bread maker.

Sprinkle yeast on top.

Set the bread maker to the Dough programme.

After it has been kneaded (about 2½ hours), lay on baking parchment which is twice the size of your pizza base, and on to which you have sprinkled a little coconut flour.

Fold the baking parchment in half, covering the dough.

Roll out inside the floured baking parchment to form a pizza shape.

Peel back the top of the baking parchment and place an upturned pizza baking tray over the top.

Holding the baking parchment to secure the dough to the pizza tray, turn over.

Remove the baking parchment.

Bake for about 10 minutes to brown slightly.

Remove from the oven and add your choice of topping and cheese.

Transfer to the oven and bake for about 25 minutes on 150ºC/300ºF/GM 2.

Serve with chopped fresh basil and freshly ground black pepper.

Fermented pizza dough – thick, soft

Ingredients:
Makes one large pizza
- 225 ml/8 fl oz ghee or butter
- 60 g/2½ oz Urban Caveman coconut yoghurt (see page 39)
- 60 g/2½ oz coconut flour
- 25 g/1 oz coconut powder
- 25 g/1 oz egg-white powder
- 2 tsp Himalayan salt
- 225 ml/8 fl oz water warmed to 25–30ºC

Whisk the ghee and yoghurt together.

Add flours to food processor with the salt, water and yoghurt and ghee mixture.

Purée until the mixture forms a dough.

Transfer to a metal or glass bowl, cover with a tea towel and leave in the airing cupboard, or equivalent, for 24 hours so that the yoghurt can partially digest the flours.

Roll out with a rolling pin between floured baking parchment (see above).

Peel the baking parchment off the top of the dough and place an upturned pizza baking tray over the dough, pressing down firmly. Any dough protruding round the edges can be removed.

Holding the baking parchment to secure the dough to the pizza tray, turn over. Peel the remaining parchment away.

Cook at 150°C/300°F/GM 2 for 10 minutes before adding topping.

Return to oven and cook for 20 to 25 minutes until browned.

The Urban Caveman Patisserie

- *Cakes*
- *Biscuits*
- *Confectionery*
- *Savoury waffles*
- *Sweet waffles*
- *Savoury pancakes*
- *Sweet pancakes*

Cakes

Cakes made with coconut flour are lower in carbs than those made with wheat flour, and are higher in fat. If you want to lower the carb content even more you could substitute egg-white protein powder for some of the coconut flour. I am indebted to Bruce Fife of www.coconutresearchcenter.org for tips on cooking with coconut flour.

Basic sponge cake mix

Ingredients:

- 75 g/3 oz ghee, butter or coconut oil – or a mixture, melted to a liquid but not too hot
- 75 ml/3 fl oz coconut milk
- 12 eggs
- Sweetener of choice to taste (see Table page 31)
- 1tsp Himalayan salt
- 1tsp vanilla extract or seeds from 1 vanilla pod
- 110g/4 oz sifted coconut flour
- 1tsp gluten-free baking powder

Pre-heat your oven to 170°C/325°F/GM 3.

Blend together the fat, coconut milk, eggs, sweetener, salt and vanilla to make a batter.

Combine the coconut flour with baking powder and, using an electric stick blender, whisk into batter.

Pour into a greased cake tin, or two small sandwich tins, and bake for 35–40 minutes or until a knife inserted comes out clean.

Cool and stand on a wire rack.

A simple, quick filling or icing can be made from softened butter to which you have added some sweetener, beaten egg and vanilla essence.

Spicy cupcakes

Ingredients:
Makes about 30

- Sweetener of choice to taste
- 1 tsp vanilla extract or seeds from 1 vanilla pod
- 9 eggs
- 1 tsp Himalayan salt
- 250 g/9 oz ghee/coconut oil, melted but not hot
- 1 tsp gluten-free baking powder
- 75 g/3 oz coconut flour, sifted
- 2 tsp ground cinnamon
- ¼ tsp ground allspice
- ¼ tsp ground cloves
- ¼ tsp ground ginger
- 1 tsp ground nutmeg

Pre-heat your oven to 170°C / 325°F / GM 3.

Add the sweetener, vanilla extract, eggs and salt to the fat and whisk well using an electric stick blender.

Stir the baking powder into the coconut flour and mix in the spices.

Sieve into the egg and fat mix and whisk in well.

Pour into paper cake cases.

Bake for 15 to 20 minutes, until a knife inserted comes out clean.

Seed fairy cakes with butter icing

Ingredients for cakes:
Makes about 36

- 75 g/3 oz melted coconut oil – not too hot
- 50 g/2 oz melted butter or ghee

- ½ tsp Himalayan salt
- 18 eggs
- Sweetener of choice to taste
- 3 tsp gluten-free baking powder
- 175 g/6 oz coconut flour
- 1 tbs caraway seeds

Pre-heat your oven to 170°C/325°F/GM 3.

Using an electric stick blender, whisk the fat, salt, eggs and sweetener together.

Stir the baking powder into the coconut flour.

Sift the flour and baking powder into the mixture and whisk again.

Using a metal spoon, stir in the caraway seeds.

Fill the cake cases and bake for 15 to 20 minutes or until a knife inserted comes out clean.

Ingredients for the icing:
- Sweetener of choice to taste
- 2 eggs
- 25 g/1 oz coconut oil
- 25 g/ 1 oz ghee or butter

Whisk the sweetener into the eggs in a glass or stainless steel bowl.

Add the oil and ghee to the egg mix.

Place the bowl over a saucepan of simmering water and stir occasionally until it thickens (about 20 minutes).

Cool slightly in the fridge and then spread over the cakes.

Fairy cakes with butter icing

Ingredients for cakes:
Makes around 36

- 75 g/3 oz melted coconut oil
- 4 tbs melted ghee
- ½ tsp Himalayan salt
- 18 eggs
- 1 tsp vanilla extract or seeds from 1 vanilla pod
- Sweetener of choice to taste
- 3 tsp gluten-free baking powder
- 175 g/6 oz coconut flour

Pre-heat your oven to 170°C/325°F/GM 3.

Using an electric stick blender, whisk the fat, salt, eggs, vanilla and sweetener together.

Stir the baking powder into the coconut flour.

Sift the flour and baking powder into the mixture and whisk again, making sure there are no lumps.

Fill cake cases and bake for 15 to 20 minutes or until a knife inserted comes out clean.

Ingredients for the icing:

- Sweetener of choice to taste
- 2 eggs
- 25 g/1 oz coconut oil
- 25 g/1 oz ghee or butter

Whisk the sweetener into the eggs in a glass or stainless steel bowl.

Add the oil and ghee to the egg mix.

Place the bowl over a saucepan of simmering water and stir frequently until it thickens (about 20 minutes).

Cool slightly in the fridge and then spread over the cakes.

Strawberry fairy cakes

Ingredients for cakes:
Makes around 36

- Fresh strawberries, sliced
- 75 g/3 oz ghee, butter or coconut oil – melted, but not too hot
- 4 tbs melted ghee
- ½ tsp Himalayan salt
- 18 eggs
- 1 tsp vanilla extract or seeds from 1 vanilla pod
- Sweetener of choice to taste
- 175 g/6 oz coconut flour
- 3 tsp gluten-free baking powder

If you have a dehydrator, place sliced strawberries on a baking tray and dehydrate at 135°C for six hours, turning once. If you are using the oven, heat to 140°C/275°F/GM 1 and bake for two hours.

Pre-heat your oven to 170°C/325°F/GM 3.

Using an electric stick blender, whisk the fat, salt, eggs, vanilla and sweetener together.

Sift the coconut flour and baking powder into the mixture and whisk again.

Then stir in the dehydrated strawberries using a metal spoon.

Fill the cake cases and bake for 15 to 20 minutes or until a knife inserted comes out clean.

Ingredients for the icing:
- Sweetener of choice to taste
- 8-10 large strawberries or 3 tbs dried strawberry powder
- 2 eggs
- 60 g/2 ½ oz ghee or butter

Whisk the sweetener and strawberries into the eggs in a glass or stainless steel bowl.

Add the oil and ghee or butter to the egg mix.

Place the bowl over a saucepan of simmering water and stir occasionally until it thickens (about 20 minutes).

Cool slightly in the fridge and then spread over the cakes.

Goji berry fairy cakes

As strawberry cakes, but stir in some goji berries and omit the icing.

Blueberry fairy cakes

As strawberry cakes, but stir in some dried blueberries and omit the icing.

Sultana fairy cakes

Ingredients:
Makes 20-24

- 75 g/3 oz melted coconut oil
- 50 g/2 oz melted ghee
- ½ tsp Himalayan salt
- 18 eggs
- 1 tsp vanilla extract or seeds from 1 vanilla pod
- Sweetener of choice to taste
- 175 g/6 oz coconut flour
- 3 tsp gluten-free baking powder
- 125 g/4½ oz sultanas (without sugar or vegetable oil)

Pre-heat your oven to 170°C/325°F/GM 3.

Using an electric stick blender, whisk the fat, salt, eggs, vanilla and sweetener together.

Sift the coconut flour and baking powder into the mixture and blend.

Then stir in the sultanas using a metal spoon.

Transfer to cake cases and bake for 15 to 20 minutes, or until a knife inserted comes out clean.

Chocolate or carob fairy cakes

Chocolate and carob are not Paleo because they are made from beans. However, occasional use is fine. Check that you are using a heat-treated carob or cocoa flour, because legumes require pre-cooking to help break down the starches.

Ingredients for cakes:
Makes 12–16
- 75 g/3 oz coconut oil or ghee or butter
- 40 g/1½ oz carob or cocoa powder
- 4 tbs coconut cream or milk
- 6 eggs
- Sweetener of choice to taste
- ¼ tsp Himalayan salt
- 1 tsp vanilla extract or seeds from 1 vanilla pod
- 40 g/1½ oz coconut flour
- 1 tsp gluten-free baking powder

Pre-heat your oven to 200°C/400°F/GM 6.

In a saucepan, blend together fat and carob powder.

Remove from the heat and allow to cool slightly.

In a bowl, mix together coconut cream, eggs, sweetener, salt and vanilla.

Using an electric stick blender, whisk in the carob mixture.

Combine the coconut flour with the baking powder and sift into the mixture.

Whisk well.

Pour into cake cases and bake for about 20 minutes.

Ingredients for the icing:

- 1-2 tbs carob or cocoa powder
- Sweetener of choice to taste
- 50 g/2 oz butter
- 2 eggs
- 1 tsp vanilla essence or seeds from 1 vanilla pod

Place all the ingredients in a glass bowl over a pan of simmering water.

Stir until the carob or cocoa has dissolved and the icing has thickened.

Leave to cool in the fridge, then spread over the cakes.

Lemon fairy cakes

Ingredients for cakes:
Makes about 24

- 225 g/8 oz ghee, butter or coconut oil, melted
- Zest and juice of 1 large lemon, unwaxed
- 9 eggs
- Sweetener of choice to taste
- ¾ tsp Himalayan salt
- 2 tsp gluten-free baking powder
- 110 g/4 oz coconut flour

Pre-heat your oven to 200°C/400°F/GM 6.

Using an electric stick blender, whisk the fat, lemon juice and zest, eggs, sweetener, and salt together.

Add the baking powder to the coconut flour and sift into the lemon mixture.

Whisk well.

Place in cake cases and bake for 15 to 20 minutes.

Remove and allow to cool on a wire rack.

Ingredients for lemon curd icing

- Zest and juice of 1 large lemon, unwaxed
- Sweetener of choice to taste
- 2 eggs
- 50 g/2 oz butter

Mix the grated lemon rind and sweetener together in a glass bowl.

In a separate bowl whizz the lemon juice into the eggs.

Pour this into the lemon mix and then add the butter and blend together.

Place the bowl over a saucepan of simmering water, bain Marie-style, stirring occasionally until thickened (about 15 to 20 minutes).

Leave to cool in the fridge, then spread over the cakes.

Savoury scones

Ingredients:
Makes about 12

- 6 eggs, plus beaten egg for glazing
- 1 tsp tamari or coconut soy-sauce substitute
- 1 tsp grated or dried horseradish (not creamed)
- 2-3 tbs coconut milk
- 90 g/3½ oz melted coconut oil, ghee or butter
- ½ tsp Himalayan salt
- ½ tsp celery salt
- 1 dsp onion powder
- 1 tsp garlic powder
- 2 tbs gluten-free baking powder
- 75 g/3 oz coconut flour plus extra for kneading

Pre-heat your oven to 170°C/325°F/GM 3.

Whisk the eggs, tamari, grated horseradish if using, and milk into the fat.

Mix the salt, celery salt, onion powder, garlic powder, baking powder and dry horse-radish if using, into the coconut flour.

Sift the dry mixture into the egg and fat mixture and using an electric stick blender, whisk in well.

Leave for a few minutes so that the coconut flour absorbs the moisture. Then knead lightly in a little coconut flour.

Roll out the scone dough and, using a pastry cutter, cut into rounds about 2 cm/¾ inch thick and 5 cm/2 inches wide.

Place on a greased baking tray and glaze with beaten egg, being careful not to let any drip down the sides as this will prevent rising.

Leave to rise for about 15 to 30 minutes.

Bake for 8 to 12 minutes.

Can be eaten hot or left to cool on a wire rack.

Cheesy scones

Ingredients:
Makes about 12

- 90 g/3½ oz melted coconut oil, ghee or butter
- 40 g/1½ oz nutritional yeast flakes
- 6 eggs, plus beaten egg for glazing
- 2-3 tbs coconut milk
- 2 tsp tamari or coconut soy-sauce substitute
- 1 tsp grated or dried horseradish (not creamed)
- ½ tsp Himalayan salt
- ½ tsp celery salt
- 1 dsp onion powder
- 1 tsp garlic powder
- 2 tbs gluten-free baking powder
- 75 g/3 oz coconut flour

Pre-heat your oven to 170°C/325°F/GM 3.

Warm the fat and add the nutritional yeast flakes, stirring until dissolved.

Remove from the heat and whisk in the eggs, milk and tamari adding grated horseradish if using, after whisking.

Add the salt, celery salt, onion powder, garlic powder, dried horseradish if using, and baking powder to the coconut flour.

Sift the flour mixture into the egg and fat mixture and using an electric stick blender, whisk in well.

Knead lightly in a little coconut flour.

Roll out the scone dough and, using a pastry cutter, cut into rounds about 2 cm/¾ inch thick and 5 cm/2 inches wide.

Place on a greased baking tray and glaze with beaten egg, being careful not to let any drip down the sides as this will prevent rising.

Leave to rise for about 15 to 30 minutes.

Bake for 8 to 12 minutes.

Can be eaten hot or left to cool on a wire rack.

Sweet scones

Ingredients:
Makes about 12
- 6 eggs
- 75 g/3 oz ghee or butter
- 1 tsp vanilla extract or seeds from 1 vanilla pod
- 1 tsp fresh lemon juice
- ½ tsp Himalayan salt
- 2-3 tbs coconut milk
- Sweetener of choice to taste
- 2 tbs gluten-free baking powder
- 50 g/2 oz coconut flour
- 50 g/2 oz desiccated coconut
- 110 g/4 oz sultanas – without vegetable oil and sugar

Preheat oven to 170°C/325°F/GM 3.

Whisk the eggs, butter, vanilla, lemon, salt, milk and sweetener together. Don't worry if it curdles.

Stir the baking powder into the coconut flour and sift into the egg mixture and whisk.

Stir in the desiccated coconut and sultanas.

Knead lightly in a little coconut flour.

Roll out the scone dough and, using a pastry cutter, cut into rounds about 2 cm/¾ inch thick and 5 cm/2 inches wide.

Place on a greased baking tray and glaze with beaten egg, being careful not to let any drip down the sides as this will prevent rising.

Leave to rise for about 15 to 30 minutes.

Bake for 8 to 12 minutes.

Can be eaten hot or left to cool on a wire rack

Serve with Urban Caveman double cream (see page 42) and mashed strawberries for an English cream tea.

Biscuits

Savoury crackers

These are great with Urban Caveman cheeses (see page 50).

Ingredients:
Makes 12

- 25 g/1 oz ghee or butter
- 4 eggs
- ½ tsp Himalayan salt
- ½ tsp fresh lemon juice
- 2 tsp tamari or coconut soy-sauce substitute
- 1 dsp onion powder
- 75 g/3 oz coconut flour

Pre-heat your oven to 190°C/375°F/GM 5.

Melt the ghee or butter and allow it to cool but still remain liquid.

Whisk in the eggs, salt, lemon juice and tamari.

Mix the onion powder into the coconut flour, sift the mix into the liquid and then whisk.

Mould into balls in your hands and flatten onto an oiled baking sheet. Using a biscuit shaper, cut away excess.

Bake for 15–20 minutes before cooling on wire rack.

Butter biscuits

Ingredients
Makes 26–30
- 175 g/6 oz fat (half ghee/half butter)
- 8 eggs
- Sweetener of choice to taste
- 1 tsp vanilla extract or seeds from 1 vanilla pod
- 225 g/8 oz coconut flour, sifted

Pre-heat your oven to 170°C/325°F/GM 3.

Melt the fat and whisk in the eggs, sweetener and vanilla extract.

Sift in the coconut flour.

Leave for five minutes to thicken.

Grease a biscuit tray.

Form into little balls in your hands and flatten onto the baking tray.

Using a round biscuit cutter, trim the edges of the flattened balls to make into biscuit shapes.

Bake for 20 minutes.

Cool on a wire rack and store in an airtight container.

Chewy strawberry biscuits

Ingredients:
Makes about 24
- 175 g/6 oz fresh strawberries, sliced
- 110 g/4 oz melted ghee, butter and/or coconut oil
- 4 eggs
- Sweetener of choice to taste
- ¼ tsp Himalayan salt

- *Optional*: 1 heaped tsp dehydrated natural strawberry powder
- 95 g/3½ oz coconut flour

If you have a dehydrator, place sliced strawberries on tray and dehydrate on 135 for six hours, turning once. If you are using the oven, heat to 140°C/275°F/GM 1 and bake for two hours.

Leave to cool and then chop into small pieces.

Pre-heat your oven to 170°C/325°F/GM 3.

Whisk the melted ghee, eggs, sweetener and salt together in a bowl.

If using strawberry powder, mix it into the flour.

Sift the flour into the mixture and leave to stand for five minutes. The consistency should be slightly stiffer than a cake mix, and firm enough to form into balls without it being too sticky.

Form into little balls in your hands and flatten onto the baking tray.

Using a round biscuit cutter, trim the edges of the flattened balls to make into biscuit shapes.

Bake for 15–20 minutes until golden and firm.

Cool on a wire rack and store in an airtight container.

Chocolate or carob biscuits

Ingredients:
Makes about 16

- 110 g/4 oz coconut oil, ghee or butter, or a mixture
- 50 g/2 oz cocoa or carob powder (not raw)
- 3 eggs
- Sweetener of choice to taste
- ¼ tsp Himalayan salt
- ¼ tsp vanilla extract or seeds from 1 vanilla pod
- 60 g/2½ oz coconut flour

Pre-heat your oven to 170°C/325°F/GM 3.

Melt the fat over low heat, and stir in cocoa or carob powder.

Remove from the heat and allow to cool slightly.

In a bowl combine eggs, sweetener, salt and vanilla.

Whisk into the carob/cocoa mixture.

Then, whisk the coconut flour into the egg mixture. Let it rest for about five minutes to thicken slightly.

Form into little balls in your hands and flatten onto the baking tray.

Using a round biscuit cutter, trim the edges of the flattened balls to make into biscuit shapes.

Bake for 15 minutes.

Cool on a wire rack and store in an airtight container.

Coconut biscuits

Ingredients
Makes about 12
- 75 g/3 oz coconut oil, ghee or butter, or a mixture
- Sweetener of choice to taste
- 4 eggs
- ½ tsp vanilla extract or seeds from 1 vanilla pod
- 50 g/2 oz coconut flour
- 50 g/2 oz desiccated coconut

Pre-heat the oven to 180°C/350°F/GM 4.

Whisk fat, sweetener, eggs and vanilla together.

Add sifted coconut flour and whisk in.

Stir in the dessicated coconut.

Form into little balls in your hands and flatten onto the baking tray.

Using a round biscuit cutter, trim the edges of the flattened balls to make into biscuit shapes.

Bake for 15 to 20 minutes.

Cool on a wire rack and store in an airtight container.

Ginger biscuits

These could be made into gingerbread man shapes using a pastry cutter.

Ingredients
Makes about 12
- 6 eggs
- 50 g/2 oz ghee, butter or coconut oil
- ¼ tsp Himalayan salt
- 110 g/4 oz blackstrap molasses
- Sweetener of choice to taste
- 1 tsp ground ginger
- ½ tsp ground cinnamon
- 110 g/4 oz coconut flour

Pre-heat your oven to 180°C/350°F/GM 4.

Using an electric stick blender, whisk the eggs, fat, salt, molasses and sweetener together.

Stir the spices into the coconut flour.

Whisk the coconut flour and spices into the mixture.

Form into little balls in your hands and flatten onto the baking tray.

Using a round biscuit cutter, trim the edges of the flattened balls to make into shapes.

Bake for 15 to 20 minutes.

Cool on a wire rack and store in an airtight container.

Lemon biscuits

Ingredients:
Makes about 24

- **4 eggs**
- **Sweetener of choice to taste**
- **¼ tsp Himalayan salt**
- **Juice of 1 lemon**
- **Grated zest of 2 lemons**
- **150 g/6 oz ghee or butter or coconut oil (or mixture), melted but not too hot**
- **125 g/5 oz coconut flour**

Pre-heat your oven to 180°C/350°F/GM 4.

Whisk the eggs, sweetener, salt, lemon juice and zest together in a food processor.

When fat has cooled but is still liquid, pour in *slowly* to prevent curdling.

Stir in the sifted coconut flour.

Form into little balls in your hands and flatten onto a baking tray.

Using a round biscuit cutter, trim the edges of the flattened balls to make into biscuit shapes.

Bake for 15 to 20 minutes.

Cool on a wire rack and store in an airtight container.

Buckwheat

Although buckwheat is a seed, it has characteristics like a grain so the body responds to it as if it were a grain. It is included here for those transitioning to a grain-free diet, but for anyone who has been off grains for a while it could provoke a reaction.

Buckwheat biscuits

Ingredients:
Makes about 12
- Sweetener of choice to taste
- 4 eggs
- 50 g/2 oz butter with 50 g/2 oz coconut oil or 100 g coconut oil – room temperature
- 110 g/4 oz buckwheat flakes
- 25 g/1 oz coconut flour
- 25 g/1 oz buckwheat flour

Pre-heat your oven to 170°C/325°F/GM 3.

Lightly grease a large baking tray.

Cream together the sweetener, eggs and fat.

Add the buckwheat flakes and flours and work them into the mixture.

Lightly knead until smooth and then roll out to a thickness of 5 mm on a lightly floured work surface.

Cut into rounds using a 6 mm cutter or cup, and place on the prepared baking tray.

Bake for about 30 minutes, until brown.

Cool on a wire rack and store in an airtight container.

Buckwheat flapjacks

Ingredients:
Makes about 12–14
- 200 g/7 oz coconut oil or 100 g/3½ oz coconut oil and 100 g/3½ oz butter
- Sweetener of choice to taste
- 1 dsp xantham gum
- 330 g/11 oz buckwheat flakes or half buckwheat flakes and half coconut flakes

Pre-heat the oven to 170°C/325°F/GM 3.

Grease a rectangular or square tin.

Melt the fat in a saucepan and stir in the sweetener.

Mix the xanthan gum into the buckwheat flakes and transfer to a bowl.

Stir in the fat/syrup mixture and make sure all the flakes are coated.

Transfer to a baking tray and flatten down the top.

Bake for about 25 minutes.

Mark into bars and cool in the fridge.

Fruit bars

Ingredients:
Makes around 12–14

- **Sweetener of choice to taste**
- **200 g/7 oz ghee, butter or coconut oil**
- **2 eggs**
- **1 tsp vanilla extract or seeds from 1 vanilla pod**
- **¼ tsp Himalayan salt**
- **110 g/4 oz coconut flour**
- **50 g/2 oz desiccated coconut**
- **Jar bought unsweetened jam**
- **Chopped pecan nuts**
- **Flaked coconut to sprinkle on top**

Pre-heat your oven to 180°C/350°F/GM 4.

Whisk the sweetener, fat, eggs and vanilla together.

Add the salt to the flour and stir in the desiccated coconut. Add to the fat and egg mixture.

Grease a rectangular or square baking tin.

Transfer the mixture to the tin and flatten down.

Spread the jam on the top (depends on size of tray but usually the whole jar)

Sprinkle with the pecan nuts and top with flaked coconut.

Bake for about 30 to 40 minutes, then leave to cool.

Cut into bar shapes.

Low-carb fruit bars

Ingredients:
Makes around 12–14

- Sweetener of choice to taste
- 200 g/7 oz ghee, butter or coconut oil
- 2 eggs
- 1 tsp vanilla extract or seeds from 1 vanilla pod
- ¼ tsp Himalayan salt
- 25 g/1 oz coconut flour
- 25 g/1 oz coconut-milk powder
- 50 g/2 oz egg-white protein powder
- 25 g/1 oz desiccated coconut
- Enough fresh organic berry fruits – e.g. strawberries or raspberries – to produce a purée that can be thinly spread over the mixture in the baking tin
- About 300 g/11 oz chopped pecan nuts, to sprinkle on top
- 1–2 handfuls flaked coconut, to sprinkle on top

Pre-heat your oven to 180°C/350°F/GM 4.

Whisk the sweetener, fat, eggs and vanilla together.

Mix the salt, flour, coconut-milk powder, egg-white powder and desiccated coconut together.

Stir into the fat and egg mixture.

Grease a rectangular or square baking tin.

Transfer the mixture to the tin and flatten down.

Purée the berries and spread on the top.

Sprinkle with the pecan nuts and top with flaked coconut.

Bake for about 30 to 40 minutes, then leave to cool.

Cut into bar shapes.

Confectionery

Some of these dishes are very sweet and are for special occasions.

Mockachoca

This provides the flavour of chocolate from the cocoa butter, but carob may be better tolerated by those sensitive to chocolate.

Ingredients:
Makes about 20

- 250 g/9 oz cocoa butter
- 75 g/3 oz butter
- 2 dsp carob powder
- Sweetener of choice to taste
- 1 tbs coconut cream
- 1 tsp vanilla extract or seeds from 1 vanilla pod

Melt the cocoa butter and butter in a small bowl over a saucepan of simmering water.

Stir in the carob powder.

When melted, whisk in the other ingredients, then transfer to a small shallow baking tray and refrigerate.

Score into small squares or rectangles.

Can be grated over Urban Caveman ice cream.

Mint mockachoca

As for mockachoca above but add mint essence when you whisk in the other ingredients. Can be grated over Urban Caveman ice cream.

Mockachoca with almonds

Ingredients:
Makes about 20
- 110 g/4 oz butter
- 110 g/4 oz cocoa butter
- 110 g/4 oz carob powder
- 1 dsp maple syrup
- Sweetener of choice to taste
- 125 g/4½ oz ground almonds
- 125 g/4½ oz flaked almonds

Melt the fats in a saucepan and stir in the carob powder, maple syrup, sweetener and ground almonds.

When the consistency is even, mix in the flaked almonds.

Transfer to a mould and refrigerate.

Score into small squares or rectangles.

Can be grated over Urban Caveman ice cream.

White chocolate

People sensitive to chocolate may tolerate white chocolate better.

Ingredients:
Makes 2–3 chocolate moulds
- 50 g/2 oz cocoa butter
- 1 tsp vanilla extract or seeds from 1 vanilla pod
- Sweetener of choice to taste
- 1 tsp coconut-milk powder (not flour)

Melt the cocoa butter in a bowl over a saucepan of boiling water.

When melted, mix in the other ingredients and pour into chocolate moulds. Refrigerate.

Carob chips

These are useful for adding to Urban Caveman cakes, biscuits, etc.

Ingredients:
- 175 g/6 oz carob powder
- Sweetener of choice to taste
- 75 g/3 oz ghee, butter or coconut oil
- 1 tsp vanilla essence
- Pinch Himalayan salt

Put the ingredients in a glass bowl and place this over a saucepan of simmering water, stirring until melted and dissolved.

Spread the mixture over a sheet of baking parchment and refrigerate until set. Then break up into pieces.

Coconut balls

Ingredients:
Makes about 12-16
- **175 g/ 6 oz desiccated coconut**
- **Sweetener of choice to taste**
- **Enough coconut oil to stick the desiccated coconut together**

Mix all the ingredients together and form into balls. Refrigerate.

Chocolate or carob coconut balls

As for coconut balls (above) but substitute half the coconut oil with melted cocoa butter.

Nut and fruit balls

Ingredients:
Makes about 10-15
- **150 g/5 oz each of dried apricots and pecan nuts, soaked in water**
- **Enough desiccated coconut to coat the balls**

Drain the soaked apricots and pecans and run them through a food processor until a dough is formed.

Shape the mixture into balls and roll in the desiccated coconut. Refrigerate.

Can be kept in the fridge for about a week.

Macaroons

Ingredients:
Makes 16

- **110 g/4 oz desiccated coconut**
- **Sweetener of choice to taste**
- **1 egg**

Pre-heat your oven to 180°C/350°F/GM 4.

Line a baking tray with greaseproof paper/baking parchment.

Mix the coconut and sweetener together.

Beat the egg and stir it into the coconut mixture.

Shape into small balls and bake for 10 to 15 minutes, until golden. Cool on a wire rack and refrigerate.

Savoury waffles

Coconut flour absorbs water, thickening the mixture. If too runny the waffles may break.

Herby yoghurt waffles

Ingredients:
Depending on size of waffle maker, makes around 6 waffles

- 1 tsp onion powder
- ¼ tsp Himalayan salt
- 75 g/3 oz coconut flour
- 2 tsp xanthan gum
- 1 tsp gluten-free baking powder
- 2 eggs
- 2 tbs ghee or butter, melted but not too hot
- 1 x 400 ml tin coconut milk, melted but not hot
- 400 ml/14 fl oz coconut yoghurt (see page 39)
- 1 tbs mixed, chopped herbs – e.g. thyme, marjoram, rosemary, parsley
- Black pepper

Sift the dry ingredients together: onion powder, salt, coconut flour, xanthan gum and baking powder.

Make a well in the centre; pour in the eggs and melted ghee and whisk.

Combine the milk and yoghurt and gradually whisk into the egg mixture until you have the consistency of a cake mix.

Stir in the finely chopped herbs and season with black pepper.

Place some ghee into the waffle iron and switch on to heat (about four minutes, until the green light goes off).

Place the egg mixture (batter) into the waffle iron and cook for about five to six minutes.

Mediterranean waffles

Ingredients:
Depending on size of waffle maker, makes around 6 waffles

- 1 dsp onion powder
- ¼ tsp Himalayan salt
- 75 g/3 oz coconut flour
- 2 tsp xanthan gum
- 1 tsp gluten-free baking powder
- 50 g/2 oz nutritional yeast flakes
- 2 eggs
- 2 tbs ghee or coconut oil, melted but not too hot
- 1 x 400 ml tin coconut milk
- 400 ml/14 fl oz coconut yoghurt
- 1 tbs chopped basil (dried)
- 2 tbs sun-dried tomatoes, chopped
- 10 olives, pitted and chopped
- Black pepper

Sift the dry ingredients together: onion powder, salt, coconut flour, xanthan gum and baking powder.

Make a well in the centre; pour in the eggs and melted ghee and whisk.

Combine the milk, nutritional yeast flakes and yoghurt and gradually whisk into the egg mixture until you have the consistency of a cake mix.

Stir in the finely chopped herbs, tomatoes and olives and season with black pepper.

Place some ghee into the waffle iron and switch on to heat (about four minutes, until the green light goes off).

Place the mixture into the waffle iron and cook for about five to six minutes.

Cheesy breakfast waffles

Ingredients:
Depending on size of waffle maker, makes around 6 waffles
- 1 tsp onion powder
- 1 tsp Himalayan salt
- 75 g/3 oz coconut flour
- 2 tsp xanthan gum
- 1 tsp gluten-free baking powder
- 2 eggs
- 1 tsp tamari or coconut soy-sauce substitute
- 2 tbs coconut oil or ghee, melted but not too hot
- 1 x 400 ml tin coconut milk
- 1 tbs nutritional yeast flakes
- *Optional*: cream cheese (see page 50) to serve

Sift the dry ingredients together: onion powder, salt, coconut flour, xanthan gum and baking powder.

Make a well in the centre; then pour in the eggs, tamari and melted coconut oil and whisk.

Heat the milk and stir in the nutritional yeast flakes until they have dissolved.

Gradually mix this into the egg mixture.

Place some ghee or coconut oil into the waffle iron and switch on to heat (about four minutes, until green light goes off).

Place the batter into the waffle iron and cook for about six to 10 minutes.

Top with the coconut cream cheese, if using, and serve with bacon. Ham, or any other cold meat, would be equally delicious.

Soured cream waffles

Ingredients:
Depending on size of waffle maker, makes around 6 waffles
- 1 tsp Himalayan salt

- 75 g/3 oz coconut flour
- 2 tsp xanthan gum
- ¼ tsp ground nutmeg
- 1 tsp gluten-free baking powder
- 2 eggs
- 2 tbs coconut oil, butter or ghee, melted but not too hot
- 1 portion soured cream (see page 41)
- ½ x 400 ml tin coconut milk

Sift the dry ingredients together: salt, coconut flour, xanthan gum, nutmeg and baking powder.

Make a well in the centre and whisk in the eggs and melted fat.

Gradually combine the soured cream, and finally enough of the coconut milk to make a thick batter consistency. Place some of the ghee, butter or coconut oil into the waffle iron and switch on to heat (about four minutes, until green light goes off).

Place the batter into the waffle iron and cook for about six to 10 minutes.

Prawn and caper waffles

Ingredients:
Depending on size of waffle maker, makes around 6 waffles
- 200 g/7 oz cooked, peeled prawns
- 1 tsp Himalayan salt
- 75 g/3 oz coconut flour
- 2 tsp xanthan gum
- ½ tsp dill
- 1 tsp gluten-free baking powder
- 3 eggs
- 1 x 400 ml tin coconut milk
- 1 tsp lemon juice, freshly squeezed
- 55 ml/2 fl oz ghee or butter, melted but not too hot
- 1 tbs capers

Drain the prawns and lay on a kitchen towel to dry.

Sift the dry ingredients together: salt, coconut flour, xanthan gum, dill and baking powder.

Make a well in the centre and whisk in the eggs.

Gradually combine enough of the coconut milk to make a thick batter consistency.

Whisk in the lemon juice and melted ghee.

Leave to stand for 10 minutes.

Place some ghee or coconut oil into the waffle iron and switch on to heat (about four minutes, until the green light goes off).

Ladle the mixture into the iron when warm and cook for about four minutes.

Open the iron, and add the prawns and capers, pushing them into the batter.

Cook for about one minute, then open the iron and turn the waffle over and cook for a further minute.

Savoury waffles with hot vegetable sauce

Ingredients for waffles:
Depending on size of waffle maker, makes around 6 waffles

- 1 tsp Himalayan salt
- 50 g/2 oz coconut flour
- 50 g/2 oz chestnut flour or egg-white protein powder
- 2 tsp xanthan gum
- 1 tsp gluten-free baking powder
- 2 eggs
- 55 ml/ 2 fl oz ghee, butter or coconut oil, melted but not too hot
- 1 x 400 ml tin coconut milk
- Black pepper
- 1 tbs tamari or coconut soy-sauce substitute
- Diced cold meat, such as ham or beef

Sift the dry ingredients together: salt, coconut flour, chestnut flour, xanthan gum and baking powder.

Make a well in the centre and whisk in the eggs and melted ghee or coconut oil.

Gradually combine with enough of the coconut milk and tamari to make a thick batter consistency. Add pepper.

Leave to stand for 10 minutes.

Place some ghee or coconut oil into the waffle iron and switch on to heat (about four minutes, until the green light goes off).

Ladle the mixture into the iron when warm, and cook for about four minutes.

Open and work cold meat in.

Cook for another four minutes.

Serve topped with vegetable sauce.

Ingredients for vegetable sauce:
- 1 large onion, finely chopped
- 1 celery stalk, finely chopped
- 300 g/11 oz mushrooms, chopped
- 2 cloves garlic, crushed
- Coconut oil for frying
- 2 tsp lemon juice
- 4 tbs vegetable stock
- Salt and pepper
- Freshly chopped parsley

Sauté the vegetables in the oil until softened.

Stir in the lemon juice and vegetable stock.

Season to taste and stir in some of the chopped parsley, reserving the rest for sprinkling on the top.

Sweet waffles

Coconut flour absorbs water, thickening the mixture. If too runny the waffles may break.

Basic sweet waffle recipe

Ingredients:
Depending on size of waffle maker, makes around 6 waffles
- ¼ tsp **Himalayan salt**
- **Sweetener of choice to taste**
- 75 g/3 oz **coconut flour**
- 25 g/1 oz **egg-white protein powder**
- 2 dsp **xanthan gum**
- 1 tsp **gluten-free baking powder**
- 2 **eggs**
- 2 tbs **coconut oil, butter or ghee, melted but not too warm**
- 1 tsp **vanilla extract or seeds from 1 vanilla pod**
- 1 x 400 ml tin **coconut millk**
- *Optional:* **Coconut yoghurt to serve (see page 39)**
- **Enough fresh berry fruits to decorate**

Sift the dry ingredients together: salt, dry sweetener if using, coconut flour, protein powder, xanthan gum and baking powder.

Make a well in the centre and whisk in the eggs and melted coconut oil and maple syrup if using.

Add the vanilla extract to the coconut milk.

Gradually combine enough of the coconut milk to make a thick batter consistency.

Place some coconut oil into the waffle iron and switch on to heat (about four minutes, until the green light goes off).

Ladle the mixture into the iron once it is warm and cook for about six to 10 minutes.

Serve with a dollop of Urban Caveman yoghurt or ice cream and top with fresh berries.

Sweet waffles with yoghurt and hot cherry sauce

Ingredients for cherry sauce:
- **Fresh cherries – stones removed**
- **1 tsp maple syrup or dash Luo Han Guo, stevia or Palmyra Jaggery**
- **1 dsp kuzu**

First make the hot cherry sauce by cooking the cherries in a little water and a dash of maple syrup.

Dissolve the kuzu in a little water and stir it into the sauce until thickened. Keep warm.

Ingredients for Urban Caveman lemon yoghurt:
- **1 tsp lemon juice**
- **1 portion Urban Caveman coconut yoghurt (see page 39)**

Stir the lemon juice into the yoghurt.

Serve the waffle with a dollop of yoghurt and hot cherry sauce poured over the top.

Pineapple and coconut waffles

Ingredients:
Depending on size of waffle maker, makes around 6 waffles
- ¼ tsp Himalayan salt
- 75 g/3 oz coconut flour
- 25 g/1 oz egg-white protein powder
- Sweetener of choice to taste
- 1 tsp gluten-free baking powder
- 1 tsp onion powder
- 2 tsp xanthan gum
- *Optional*: Small piece grated ginger
- 2 eggs
- 2 tbs coconut oil, butter or ghee, melted but not too hot
- 1 x 400 ml tin coconut milk
- 2 pineapple rings, core removed, finely chopped
- 2 tbs desiccated coconut

Sift the dry ingredients together: salt, coconut flour, protein powder, dry sweetener if using, baking powder, onion powder, xanthan gum and ginger, if using.

Make a well in the centre and whisk in the eggs and melted coconut oil and maple syrup if using.

Gradually whisk milk into the egg mixture until you have the consistency of a cake mix.

Stir in the finely chopped pineapple and desiccated coconut.

Place some ghee into the waffle iron and switch on (about four minutes, until the green light goes off).

Ladle the mixture into the waffle iron once warm and cook for about six to 10 minutes.

Lemon waffles

Ingredients:
Depending on size of waffle maker, makes around 6 waffles

- ¼ tsp Himalayan salt
- 75 g/3 fl oz coconut flour
- Sweetener of choice to taste
- 2 dsp xanthan gum
- 1 lemon (unwaxed), juice and zest
- 1 tsp gluten-free baking powder
- 2 eggs
- 2 tbs ghee or butter, or coconut oil, melted but not warm or it may curdle the lemon juice
- 1 x 400 ml tin coconut milk
- *Optional:* Coconut yoghurt to serve (see page 39)

Sift the dry ingredients together: salt, coconut flour, dry sweetener if using, xanthan gum, lemon zest and baking powder.

Make a well in the centre and whisk in the eggs, melted ghee and lemon juice and maple syrup if using.

Gradually combine with enough of the coconut milk to make a thick batter consistency.

Place some coconut oil into the waffle iron and switch on to heat (about four minutes, until the green light goes off).

Ladle the mixture into the iron once it is warm and cook for about six to ten minutes.

Serve with a dollop of Urban Caveman yoghurt.

Fruit and rosewater waffles

Ingredients for waffles:
Depending on size of waffle maker, makes around 6 waffles

- ¼ tsp Himalayan salt
- 75 g/3 oz coconut flour
- Sweetener of choice to taste
- 25 g/1 oz egg-white protein powder
- 2 dsp xanthan gum
- 1 tsp dried cardamom
- 1 tsp gluten-free baking powder
- 2 eggs
- 2 tbs ghee or butter, melted but not warm
- 1 tsp lemon juice
- 1 x 400 ml tin coconut milk
- 50 g/2 oz dried fruits – raisins, sultanas, cranberries, etc
- 2 tsp rosewater

Ingredients for topping
- 1 dsp maple syrup or Palmyra Jaggery
- 1 portion Urban Caveman coconut yoghurt (see page 39)
- Rosewater to taste

Sift the dry ingredients together: salt, coconut flour, dry sweetener if using, egg-white protein powder, xanthan gum, cardamom and baking powder.

Make a well in the centre and whisk in the eggs, melted ghee, maple syrup if using and lemon juice, adding enough coconut milk to make a thick batter consistency. Leave to stand for 15 mins.

Stir in the dried fruits.

Place some coconut oil into the waffle iron and switch on to heat (about four minutes, until the green light goes off).

Ladle the mixture into the iron once it is warm and cook for about six to 10 minutes.

Blend the topping ingredients together and serve, with rosewater drizzled over the top.

Spicy apple waffles

Ingredients
Depending on size of waffle maker, makes around 6 waffles

- 2 tsp ground cinnamon
- ¼ tsp Himalayan salt
- 75 g/3 oz coconut flour
- 25 g/1 oz egg-white protein powder
- Sweetener of choice to taste
- 2 tsp xanthan gum
- 1 tsp gluten-free baking powder
- 3 eggs
- 2 tbs ghee or butter, melted but not too hot
- ½ x 400 ml tin coconut milk
- 2 eating apples, finely chopped and sprinkled with lemon juice
- *Optional*: Urban Caveman coconut yoghurt to serve (see page 39)

Sift the dry ingredients together: cinnamon, salt, coconut flour, egg-white protein powder, dry sweetener if using, xanthan gum and baking powder.

Make a well in the centre and whisk in the eggs and melted ghee.

If using maple syrup, add to the coconut milk.

Gradually whisk the milk and maple syrup into the egg mixture until you have the consistency of a cake mix. Leave to stand for 15 mins.

Stir in the finely chopped apple.

Place some ghee into the waffle iron and switch on (about four minutes, until the green light goes off).

Place the mixture into the waffle iron once warm and cook for about six to eight minutes.

Serve with Urban Caveman coconut yoghurt, if using.

Savoury pancakes

Coconut flour absorbs water, thickening the mixture. If too runny the pancakes may break.

Basic savoury pancakes

Ingredients:
Makes 4

- 2 tbs coconut flour, sifted
- ⅛ tsp gluten-free baking powder
- 2 eggs
- 2 tbs coconut oil, ghee or butter, melted but not too hot.
- 3–4 tbs coconut milk
- Dash tamari or coconut soy-sauce substitute
- ¼ tsp Himalayan salt

Combine the coconut flour and baking powder.

Blend together the eggs, 1 tbs of the fat, coconut milk, tamari and salt.

Mix flours into egg and milk mixture and leave to stand for 15 minutes.

Heat the rest of the fat in an omelette pan or skillet.

Spoon the mixture into the hot pan and cook.

Breakfast pancakes

Ingredients for pancakes:
Makes 4

- 2 tbs coconut flour, sifted
- Black pepper
- ⅛ tsp gluten-free baking powder
- 2 eggs
- 2 tbs coconut oil, ghee or butter, melted but not too hot.
- 3-4 tbs coconut milk
- Dash tamari or coconut soy-sauce substitute
- ¼ tsp Himalayan salt
- Finely chopped fresh parsley

Ingredients for the filling:

- Diced bacon
- Chopped mushrooms
- Coconut oil or ghee for scrambling
- 2 eggs per person for scrambling
- Seasoning

Make the pancakes first:

Combine the coconut flour, pepper and baking powder.

Blend together the eggs, 1 tbs of the fat, coconut milk, tamari and salt.

Mix flour into egg/milk mix and leave to stand for 15 minutes.

Heat the rest of the fat in an omelette pan or skillet.

Spoon the mixture into the hot pan and cook. Keep warm while you make the filling.

Then make the filling:

Sauté the diced bacon and chopped mushrooms in the oil or ghee.

Beat the eggs together and season.

Pour the eggs over the bacon and mushrooms and scramble.

To serve, spoon the egg mixture on to each pancake, fold in half and sprinkle with chopped parsley.

Beetroot pancakes with vegetables

Ingredients for pancakes:
Makes 4
- 2 tbs coconut flour, sifted
- ½ small beetroot, grated
- ⅛ tsp gluten-free baking powder
- 2 eggs
- 2 tbs coconut oil, ghee or butter, melted but not too hot.
- 3-4 tbs coconut milk
- Dash tamari or coconut soy-sauce substitute
- ¼ tsp Himalayan salt

Ingredients for vegetable sauce:
- 1 onion, diced
- 1 pepper, diced
- 1 stalk celery, diced
- 8 mushrooms, chopped
- 1-2 cloves garlic, crushed
- 1 tbs coconut oil, ghee or butter for frying
- 1 tsp mustard
- A little water
- 1 tsp vegetable bouillon powder
- Seasoning

To serve:
- Urban Caveman soured cream (see page 41)

Make the sauce first:

Sauté the vegetables in the garlic and oil.

Stir in the mustard.

Add the water and bouillon.

Season.

Leave to simmer until the vegetables are soft and the water has mostly evaporated.

Then, make the pancakes:

Combine the coconut flour, grated beetroot and baking powder.

Blend together the eggs, 1 tbs of the fat, coconut milk, tamari and salt.

Whisk flour and egg mixtures together and leave to stand for 15 minutes.

Heat the rest of the fat in an omelette pan or skillet.

Spoon the mixture into the hot pan and cook.

To serve, ladle the thickened vegetable mixture on to the pancakes and top with soured cream.

Liver paté pancakes

Ingredients for pancakes:
Makes 4
- 2 tbs coconut flour, sifted
- ⅛ tsp gluten-free baking powder
- 2 eggs
- 2 tbs coconut oil or ghee or butter, melted but not too hot
- 3-4 tbs coconut milk
- Dash tamari or coconut soy-sauce substitute
- ¼ tsp Himalayan salt

Ingredients for filling:
- Urban Caveman liver paté to spread (see page 170)

To serve:
- Mustard
- Urban Caveman cream cheese with chives (see page 51)
- Sliced cucumber
- Bunch watercress
- Sliced tomatoes
- Balsamic vinegar

Combine the coconut flour and baking powder.

Blend together the eggs, 1 tbs of the fat, coconut milk, tamari and salt.

Whisk flour and egg mixtures together and leave to stand for 15 minutes.

Heat the rest of the fat in an omelette pan or skillet.

Spoon the mixture into the hot pan and cook.

Spread each pancake with the liver paté and roll up.

Slice into rings.

Stir the mustard into the cream cheese.

Arrange the sliced cucumber, watercress and tomatoes on a plate and put the cream cheese and mustard mix on top.

Drizzle the cheese salad with balsamic vinegar.

Place the warm pancakes beside the salad and serve.

Salmon and cream cheese pancakes

Ingredients for pancakes:
Makes 4
- **2 tbs coconut flour, sifted**
- **⅛ tsp gluten-free baking powder**
- **2 eggs**
- **2 tbs coconut oil or ghee or butter, melted but not too hot**
- **3-4 tbs coconut milk**
- **Dash tamari or coconut soy-sauce substitute**
- **¼ tsp Himalayan salt**

Ingredients for filling:
- **Urban Caveman cream cheese (see page 50) or soured cream (see page 41)**
- **Watercress**
- **Smoked salmon**

- **Black pepper to season**
- **Fresh dill**
- **Lemon wedges to serve**

Combine the coconut flour and baking powder.

Blend together the eggs, 1 tbs of the fat, coconut milk, tamari and salt.

Whisk flour and egg mixtures together and leave to stand for 15 minutes.

Heat the rest of the fat in an omelette pan or skillet.

Spoon the mixture into the hot pan and cook.

Spread the Urban Caveman cream cheese over each pancake and arrange the watercress and smoked salmon over that, and top with freshly milled black pepper and dill.

Serve with lemon wedges.

Lemon pancakes with trout

Ingredients for pancakes:
Makes 4
- **2 tbs coconut flour, sifted**
- **Zest of 1 lemon, unwaxed**
- **⅛ tsp gluten-free baking powder**
- **2 eggs**
- **2 tbs coconut oil or ghee or butter, melted but not too hot**
- **3-4 tbs coconut milk**
- **¼ tsp Himalayan salt**

Ingredients for filling:
- **1 trout fillet, flaked**
- **Urban Caveman coconut yoghurt to which you have added 1 tsp mustard, black pepper to taste, horseradish (either fresh or dried) and 1 jar of capers in a little of their vinegar to make a sauce**

Steep the trout flakes in the sauce and chill.

Combine the coconut flour, lemon zest and baking powder.

Blend together the eggs, 1 tbs of the fat, coconut milk and salt.

Whisk both mixtures together and leave to stand for 15 minutes.

Heat the rest of the fat in an omelette pan or skillet.

Spoon the mixture into the hot pan and cook.

Serve warm with the cooled trout sauce and season with black pepper.

Pancakes with avocado sauce

Ingredients for pancakes:
Makes 4

- 2 tbs coconut flour, sifted
- ½ lime zest
- ⅛ tsp gluten-free baking powder
- 2 eggs
- 2 tbs coconut oil or ghee or butter, melted but not too hot
- 3-4 tbs coconut milk
- ¼ tsp Himalayan salt

Ingredients for filling:

- 2 avocados
- 1 tbs freshly squeezed lime juice
- 1 small onion, diced
- 2 cloves garlic, crushed
- 1 tsp coriander, ground
- 2 tbs olive oil
- Seasoning

To serve:

- Lemon or lime wedges and freshly chopped parsley, to serve

Mash the avocados in with the lime juice and keep in the fridge.

Chop the onion, garlic and coriander and stir into the avocado with the olive oil and season.

Combine the coconut flour, lime zest and baking powder.

Blend together the eggs, 1 tbs of the fat, coconut milk and salt.

Whisk into the flour mixture and leave to stand for 15 minutes.

Heat the rest of the fat in an omelette pan or skillet.

Spoon the batter into the hot pan and cook.

Spread the avocado mixture over the pancakes and serve with lemon or lime wedges, freshly milled black pepper and chopped fresh parsley.

Sausage breakfast pancakes

Ingredients for pancakes:
Makes 4

- 2 tbs coconut flour, sifted
- ⅛ tsp gluten-free baking powder
- 2 eggs
- 2 tbs coconut oil or ghee or butter, melted but not too hot
- 3-4 tbs coconut milk
- Dash tamari or coconut soy-sauce substitute
- ¼ tsp Himalayan salt

Ingredients for filling:

- 4 gluten-free/grain-free sausages
- Urban Caveman tomato ketchup (see page 327)
- Chopped fresh basil

Cook the sausages and keep warm.

Combine the coconut flour and baking powder.

Blend together the eggs, 1 tbs of the fat, coconut milk, tamari and salt.

Whisk both mixtures together and leave to stand for 15 minutes.

Heat the rest of the fat in an omelette pan or skillet.

Spoon the mixture into the hot pan and cook.

Spread each pancake with the Urban Caveman tomato ketchup and sprinkle basil on top.

Roll each pancake around a sausage and serve hot.

Cheese and ham breakfast pancakes

Ingredients:
Makes 4
- **2 tbs coconut flour, sifted**
- **⅛ tsp gluten-free baking powder**
- **1 tbs nutritional yeast flakes**
- **3–4 tbs coconut milk**
- **2 eggs**
- **2 tbs coconut oil or ghee or butter, melted but not too hot**
- **Dash tamari or coconut soy-sauce substitute**
- **¼ tsp Himalayan salt**

To serve:
- **Finely diced ham from good butcher**
- **Black pepper**

Combine the coconut flour and baking powder.

Dissolve the nutritional yeast flakes into the coconut milk.

Blend together the eggs, 1 tbs of the fat, coconut milk, tamari and salt.

Whisk both mixtures together and leave to stand for 15 minutes.

Heat the rest of the fat in an omelette pan or skillet.

Spoon the mixture into the hot pan and cook.

Sprinkle the ham and pepper on top.

Once cooked, fold the pancake in half and serve hot.

Watercress and cream cheese pancakes

Ingredients for pancakes:
Makes 4

- 2 tbs coconut flour, sifted
- ⅛ tsp gluten-free baking powder
- 2 eggs
- 2 tbs coconut oil or ghee or butter, melted but not too hot
- 3–4 tbs coconut milk
- Dash tamari or coconut soy-sauce substitute
- ¼ tsp Himalayan salt

Ingredients for filling:

- 1–2 tomatoes per pancake, sliced
- Bunch watercress
- 1 portion Urban Caveman cream cheese (see page 50)
- Olive oil
- Himalayan salt and pepper

Combine the coconut flour and baking powder.

Blend together the eggs, 1 tbs of the fat, coconut milk, tamari and salt.

Whisk both mixtures together and leave to stand for 15 minutes.

Heat the rest of the fat in an omelette pan or skillet.

Spoon the mixture into the hot pan and cook.

To serve, fold each pancake in half, filling it with sliced tomato and watercress and top-ping with cream cheese, over which you have drizzled a little olive oil and seasoning.

Sweet pancakes

Coconut flour absorbs water, thickening the mixture. If too runny the pancakes may break.

Basic sweet pancakes

Ingredients:
Makes 4

- 2 tbs coconut flour, sifted
- A little sweetener of choice
- ¼ tsp Himalayan salt
- ⅛ tsp gluten-free baking powder
- 2 eggs
- 2 tbs coconut oil or ghee or butter, melted but not too hot, plus oil for frying
- 3–4 tbs coconut milk
- 1tsp vanilla extract or seeds from 1 vanilla pod

Combine the coconut flour with the dry sweetener if using, plus the salt and baking powder.

Blend together the eggs, 1 tbs of the fat, coconut milk, vanilla extract and maple syrup, if using.

Whisk both mixtures together to form a batter, which may appear thick but this is fine.

Heat the rest of the fat in an omelette pan or skillet.

Spoon the batter into the hot pan and cook.

Fruit and cream cheese pancakes

Ingredients for pancakes:
Makes 4

- 2 tbs coconut flour, sifted
- A little sweetener of choice
- 1–2 tsp ground cinnamon or allspice
- ¼ tsp Himalayan salt
- ⅛ tsp gluten-free baking powder
- 2 eggs
- 2 tbs coconut oil or ghee or butter, melted but not too hot
- 3–4 tbs coconut milk
- 1 tsp vanilla extract or seeds from 1 vanilla pod
- 2–3 apples, diced and drizzled with a little freshly squeezed lemon juice to prevent browning
- Sultanas

To serve:

- Urban Caveman yoghurt or cream cheese to serve (see pages 39 and 50)

Combine the coconut flour, dry sweetener if using, cinnamon or allspice, salt and baking powder in a bowl.

Blend together the eggs, 1 tbs of the fat, coconut milk, vanilla extract, and maple syrup, if using.

Whisk the two mixtures together to form a batter, which may appear thick but this is fine.

Stir in the apples and sultanas.

Heat the rest of the fat in an omelette pan or skillet.

Spoon the batter into the hot pan and cook.

Serve with Urban Caveman cream cheese or yoghurt.

Fruit and ice-cream pancake stacks

Ingredients for pancakes:
Serves 4
- 2 tbs coconut flour, sifted
- A little sweetener of choice
- ¼ tsp Himalayan salt
- ⅛ tsp gluten-free baking powder
- 2 eggs
- 2 tbs coconut oil or ghee or butter, melted but not too hot
- 3–4 tbs coconut milk
- 1 tsp vanilla extract or seeds from 1 vanilla pod

To serve:
- Fresh berry fruits to cover
- Urban Caveman ice cream (see page 44)

Combine the coconut flour, dry sweetener if using, salt and baking powder.

Blend together the eggs, 1 tbs of the fat, coconut milk, vanilla extract, and maple syrup, if using

Whisk the two mixtures together to form a batter, which may appear thick, but this is fine.

Heat the rest of the fat in an omelette pan or skillet.

Spoon the batter into the hot pan and cook.

To serve, stack the pancakes with a layer of ice cream and berries in between each.

Optional: Drizzle maple syrup on the top pancake.

Grape and cream-cheese pancake

Ingredients for pancakes:
Makes 4
- 2 tbs coconut flour, sifted

- A little sweetener of choice
- Zest of ½ a lemon
- ¼ tsp Himalayan salt
- ⅛ tsp gluten-free baking powder
- 2 eggs
- 4 tbs coconut milk
- 2 tbs coconut oil or ghee or butter, melted but not too hot

Ingredients for filling:
- 2 tbs coconut milk
- Juice and zest of ½ a lemon
- 1 portion Urban Caveman cream cheese (see page 50)
- *Optional*: Maple syrup

To serve:
- Grapes

To make the filling:

Stir coconut milk, zest and lemon juice and maple syrup, if using, into the cream cheese.

Refrigerate while you make the pancakes.

To make the pancakes:

Combine the coconut flour, dry sweetener if using, lemon zest, salt and baking powder in a bowl.

Make a well in the centre and whisk in the eggs, milk and 1 tbs of the fat, forming a batter, adding more milk if necessary.

Heat the rest of the fat in a skillet or omlette pan.

Spoon in the batter and cook.

To serve, dollop the cream cheese mixture onto each pancake and serve with grapes.

Strawberry and balsamic vinegar pancakes

Ingredients for pancakes:
Makes 4

- 2 tbs coconut flour, sifted
- A little sweetener of choice
- ¼ tsp Himalayan salt
- ⅛ tsp gluten-free baking powder
- 2 eggs
- 2 tbs coconut oil or ghee or butter, melted but not too hot plus oil for frying
- 3–4 tbs coconut milk
- 1 tsp vanilla extract or seeds from 1 vanilla pod

Ingredients for filling:

- A little sweetener of choice
- 3 tbs balsamic vinegar
- Strawberries – about 10–12, depending on size

To make the filling:

Stir the sweetener into the vinegar, bring to the boil. Simmer for about 15 minutes until reduced and slightly thickened.

Cut the strawberries into quarters and add to the sweetened vinegar. Put to one side.

To make the pancakes:

Combine the coconut flour, dry sweetener if using, salt and baking powder.

Blend together the eggs, 1 tbs of the fat, coconut milk, vanilla extract and maple syrup, if using.

Whisk the two mixtures together to form a batter, which may appear thick, but this is fine.

Heat the rest of the fat in an omelette pan or skillet.

Spoon the batter into the hot pan and cook.

To serve, top each pancake with the strawberry and balsamic vinegar mix.

The Urban Caveman Meals

Breakfasts

Soups and stocks

Starters

Main courses

Side dishes

Sauces and gravies

Desserts

Pickles and chutneys

Breakfasts

Our Paleo ancestors most probably ate one main meal each day, and breakfast may have consisted of the remains of the previous evening's dinner, such as cold meat. They may also have enjoyed any seasonal fruits that were available.

Nuts would have been eaten rarely and do present similar problems to grains as far as digestion and nutrition are concerned. They are also high in polyunsaturated fats so are best not heated. However, I have included a couple of breakfast recipes that contain nuts, simply because they may ease the transition to the Paleo diet and can help fill the gap left by cereals.

Include fat and protein at breakfast to set your blood sugar level up for the day, reduce cravings and keep you going until lunch time – without an attack of the elevensies!

Breakfast energy shake

Quick to make and nutritious, this shake is an excellent start to the day, providing sustaining fat and protein. It is also low in carbs. It can be made up the previous evening, stored in the fridge and taken to work in a flask. Great if you are short of time and need to have breakfast on the hoof! The addition of coconut oil helps you feel full, is good for immunity and increases energy levels. If you find it too fatty, simply reduce or omit the oil.

Ingredients:
- 1-2 tbs undenatured whey protein or egg-white protein powder
- 2 raw eggs
- ½ x 400 ml tin coconut milk or 100 ml coconut cream
- 2 tbs desiccated coconut
- 1 dsp coconut oil, melted if too hard
- Generous portions of fruits (fresh and preferably organic) – strawberry, pineapple, mango, raspberry, blueberry and 1 tbs baobab powder for extra vitamin C
- *Optional*: A little sweetener of choice

Whisk all the ingredients together with an electric handwhisk, or in the smoothie at-tachment of a food processor.

Any leftovers can be run through an ice-cream maker later in the day to make a deli-cious high-protein dessert.

No-fruit breakfast shake

If you are restricting your fruit intake to help regulate your blood sugar, this is a delicious low-fruit shake.

Ingredients:

- 1–2 tbs undenatured whey protein or egg-white protein powder
- 2 raw eggs
- ½ x 400 ml tin organic coconut milk or 100 ml coconut cream
- 2 tbs desiccated coconut
- 1 dsp coconut oil or butter, melted if too hard
- A little sweetener of choice
- *Optional*: Pinch of cinnamon or nutmeg

Whisk all the ingredients together with an electric handwhisk, or in the smoothie at-tachment of a food processor.

Baked egg and vegetable muffins

Ingredients:
Makes six

- 1-2 tbs coconut milk
- 3 tbs nutritional yeast flakes
- 6 eggs
- Green vegetables in season – e.g. broccoli florets, shredded cabbage, diced

- **peppers**
- **Finely chopped onions, lightly sautéed in coconut oil or butter**
- **Cold meat – either diced bacon, or ham from a good butcher, or chicken or beef**
- **1 tbs Urban Caveman mayonnaise (see page 296)**
- **Salt and pepper**

Heat the oven to 180°C/350°F/GM 4.

Place six muffin cases in a muffin tin.

Warm the coconut milk and dissolve the nutritional yeast flakes into it.

Beat the eggs and mix all the remaining ingredients together, seasoning well.

Fill the muffin cases and bake for about 15 to 20 minutes, until set in the middle.

Best eaten warm from the oven, but can be made in advance.

Eggs Benedict

Ingredients:

- **2 eggs per person**
- **Coconut oil, ghee or butter for poaching the eggs**
- **2 stalks asparagus per person**
- **Thinly sliced salt beef or ham from a good butcher**
- **1 dsp Urban Caveman mayonnaise or Hollandaise sauce per person (see pages 296 and 291)**

Place the eggs in an egg poacher with a little melted coconut oil, ghee or butter.

Steam the asparagus and wrap it in one slice of salt beef per stalk.

Arrange these on a plate, then place the eggs on the asparagus and top with mayonnaise.

How to cook the perfect omelette

The recipes mention butter, but ideally you should use fat from a roast, or bacon fat for flavour. To prevent the omelette sticking to the pan, use enough fat to generously coat the pan, and get it really hot. Pour in the omelette mix and cook on high for a few seconds, until the base is starting to firm. Place a plate over the top and turn the heat down to its lowest setting. This way, you cook the top of the omelette without having to grill it, which dries it out, and you also have a warm plate to serve it on!

Savoury omelette

Ingredients:
Serves 4

- 4 onions, chopped into rings
- 2 red peppers, chopped finely
- 8 mushrooms, chopped finely
- Butter for frying
- 8 eggs
- Seasoning
- Dash tamari
- Chopped flat-leaf parsley
- Tomatoes, quartered to serve

Fry the onions, peppers and mushrooms in the butter with a lid on for about 20 minutes.

Beat the eggs in a large bowl and add the seasoning.

Turn the vegetables into the eggs and add a dash of tamari.

Add the parsley.

Pour the egg and vegetable mixture into the pan and fry in the butter. Turn off and cover with a plate. It will cook by itself.

Serve with chopped tomatoes.

Hearty breakfast scramble

Ingredients:
- Butter for frying
- Chopped vegetables – e.g. broccoli florets, sprouts, shredded cabbage, peppers, diced onions and chopped tomatoes
- Diced cold meat (e.g. beef, chicken, or raw bacon, cut into lardons)
- 3 eggs per person
- Chopped fresh chives and/or parsley
- Seasoning

Sauté the vegetables and meat.

Either break the eggs in or beat them first in a separate dish, and add to the vegetables and meat in the pan.

Toss, using two small flexible palate knives or fish slices.

Sprinkle with fresh herbs and season to taste.

Bacon omelette

Ingredients:
- Butter for frying
- 1–2 rashers streaky bacon per person
- Chopped green vegetables
- Chopped spring onions
- Diced tomato
- 2–3 eggs per person
- Seasoning to taste

Sauté the bacon and vegetables in the butter until lightly cooked.

Mix the eggs and seasoning together in a bowl.

Pour the egg mixture into the pan and as soon as the base is starting to form, place a plate over the pan and turn off. It will cook by itself.

Serve on the warmed plate.

'Cheesy' flavour tomato omelette

The nutritional yeast flakes provide a cheesy flavour.

Ingredients:

- **Butter for frying**
- **1 tbs nutritional yeast flakes**
- **2–3 eggs per person**
- **2 large tomatoes, diced, per person**
- **Seasoning**

Melt the butter in an omelette pan.

Beat the nutritional yeast flakes into the eggs.

Add the tomatoes to the eggs and season to taste.

Pour into the hot butter and cook on high before reducing the heat to the lowest setting, allowing to cook for a few minutes.

Then turn off and place a serving plate on top to warm.

Bacon and eggs

This can be a Paleo-inspired dish if you take into account the following:

Only use bacon cured in Himalayan salt.

Fry the bacon in coconut oil.

Set aside to keep warm.

Then lightly scramble the eggs in the bacon fat and serve.

You can soak the bacon overnight in water to remove the sugar that was used to cure it.

Eggy bread

Ingredients:

- 1 egg per 2 slices of bread
- Salt and pepper
- 2 slices of Urban Caveman bread (see page 64) per person
- Ghee, butter or coconut oil for frying

Beat the eggs and season.

Soak the bread in the eggs, getting them completely coated.

Fry lightly, or for longer depending upon how well done you like your eggs.

Can be served with bacon or ham.

Variation:

For a cheesy flavour add 2 tbs of nutritional yeast flakes to the eggs.

Full English

Ingredients:

- 2 rashers of bacon per person
- Ghee, butter or coconut oil, for frying
- Slice Urban Caveman bread (see page 64) per person
- Sliced tomatoes
- Flat mushrooms, chopped
- 2 eggs per person

Fry the bacon and set aside in the oven to keep warm.

Fry the bread in the bacon fat and add to the bacon.

Fry the tomatoes and mushrooms, and finally the eggs.

Arrange on a plate and enjoy!

Full English on the run

Ingredients:

- 1–2 eggs, hard boiled, per person
- 2 rashers streaky bacon, grilled and diced
- 1 tomato, finely chopped
- 1 tbs Urban Caveman mayonnaise (see page 296)
- 2 slices of Urban Caveman bread (see page 64) per person
- Butter or ghee for spreading

In a bowl mash the egg, bacon and tomato into the mayonnaise.

Spread the slices of bread with butter.

Place the mayonnaise mixture on one slice and top with the other.

Wrap in kitchen paper and enjoy!

Trout and scrambled eggs

Ingredients:

- Dried dill
- Salt and pepper
- ½ trout, filleted and opened out, per person
- Coconut oil for frying
- 2 eggs per person

Sprinkle the dill and salt and pepper on to the trout and fry in the coconut oil until cooked.

Set aside to keep warm.

Beat the eggs.

Lightly scramble the eggs in the coconut oil, adding more if necessary to prevent sticking.

Add to the trout and serve warm.

Kedgeree

Developed from Indian cooking during the time of the Raj, this makes a filling and different breakfast.

Ingredients:
Serves 6–8
- 3 eggs
- 650 g/1¼ lb smoked, undyed haddock
- 2 bay leaves
- 3 packets Konjac rice, or florets from 1 large cauliflower, ground in food processor (see page 268)
- 110 g/4 oz ghee or butter
- 1 onion, chopped
- Small piece fresh ginger, grated
- 1 clove garlic, crushed
- 1 dsp medium curry powder
- 1 dsp mustard seeds
- 2 tomatoes, chopped
- Juice of 2 lemons
- Fresh coriander
- 1 fresh chilli, chopped
- Himalayan salt to taste
- Urban Caveman coconut yoghurt (see page 39)

Boil the eggs for 10 minutes and then place in a bowl of cold water.

Put the fish and bay leaves in small frying pan and cover with water. Boil, cover and simmer for about five minutes, until cooked through.

Drain and cool and cut into large chunks.

Rinse the konjac rice and leave to drain or use cauliflower florets instead.

Melt the ghee or butter and sauté the onion with the ginger and garlic.

Stir in the curry powder and mustard seeds and cook for a few more minutes.

Add the tomatoes and lemon juice.

Shell the eggs and cut into quarters.

Stir the fish and 'rice' into the pan and heat gently.

Add the eggs, three-quarters of the coriander and the chilli, stirring well. Add salt.

Mix the remaining coriander into the Urban Caveman coconut yoghurt and serve with the warm kedgeree.

Grain-free breakfast nutmeal

Nuts aren't very high in protein, so have some additional protein with this if it is all you are having for breakfast. This recipe has been included for those having a hard time weaning off breakfast cereals.

Ingredients:
Serves 4-6
- **About 450 g/1 lb mixed nuts – e.g. walnuts, cashews, brazils, pecans, almonds**
- **Enough coconut cream to cover the nuts**
- **1 tsp ground cinnamon**
- **½ tsp ground nutmeg**
- **4 eggs**
- **1 tbs melted butter or ghee**
- **Fresh fruit**

Roughly grind the nuts in a food processor.

In a bowl, cover the ground nuts with the coconut cream to which you have added the cinnamon and nutmeg.

Cover the bowl with clingfilm and leave in a cool place overnight.

The next morning, beat the eggs and stir them in together with the melted ghee or butter, adding more coconut cream if too thick.

If you have a dehydrator, heat the mixture on 135 for an hour, or until warmed. If not, transfer to a saucepan and warm gently, stirring to prevent burning, but do not heat too much.

Pour into a serving bowl and garnish with chopped fresh fruit or berries and eat warm.

Optional: you may like to serve with extra coconut cream or yoghurt.

Knickerbocker glory

Ingredients:
- **Approx 110 g/4 oz mixed berry fruits**
- **Grain-free breakfast nutmeal (see above)**
- **Urban Caveman coconut yoghurt (see page 39)**

Place half the berry fruits in the bottom of a glass and cover with the yoghurt.

Purée the rest of the berry fruits and place in a layer on top of the yoghurt.

Add another layer of yoghurt.

Top with the nutmeal.

Winter warmer stewed apples

This is good for gut health and for soothing an inflamed digestive system.

Ingredients:
Serves 4-6
- **6 cooking apples, diced**
- **2 tsp ground cinnamon**
- **A little sweetener of choice**
- **A little water**
- **Urban Caveman coconut yoghurt (see page 39), to serve**

Add all the ingredients except the yoghurt to a saucepan and stew until the apples are softened.

Serve warm with the yoghurt.

Soups and stocks

In the winter, soups and slow-cooked casseroles are a nourishing and convenient way of eating. Slow cooking more closely represents the way indigenous cultures prepared their meats, and both casseroles and soups optimise flavour and nutrient content. It is worth investing in the largest slow cooker available and a catering-sized soup tureen so that any meals you prepare will last several days or can be frozen for future use. Although you can buy ready-made meat stocks from the chilled meat cabinet in supermarkets, it is quick and easy to make your own and freeze them.

Cooking with bones provides nutrients like glucosamine, collagen and gelatine – all of which are important for strengthening connective tissues such as bones, joints and muscles. If you add a dash of vinegar to the pot, the acid will help draw the nutrients out of the bones.

To avoid the development of bacteria, stock should be cooled quickly before refrigeration. This can easily be done by placing the saucepan in a sink of cold water.

Chicken stock

If you don't have a carcass, just make stock using the other ingredients.

Ingredients:
- 1 chicken carcass (save after a roast)
- Chicken giblets (your butcher will provide these if they are not in the carcass)
- 2 cloves garlic, peeled
- 10 black peppercorns
- 2 onions, quartered
- 1 carrot, cut into large chunks
- 2 stalks celery, broken in two
- Parsley stalks
- 2 bay leaves
- *Optional, if available:* juices from the roasting tin

Place all the ingredients in a saucepan, cover with water and bring to the boil. Simmer for two hours.

Drain stock through a sieve into a jug and leave to cool, discarding the other ingredients. Once cooled, either freeze or add to your recipe.

Turkey stock

Make as for chicken stock.

Beef stock

Ingredients:
- 1.3 kg/3 lb approx beef marrowbones
- 2 onions, quartered
- 2 carrots, chopped roughly into chunks
- 2 stalks celery, broken in half
- 1 bay leaf
- 10 black peppercorns
- ¼ tsp dried thyme

Place the marrowbones, onion, carrot and celery in a roasting tin and roast for 45 minutes on 230°C/450°F/GM 8, basting occasionally.

Transfer to a large soup tureen and add the rest of the ingredients.

Cover with water, place a lid on top and bring to the boil.

Remove any scum that forms and leave to simmer for four hours.

To concentrate the stock, leave a little gap between the lid and the pot to allow the steam to evaporate.

Cool quickly, and remove any fat that forms on the surface.

Drain stock through a sieve into a jug and leave to cool, discarding the other ingredients. Once cooled, either freeze or add to your recipe.

Fish stock

Ingredients:
- 450 g/1 lb fish trimmings from the fishmonger
- 1 onion, quartered
- 2 stalks celery, broken in half
- Parsley stalks
- 1 bay leaf
- ¼ tsp dried thyme or slightly more if fresh
- 1 tsp white wine vinegar
- Seasoning to taste

Add all the ingredients to a saucepan and cover with water.

Simmer for about half an hour, but without a lid.

Drain stock through a sieve into a jug and leave to cool, discarding the other ingredients. Once cooled, either freeze or add to your recipe.

Vegetable stock

Ingredients:

- 1 onion, quartered
- 1 leek, roughly chopped
- 2 stalks celery, broken in half
- 2 bay leaves
- 12 peppercorns
- Parsley stalks
- 1 clove garlic, peeled
- 2 carrots, chopped into chunks

Place all ingredients in a saucepan, cover with water and simmer for about half an hour.

Drain stock through a sieve into a jug and leave to cool, discarding the other ingredients.

Once cooled, either freeze or add to your recipe.

Potassium broth

This is a therapeutic broth which can be taken twice daily during an infection. It helps reduce aches and pains and is also good for fluid balance.

Ingredients:

- 2–3 carrots, washed and unpeeled
- Peelings from about 4 potatoes
- Bunch parsley including the stalks
- 2 onions, quartered
- 2–6 cloves garlic
- Cabbage and any other green vegetables except spinach or asparagus, chopped
- 2-4 stalks celery
- 10 peppercorns
- *Optional, for flavouring*: sea vegetables, such as kelp

Simmer all the ingredients in a large covered pot of water for no longer than 30 minutes. Using a sieve, strain off the vegetables and drink the broth.

Vegetable soup

Ingredients:
Serves 6

- 2 onions, finely chopped
- 1 leek, finely chopped
- 1–2 cups of seasonal vegetables, finely chopped
- Goose fat, coconut oil, butter or ghee for sautéing
- 1–1½ l/1¾–2½ pt meat stock
- 2 bay leaves
- Chopped fresh garlic
- Chopped parsley
- Dash tamari or coconut soy-sauce substitute
- Himalayan salt to taste
- Freshly ground black pepper
- *Optional*: Marigold Swiss vegetable bouillon powder*

Sauté the vegetables in the fat.

Add the stock, boiling water to cover and bay leaves.

Cook for about half an hour.

Add the garlic, parsley and tamari or coconut soy-sauce substitute and season to taste. Add bouillon powder if using.

This can be eaten as it is, or puréed.

* Contains organic vegetables, yeast extract and rice flour. Although not Paleo, a spoonful added to several litres of soup is not going to provide enough rice or yeast to upset the digestion, and it does enhance the flavour.

Tomato and vegetable soup

As for the vegetable soup, but add some chopped tomatoes or a tin of organic tomatoes, and reduce the amount of stock.

Root vegetable soup

This can be made in a pressure cooker.

Ingredients:
Serves 6

- 2 onions, finely chopped
- Coconut oil, goose fat, butter or ghee
- 2 leeks, finely chopped
- 1 swede, diced
- 2 carrots, diced
- 4 stalks celery, sliced
- 2 bay leaves
- 1 l/2 pt meat stock, to cover
- 2 cloves garlic, roughly chopped
- Dash tamari or coconut soy-sauce substitute to flavour
- Seasoning
- Chopped parsley

If using a pressure cooker, sauté the onions in the fat for two to three minutes and then add all the ingredients saving some parsley, and cook as instructed by manufacturer.

If you don't have a pressure cooker, proceed as follows:

In a large saucepan, sauté the onions in the fat for about five minutes.

Add the other vegetables, the bay leaves and the stock.

Cover and cook for about half an hour.

Then add the garlic, tamari, seasoning and most of the parsley, and purée in the food processor.

Check the seasoning and sprinkle with remaining chopped parsley to serve.

Avocado soup

Ingredients:
Serves 4-6

- 200 ml/7 fl oz chicken stock
- 1 tsp Marigold Swiss vegetable bouillon powder (see footnote on page 151)
- 1 l/1¾ pt water
- 2 leeks, thinly sliced
- 1 large, ripe avocado
- 150 ml/5 fl oz coconut cream
- 1 tbs lemon juice
- ½ tsp paprika
- Seasoning
- Chopped parsley

Bring the chicken stock, bouillon powder and water to the boil and add the leeks.

Cook for about 10 minutes.

Blend the avocado flesh in a food processor with the coconut cream and lemon juice.

Add the leek stock to the food processor and purée.

Return to the saucepan and bring to the boil, then add the paprika and seasoning.

Serve with chopped parsley sprinkled on top.

Can be eaten hot or chilled.

Watercress soup

Ingredients:
Serves 6-8

- 2 onions, chopped
- Ghee or butter, for frying, or coconut oil but it gives a less creamy flavour
- 2 white or sweet potatoes, diced
- 1½ l/2½ pt meat stock
- Large bunch watercress
- ½ x 400 ml tin coconut cream or Urban Caveman yoghurt (see page 39)
- Seasoning
- Chopped fresh chives

Sauté the onions in the ghee or butter until softened.

Add the potatoes to the onions, making sure they are coated with the fat.

Add the stock and the watercress and cook for about 15 minutes.

Cool slightly and add the coconut cream.

Transfer to food processor and purée.

Season to taste and serve with chopped chives and a swirl of coconut cream.

Cock-a-leekie soup

Ingredients:
Serves 4–6

- 2 onions, chopped
- 4 leeks, chopped
- Ghee, goose fat or butter, for frying
- 2–3 large potatoes or sweet potatoes, diced
- 1 l/1¾ pt meat stock
- Tamari or coconut soy-sauce substitute or Marigold Swiss vegetable bouillon powder (see footnote on page 151)

- **Seasoning**
- **Spoonful coconut cream**
- **Chopped fresh chives, to serve**

Sauté the onions and leeks in the fat.

Add the diced potatoes and coat in fat.

Add the stock and tamari, cover and simmer for about 45 minutes.

Purée with an electric stick blender or in a food processor.

Season to taste.

Serve with a swirl of coconut cream and chopped chives.

Gazpacho

Ingredients for the soup:
Serves 6

- **250 ml/9 fl oz boiling water**
- **600 g/1¼ lb tomatoes, scored**
- **1 cucumber, diced**
- **3 spring onions, chopped**
- **2 cloves garlic, crushed**
- **Fresh basil, chopped**
- **4 tbs olive oil**
- **2 tbs balsamic vinegar**
- **1 dsp lemon juice**
- **1 pepper, chopped**
- **Seasoning**

Ingredients to serve:
- Selection of diced pepper, cucumber, spring onions and chopped tomatoes
- *Optional*: 2 hard-boiled eggs
- Seasoning
- Chopped parsley
- Lemon wedges

Pour boiling water over the scored tomatoes and then remove the skins. Keep the hot water.

Liquidise the tomatoes, cucumber, spring onions, garlic, basil, olive oil, balsamic vinegar, lemon juice and pepper.

Season and add the water.

Cover and chill in the fridge.

Before serving, stir in the chopped vegetables and egg and check the seasoning.

Serve with the chopped fresh parsley and lemon wedges and two ice cubes floating in each bowl.

Chicken soup

Ingredients:
Serves 10–12
- 1 chicken with giblets
- 3 bay leaves
- 2 leeks, chopped small
- 2 onions, diced
- Dash balsamic vinegar or 1 tsp lemon juice
- 2 large carrots, diced
- 2 stalks celery, chopped
- 1 small cabbage, shredded
- Tamari or coconut soy-sauce substitute, to taste
- *Optional*: Marigold Swiss vegetable bouillon powder (see footnote on page 151)

- **Seasoning**
- **Lots fresh parsley**

Place the chicken in a large cooking pot and cover with water.

Add the bay leaves, leeks and onions, and a dash of vinegar (balsamic has a good flavour) or lemon juice to release the minerals from the bones.

Bring to the boil and simmer for one-and-a-half to two-and-a-half hours, depending on the size of the chicken.

Remove the chicken to cool.

Add the carrots and celery to the water and cook for about 10 minutes. You may need to add more water during cooking.

Using an electric hand blender, purée the contents of the pot.

Once cooled, remove the skin from the cooked chicken, and break off the meat, discarding bones, gristle, giblets, skin etc.

Add the meat to the pot.

Add the shredded cabbage and tamari, and cook for 5 minutes, flavouring with the bouillon if using.

Season well.

Serve with chopped parsley.

Can be frozen.

Greek avgolemeno chicken soup

This is a traditional Greek recipe.

Ingredients:
Serves 8

- 1 chicken
- 6 peppercorns
- Himalayan salt
- 2 bay leaves
- Dash balsamic vinegar or 1 tsp lemon juice
- 2 onions, chopped
- 2 stalks celery, chopped
- 3 eggs
- Fresh parsley
- Ground black pepper

Add the chicken, peppercorns, salt, bay leaves, vinegar and vegetables to a large saucepan and cover with water.

Boil for one-and-a-half to two hours, depending on the size of the chicken, until the chicken is tender.

Remove the chicken and leave it to cool enough to remove the skin and break meat off, setting the meat aside for adding back to the soup later.

Whisk the eggs together in a large bowl.

Add a small amount of the warm (not hot) soup to the eggs and whisk with an electric stick blender.

Continue adding more of the soup until you have puréed about half.

Return the soup and egg mix to the pan and add the meat.

Adjust the seasoning and serve with the chopped parsley and freshly ground black pepper.

Oxtail soup

Ingredients:
Serves 6–8

- Approx 1–1½ kg/2–3 lb oxtails
- Coconut oil or butter/goose fat/ghee, for frying
- 2 onions, diced
- 2 leeks, diced
- 570 ml/1 pt beef stock
- 2 bay leaves
- Dash balsamic vinegar
- 2 tbs tomato purée
- Several sprigs thyme
- Chopped chives
- 2 heaped dsp Marigold Swiss vegetable bouillon powder (see footnote on page 151) or tamari or coconut soy-sauce substitute
- 1 swede, chopped
- 2 carrots, thickly diced
- 3 stalks celery, chopped
- 1 cabbage, shredded
- Seasoning
- Chopped parsley

Sauté the oxtails in the fat in a large soup tureen.

Add the onions and leeks.

Add the stock, bay leaves, vinegar and water to cover and simmer for one hour.

Then add the tomato purée, thyme, chives and bouillon.

Simmer for a further three hours.

Then add the vegetables and seasoning and simmer for another one to two hours, until the meat falls off the bone.

Check the seasoning and serve with chopped parsley.

Bacon and vegetable soup

Ingredients:
Serves 10–12
- Coconut oil, ghee or goose fat
- About 10 rashers bacon, diced
- 2 onions, chopped
- 2 sticks celery, sliced
- 2 carrots, sliced
- Swede or turnip, diced
- 1½ l/2½ pt meat stock (see above)
- 2 bay leaves
- 4 cloves garlic
- Dash tamari or coconut soy-sauce substitute, or Marigold Swiss vegetable bouillon powder (see footnote on page 151)
- Green cabbage, finely shredded
- Seasoning
- Chopped, fresh parsley

Sauté the diced bacon in the fat.

Add the chopped vegetables, except the cabbage.

Pour in the meat stock and add more water to cover generously.

Add the bay leaves and garlic and tamari.

Bring to the boil and simmer for about half an hour.

Then add the shredded cabbage and cook for a further 5 minutes.

Add the seasoning and parsley and serve hot.

Ham soup

Ingredients:
Serves 10–12
- 1 large ham (raw)
- Large bunch mint
- 2 bay leaves
- 2 onions, chopped
- 2 carrots, diced
- 2 stalks celery, sliced
- Chopped, fresh parsley
- Dash tamari or coconut soy-sauce substitute, or Marigold Swiss vegetable bouillon powder (see footnote on page 151)
- Black pepper
- Green cabbage, thinly sliced
- *Optional*: Packet frozen peas (not strictly Paleo as peas are a legume)

Soak the ham in a tureen of water overnight to remove salt, then drain and rinse.

Place the ham back in the tureen and cover with fresh water, add the bunch of mint.

Add the bay leaves and boil the ham for about one-and-a-half hours.

Add the vegetables, except the cabbage, and boil for about 10 minutes.

Remove the ham and mint and leave soup to cool slightly before part-puréeing with an electric stick blender. Add parsley and tamari until stock is slightly creamy.

Add black pepper and check if salt is needed. Add the cabbage and peas and the chopped ham.

You can save some ham and keep it cold in the fridge, if desired.

Beetroot soup

Beetroot helps stimulate the flow of bile, aiding digestion of fats. It also helps to lower levels of homocysteine, a by-product of protein breakdown linked to cardiovascular disease.

Ingredients:
Serves 6

- 2 onions, diced
- 4 cloves garlic, minced
- 1 leek, chopped small
- Coconut, goose fat, ghee or butter to sauté
- 6 medium-sized beetroots, diced
- 1 bay leaf
- 1 l/1¾ pt meat stock
- Seasoning
- Coconut yoghurt for serving (see page 39)
- Fresh flatleaf parsley, chopped

In a large tureen, sauté the onion, garlic and leek in the fat.

After about five minutes, when they are starting to soften, stir in the diced beetroot and sauté for a few more minutes.

Add the bay leaf and stock and bring to the boil.

Simmer for about 30–40 minutes, until the beets are cooked.

Allow to cool and remove the bay leaf.

Purée with a stick blender and season to taste.

Serve with swirls of coconut cream and chopped parsley.

Minestrone soup

Ingredients:
Serves 6

- 1 large onion, diced
- 1 leek, diced
- 2 stalks celery, chopped
- 2 carrots, diced
- 10 rashers bacon, diced
- Coconut oil, goose fat, butter or ghee to sauté
- 1 x 400 g tin organic tomatoes
- 6 cloves garlic, crushed
- Seasoning
- 1 1/2 pt meat stock and extra water if needed
- 1 dsp dried basil
- 110 ml/4 fl oz tomato purée
- 1 cabbage, shredded
- 2 packets konjac or kelp noodles
- Chopped parsley

Sauté the onion, leek, celery, carrots and bacon in the oil.

Add the tinned tomatoes, crushed garlic and seasoning.

Cook for about 15 minutes, stirring occasionally.

Then add the stock and basil and simmer, covered, for about an hour.

Stir in the tomato purée, shredded cabbage and the noodles.

Stir in most of the chopped parsley and check the seasoning.

Serve with the remaining chopped parsley and black pepper. Great with Urban Caveman bread.

Fish chowder

Ingredients:
Serves 4

- 4 rashers bacon, diced
- Ghee or butter for frying
- 2 leeks
- 1 bay leaf
- Fresh or dried dill
- 4 stalks celery, chopped
- 1 swede, diced
- 1 1/2 pt fish stock
- Zest of 1 lemon
- 250 g/9 oz salmon, cut into chunks
- 250 g/9 oz white fish (e.g. halibut, haddock) cut into chunks
- 500 g/1¼ lb raw prawns or shrimps
- 1 x 400 ml tin coconut cream
- Seasoning
- Chopped fresh chives

Sauté the bacon in a little of the fat.

Add the leeks, bay leaf, dill, celery and swede and continue cooking until the bacon is crispy.

Add the fish stock and lemon zest, and simmer for about 10 minutes.

Add the fish and prawns and bring to the boil, simmering for a further 10 minutes, until the fish is cooked.

Stir in coconut cream.

Season to taste and serve with chopped fresh chives and extra dill.

Starters

Rocket and ham salad

Ingredients:
Serves 4

- 1 packet rocket leaves, washed and dried
- Parma ham from good butcher or organic charcuterie online (see Resources)
- Avocado
- Seasoning
- Dash balsamic vinegar

Place the rocket in a salad bowl.

Making sure your hands are clean, tear the parma ham into strips and mix into the rocket by hand.

Slice the avocado lengthways and mix into the salad.

Season and sprinkle a little balsamic vinegar over the top.

Egg mayonnaise

Ingredients:
- 1 hard-boiled egg per person
- Portion of Urban Caveman mayonnaise (see page 296)
- 1–2 tsp mustard
- Seasoning
- Small jar capers, drained
- Bed of lettuce or watercress
- Fresh parsley
- Paprika
- Lemon wedges
- Quartered tomatoes

Cut the eggs in half and scoop out the yolks.

Mash the mayonnaise, mustard and seasoning into the yolks. Stir in the capers.

Place the egg whites on to the lettuce or watercress.

Dollop the mixture into the egg whites.

Decorate with sprigs of the parsley and a little paprika.

Serve with lemon wedges and tomato quarters.

Chicken wings

This recipe can be served cold as a starter or hot straight from the barbecue.

Ingredients:
Serves 4-6
- 1 dsp tomato purée
- 1 tbs olive oil
- 1 tbs balsamic vinegar
- 1 dsp lemon juice
- 1 tsp mustard

- 1 dsp tamari or coconut soy-sauce substitute
- Seasoning
- Chopped fresh sage leaves, or 1 tsp dried sage
- 12 chicken wings
- Parsley, to decorate

Mix the marinade ingredients together and steep the chicken wings.

Refrigerate for two hours.

Barbecue or bake in the oven for about half an hour.

If using the oven, set the temperature to 200°C/400°F/GM 6, but turn down to 170°C/325°F/GM 3 as you put the meat in.

Serve in a basket lined with kitchen roll and sprinkle parsley on the top.

Light fruit salad and mint starter

Ingredients for fruit salad:
Serves 4–6

- Juice of ½ lemon
- 2 eating apples, chopped
- 2 pears, chopped
- Small bunch grapes, halved and with seeds removed
- 2 nectarines, peaches or mangoes, diced and stoned
- 10 strawberries, cut in half
- Fresh mint, chopped

Ingredients for dressing:

- 1 tsp Himalayan salt
- 2 tbs balsamic vinegar
- 6 tbs olive oil
- 4 tbs coconut cream
- Fresh mint

Pour the lemon juice over the apples and pears to prevent browning.

Add the rest of the fruit and mint, cover and refrigerate.

Dissolve the salt in the vinegar and add the olive oil and coconut cream.

Whisk well to form a creamy consistency.

Divide the fruit into glasses and pour the dressing over, and top with fresh sprigs of mint.

Avocado mousse with prawns

Ingredients:
Serves 4–6

- 3 strips unsulphured gelatine
- 150 ml/5 fl oz chicken stock, hot
- 2 avocados
- Juice of ½ lemon
- 2 cloves garlic, crushed
- 150 ml/5 fl oz Urban Caveman mayonnaise (see page 296)
- 150 ml/5 fl oz coconut yoghurt (see page 39) or coconut cream
- Seasoning
- 250 g/9 oz cooked organic prawns
- 1 quantity vinaigrette (see page 301)
- Flatleaf parsley and lemon wedges to garnish

Oil 4-6 serving ramekins.

Soften the gelatine in a little cold water for five minutes.

Discard the water and warm the softened gelatine in a saucepan, stirring until it liquefies.

Transfer to a food processor and whizz together with the chicken stock, avocados, lemon juice, garlic and mayonnaise.

Stir in the cream or yoghurt and season to taste.

Pour into the prepared ramekins, cover with clingfilm, making sure the clingfilm does not touch the mixture, and refrigerate until set.

When ready, remove from the ramekins with a knife and turn out on to serving plates.

Top with prawns and sprinkle some vinaigrette over them.

Season and serve with parsley and lemon wedges.

Smoked mackerel paté

Ingredients:
Serves 8–10

- 2 smoked mackerel fillets, skinned
- 110 g/4 oz Urban Caveman cream cheese (see page 50)
- 150 ml/5 fl oz Urban Caveman coconut yoghurt (see page 39)
- Juice of ½ lemon
- Seasoning
- Pinch nutmeg
- Pinch cayenne pepper
- Watercress
- Lemon wedges

Place the mackerel flakes in a liquidiser with the cream cheese, coconut yoghurt and lemon juice and whizz until smooth.

Spoon into a bowl and season, also adding the nutmeg.

Add more lemon juice if you need to.

Place in ramekins and chill.

To serve, sprinkle on a pinch of cayenne pepper, and garnish with the watercress and lemon wedges.

Liver paté

This is delicious on celery or cucumber, or with Urban Caveman toast (see page 64).

Ingredients:
Serves 6

- 450 g/1 lb chicken or calf livers
- Generous amount of butter, ghee or coconut oil
- 1 large onion, chopped
- 6–8 mushrooms, roughly chopped
- 2 cloves garlic, crushed
- Dash tamari or coconut soy-sauce substitute
- 1 tsp ground mustard
- Dried dill
- Rosemary (dried or fresh)
- Juice of ½ lemon
- Seasoning
- Flatleaf parsley and lemon wedges to garnish

Fry the livers in the fat until nearly cooked.

Add the onion, mushrooms and garlic.

Continue frying until the livers are done.

Add all the other ingredients, except the seasoning, and cook until the lemon juice and tamari have nearly evaporated.

Season and transfer to a food processor.

Process lightly for a chunkier paté and more intensely for a smoother paté.

Serve with chopped flatleaf parsley and lemon wedges, or store in an airtight container in the fridge.

Chunky paté

This recipe requires a slow cooker and a heat-resistant dish for the paté mould.

Ingredients:
Serves 8–10

- 6 rashers streaky bacon
- 4 cloves garlic, crushed
- 1 onion, finely chopped
- Ghee or butter, unsalted
- 150 g/5 oz chicken liver, chopped
- 275 g/10 oz minced pork
- 1 tsp dried mustard
- Chopped parsley
- Chopped rosemary
- 2 eggs, beaten
- 2 tbs tamari
- Zest of 1 lemon
- Seasoning
- Watercress and lemon wedges to garnish

Set the slow cooker to High.

Grease a paté mould and line with half the bacon rashers.

Sauté the garlic and onion in ghee or butter for a few minutes.

Add the liver, pork and dried mustard and cook for a few more minutes.

Stir in the herbs, beaten egg, tamari and lemon zest and season well.

Press the mixture down into the mould, arranging the remaining bacon over the top.

Cover with baking parchment and foil on top, and place in the slow cooker.

Pour boiling water around it and cook on high for five hours.

Remove and leave to cool.

Turn out onto serving plate and garnish with watercress and lemon wedges.

Avocados and prawns

Ingredients:

- ½ avocado per person
- Prawns, cooked and peeled
- Coconut mayonnaise (see page 296) to which you have added enough tomato purée to colour
- Watercress/rocket
- Dash balsamic vinegar
- Lemon, to serve
- Chopped parsley
- Black pepper

Slice the avocados in half, removing the stones, and place on a flat plate.

Fill the centres with prawns, with a dollop of mayonnaise on the top.

Arrange salad leaves next to the avocado.

Drizzle a dash of vinegar over the top.

Thinly slice the lemon and cut through the middle of each slice as far as the rind. Twist and position on the prawns and mayonnaise.

Sprinkle with the parsley and serve with freshly ground black pepper.

Urban Caveman mozzarella and tomato salad

Ingredients:

- 2 packets tomatoes on the vine (Capri are good)
- Spring onions
- Seasoning
- Fresh basil leaves, thinly sliced
- Olive oil
- Tamari or coconut soy-sauce substitute
- Urban Caveman mozzarella rolled into small balls (see page 52)

Slice the tomatoes and spring onions and place in a bowl with salt and lots of black pepper and half the basil leaves.

Place the remaining basil leaves, olive oil and tamari in a jug and whisk well.

Stir into the salad.

Add the mozzarella balls.

Main courses

Pies, pizzas and quiches

Before we start, my general recommendations for this section are:
- If making a sweet pastry, add a little Luo Han Guo, stevia or Palmyra Jaggery to the coconut flour, or maple syrup into beaten eggs.
- If making a savoury pastry, add a dash of tamari to the beaten eggs.
- If the pastry is for a meat pie, you may like to substitute suet for some of the other types of fat I've listed.
- Coconut flour, egg-white protein powder and coconut milk powder are used in place of wheat flour.

Single-crust pastry

Ingredients:
- **50 g/2 oz coconut flour**
- **50 g/2 oz egg-white protein powder**
- **50 g/2 oz coconut milk powder**
- **¼ tsp Himalayan salt**
- **½ tsp xanthan gum**
- **90g/3½ oz butter, cut into little squares**
- **2 eggs, beaten; save a little for painting over the pastry**

Mix the flours, salt and xanthan gum together.

Rub the butter into the flours, either by hand or in a food processor.

If making a sweet pastry, add a little sweetener (see above) to the flour mix.

If making a savoury pastry, add a dash of tamari to the beaten eggs.

Add the eggs and combine all ingredients together well to form the pastry.

Roll the pastry out between two sheets of floured greaseproof paper/baking parchment.

Peel the top sheet of baking parchment off and turn a pie dish upside down over the pastry. The bottom sheet of parchment will provide support as you then flip the dish with the pastry under it back over.

Remove the baking parchment and shape the pastry in the pie dish, covering any cracks or holes. Paint with a little beaten egg.

Prick the pastry with a fork to prevent distortion when cooking and rub water around the edge to prevent burning.

Bake for 12 to 15 minutes at 180°C/350°F/GM 4.

Double-crust pastry

Ingredients

- 110 g/4 oz coconut flour
- 110 g/4 oz egg-white protein powder
- 110 g/4 oz coconut powder
- ½ tsp Himalayan salt
- 1 level tsp xanthan gum
- 175 g/6 oz butter, cut into little squares
- 4 eggs, beaten; save a little for painting over the pastry

Mix the flours, salt and xanthan gum together.

Rub the butter into the flours, either by hand or in a food processor.

If making a sweet pastry, add a little sweetener to the flour mix.

If making a savoury pastry, add a dash of tamari to the beaten eggs.

Add the eggs and combine all the ingredients together well to form the pastry.

Roll the pastry out between two sheets of floured greaseproof paper/baking parchment.

Peel the top sheet of baking parchment off and turn a pie dish upside down over the pastry. The bottom sheet of parchment will provide support as you then flip the dish with the pastry under it back over.

Remove the baking parchment and shape the pastry in the pie dish, covering any cracks or holes. Paint with a little beaten egg.

Prick the pastry with a fork to prevent distortion when cooking and rub water around the edge to prevent burning.

Bake for 12 to 15 minutes at 180°C / 350°F / GM 4.

Steak and kidney pie

Make this using the savoury double-crust pastry described above.

Ingredients for the filling:
Serves 4–6

- 2 onions, chopped
- 1 tbs dripping, or fat from bacon, or goose fat
- 1 tsp dried mixed herbs
- 700 g/1½ lb steak, diced
- 175 g/6 oz ox kidney, diced
- 1½ tsp Worcester sauce (from health-food shops, without sugar or gluten)
- 1 dsp Urban Caveman tomato ketchup
- Seasoning
- 425 ml/¾ pt beef stock
- 1 tbs kuzu or arrowroot
- 250 g/9 oz mushrooms, sliced

Line a pie dish with baking parchment.

Transfer two-thirds of the pastry dough to the dish, using the bottom sheet of baking parchment to support it, leaving a lip of pastry around the edge to which you can attach the pastry topping.

Leave the pastry to 'rest' and make the filling.

Sauté the onions in the fat and herbs.

Add the meats and cook until browned.

Stir in the Worcester sauce and ketchup and season well.

Pour most of the stock into the pan, reserving a little in which to dissolve the kuzu or arrowroot.

When the mixture is nearly boiling, stir in the remaining stock with the blended kuzu or arrowroot.

Stir until thickened.

Add the mushrooms and cover, simmering for about two hours.

Check seasoning.

Pour the mixture into the prepared pastry base.

Pre-heat the oven to 220°C / 425°F / GM 7.

Roll out the remaining third of the pastry on floured greaseproof paper to fit over the top of the pie dish.

Dampen the lip of the pastry in the pie dish and lay the pastry lid on top, making a few dashes in the top to allow steam to escape.

Press the edges down well and flute with a fork.

Bake in the oven for about 30 to 45 minutes, until golden brown.

Slow-cooked suet pudding

Ingredients for the pastry:
Serves 4–6

- 3 eggs, beaten
- 2 tbs suet, melted
- Dash tamari or coconut soy-sauce substitute
- 150 g/5 oz coconut flour
- 25 g/1 oz egg-white protein powder
- 2 tsp xanthan gum
- 2 tsp gluten-free baking powder
- Himalayan salt to taste

Ingredients for the filling:

- 1 dsp arrowroot
- 450 g/1 lb steak, diced
- 225 g/8 oz ox kidneys, diced
- Seasoning
- 1 onion, chopped
- 1 tsp Worcester sauce (from health-food shops, without sugar or gluten)
- Enough home-made beef stock to cover the meat in the pie dish

To make the pastry:

Whisk the eggs into the melted suet in a food processor. Add tamari.

Mix the flour, egg-white protein powder, xanthan gum, baking powder and salt together.

Add to the mixture in the food processor and blend to form a pastry dough. Add water if necessary.

Sprinkle coconut flour onto greaseproof paper/baking parchment.

Place two thirds of the pastry dough on the paper, sprinkle coconut flour on top of the dough and fold the paper over the top leaving room for rolling out. (Coconut flour absorbs moisture so can be flaky and tricky to roll out.) Roll out the pastry. Roll out the remaining third and put aside for the lid.

Generously grease a 1 litre Pyrex bowl – this is important as you need it well oiled so that the pie can be turned out.

Line the bowl with the pastry, leaving a lip to attach the pastry lid.

Preheat your slow cooker to high.

To make the filling:

In a fresh bowl place enough arrowroot to roll the meats in. Season well.

Make sure the meats are well covered with the arrowroot and seasoning and place in the lined pie dish with the chopped onion.

Add the Worcester sauce to the beef stock and check the seasoning.

Warm the stock to almost boiling and pour in enough to cover the meat.

Attach the remaining third of the pastry to the lip and seal well.

Cover with a sheet of greaseproof paper/baking parchment, with a fold down the centre, and cover with foil or Roastcosy. If using foil, secure well with string.

Line the slow cooker with foil, which will help you lift the hot bowl out when cooked.

Place the pie in the centre of the slow cooker.

Pour boiling water to around half way up the sides of the bowl.

Cover and cook for six to eight hours, checking the water level.

Turn out on to a warm plate to serve.

Chicken pie

This pie can be eaten hot or cold.

   Use the savoury double-crust pastry described on page 175.

Ingredients for the filling:
Serves 8–10

- 3 chicken breasts, diced
- 1 tsp ground mace
- ¼ tsp ground nutmeg
- Seasoning
- 450 g/1 lb sausage meat, gluten free
- 6 spring onions, finely chopped
- 1 tsp fresh thyme, chopped /½ tsp dried
- 1 tsp fresh sage leaves, chopped /½ tsp dried
- Zest and juice of ½ lemon
- 3 tbs coconut cream
- 1 egg, beaten

Line a pie dish with baking parchment.

Make the double-crust pasty dough. Transfer two thirds of the rolled-out pastry into the pie dish, leaving a lip around the edges to which you can attach the pastry topping.

Prick the pastry base with a fork to prevent distortion when cooking, and rub water around the edge to prevent burning.

Pre-heat your oven to 200°C/400°F/GM 6.

Place the diced chicken breasts in a bowl and roll them in the mace, nutmeg and seasoning.

In a separate bowl, mix the sausage meat, spring onions, thyme and sage, lemon zest and two teaspoons of the lemon juice.

Pour in the coconut cream and mix together, forming a soft texture. You may need to add a little extra coconut cream.

Place one third of the sausage-meat mixture on to the pastry base.

Then put half the chicken pieces on top and sprinkle with the remaining lemon juice.

Place another third of the sausage meat on the top, followed by another layer of chicken and top with the remaining sausage meat.

Roll out the remaining third of the pastry and top the pie, sealing the edges with water.

Glaze with the beaten egg and make little scores to allow steam out.

Bake for half an hour.

Reduce the oven temperature to 180°C/350°F/GM 4 and bake for a further one-and-a-quarter hours.

Pizza with chicken or ham

Ingredients:
Makes one large pizza

- **Urban Caveman pizza dough (see page 74) and a little coconut flour**
- **Coconut oil, butter or ghee**
- **110 ml/4 fl oz passata**
- **Fresh or dried oregano, to taste**
- **Fresh or dried basil, to taste**
- **Seasoning**
- **Onions, sliced into rings**
- **Garlic, sliced**
- **Pepper, sliced into rings**
- **Mushrooms, sliced**
- **Cold, cooked chicken or ham, chopped into chunks**
- **1 portion Urban Caveman mozzarella (see page 52)**
- **Olive oil and fresh chopped basil leaves to serve**

Pre-heat your oven to 220°C/425°F/GM 7.

Make the pizza base and grease a pizza baking tray with butter, ghee or coconut or olive oil, and sprinkle with coconut flour.

Spread the pizza dough on the baking tray.

Mix the passata and half the oregano and basil together and season.

Spread the passata mix onto the dough.

Arrange the vegetables and chicken or ham on top and sprinkle on the remaining oregano and basil.

If your Urban Caveman mozzarella is hardened, place slices on top. If it has just been made, pour the unset mixture over the pizza.

Bake for about 25 minutes until the cheese has browned.

Serve with drizzled olive oil and chopped fresh basil leaves and lashings of black pepper.

Margherita pizza

Ingredients:
Makes one large pizza
- Urban Caveman pizza dough (see page 74) and a little coconut flour
- Coconut oil, butter or ghee
- 100 ml/4 fl oz passata
- Fresh basil leaves, saving a few to decorate
- 2 cloves garlic, peeled and roughly chopped
- Seasoning
- Cherry tomatoes, sliced
- 1 portion Urban Caveman mozzarella (see page 52)
- Olive oil, black pepper and fresh, chopped basil leaves, to serve

Pre-heat your oven to 220°C/425°F/GM 7.

Make the pizza base and grease a pizza baking tray with butter, ghee or coconut or olive oil, and sprinkle with coconut flour.

Spread the pizza dough on the baking tray.

Roughly blend the passata, fresh basil leaves and garlic together and season.

Spread over the pizza base.

Arrange the sliced tomatoes over the topping.

Place mozzarella on top and bake for about 25 minutes until the top is browned.

Serve with olive oil drizzled over the top, chopped fresh basil leaves and lashings of black pepper.

Sausage pizza

Ingredients:
Makes one large pizza

- **Urban Caveman pizza dough (see page 74) and a little coconut flour**
- **110 ml/4 fl oz passata**
- **Fresh or dried basil, to taste**
- **Fresh or dried oregano, to taste**
- **2 cloves garlic, peeled and roughly chopped**
- **Seasoning**
- **Cherry tomatoes, sliced**
- **1 onion, cut into rings**
- **2–3 gluten-free sausages, sliced**
- **1 portion Urban Caveman mozzarella (see page 52)**
- **Olive oil, black pepper and fresh, chopped basil leaves, to serve**

Pre-heat your oven to 220°C/425°F/GM 7.

Make the pizza base and grease a baking tray with butter, ghee or coconut or olive oil, and sprinkle with coconut flour.

Spread the pizza dough on the baking tray.

Roughly blend the passata, herbs, garlic and seasoning together.

Spread over the pizza base.

Arrange the sliced tomatoes, onion rings and sausages over the pizza.

Place the mozzarella on the top and bake for about 25 minutes until the top is browned.

Serve with olive oil drizzled over the top, chopped fresh basil leaves and lashings of black pepper.

Olive and artichoke pizza

Ingredients:
Makes one large pizza

- Urban Caveman pizza dough (see page 74) and a little coconut flour
- ½ x 400 ml tin coconut cream
- 2 tbs nutritional yeast flakes
- 3 tbs green pesto (see page 306)
- 2 cloves garlic, peeled and roughly chopped
- 1 tsp onion powder
- Fresh or dried basil, to taste
- Seasoning
- Cherry tomatoes, sliced
- ½ small jar capers, drained
- Ham or chicken, diced
- 1–2 artichoke hearts, drained
- Fresh olives
- 1 portion Urban Caveman mozzarella (see page 52)
- Olive oil, black pepper and fresh, chopped basil leaves, to serve

Make the pizza base and grease a baking tray with butter, ghee or coconut or olive oil, and sprinkle with coconut flour.

Spread the pizza dough on a baking tray and pre-heat your oven to 220°C/425°F/GM 7.

Roughly mix the coconut cream, nutritional yeast flakes, pesto, garlic, onion powder, basil and seasoning together.

Spread over the pizza base.

Arrange the sliced tomatoes, capers, meat, artichoke hearts and olives over the pizza.

Cover with the mozzarella and bake for about 25 minutes until the top is browned.

Serve with drizzled olive oil, chopped fresh basil leaves and lashings of black pepper.

Olive and caper pizza

Ingredients:

Makes one large pizza

- Urban Caveman pizza dough (see page 74) and a little coconut flour
- 110 ml/4 fl oz passata
- Fresh or dried basil, to taste
- 3 tbs green pesto (see page 304)
- 2 cloves garlic, peeled and roughly chopped
- Seasoning
- 6–8 cherry tomatoes, sliced
- 1 onion, sliced into rings
- Fresh olives
- ½ jar capers, drained
- Ham or chicken, diced
- 1 portion Urban Caveman mozzarella (page 52)
- Olive oil, black pepper and fresh, chopped basil leaves, to serve

Pre-heat your oven to 220°C/425°F/GM 7.

Make the pizza base and grease a baking tray with butter, ghee or coconut or olive oil, and sprinkle with coconut flour.

Roughly blend the passata, basil, pesto, garlic and seasoning together.

Spread over the pizza base.

Arrange the sliced tomatoes, onion rings, olives, capers and meat over the pizza.

Place the mozzarella on top and bake for about 25 minutes, until top is browned.

Serve with olive oil drizzled over the top, chopped fresh basil leaves and lashings of black pepper.

Chicken quiche

Use the savoury double-crust pastry described on page 175.

Ingredients for the filling:
Serves 8–10

- 1 small onion, diced
- ¼ leek, sliced
- 1 small courgette, sliced and quartered
- Butter, ghee, coconut oil or goose fat for sautéing
- 1 tsp mustard powder
- 2 cloves garlic, crushed
- 2 cooked chicken breasts, diced
- 2 large eggs, plus 1 yolk
- 1 x 400 ml tin coconut cream
- 1 tsp onion powder
- 1 tsp garlic powder
- Nutmeg to taste
- 1 tsp tamari or coconut soy-sauce substitute
- Seasoning

Pre-heat your oven to 180°C/350°F/GM 4.

Make the pastry and bake for 10 to 15 minutes, then remove.

To make the filling:

Turn up the oven to 200°C/400°F/GM 6.

Sauté the onion, leek and courgette in the melted butter, mustard powder and crushed garlic.

Add the diced chicken and sauté then transfer to the cooked pastry base.

Whisk the eggs, including the extra yolk, coconut cream, onion powder, garlic powder, nutmeg and tamari together and season well.

Pour the mixture into the prepared pastry base.

Bake in the oven for about 30 to 45 minutes until golden.

Cheese and tomato quiche

Use the double-crust pastry described on page 175.

Ingredients for the filling:

- 1 onion, diced
- 1 red pepper, diced
- 2 cloves garlic, crushed
- 25 g butter or ghee or coconut oil
- 2 large eggs, beaten, plus 1 yolk
- 1 dsp onion powder
- 40 g/1½ oz nutritional yeast flakes
- 1 tsp tamari or coconut soy-sauce substitute
- Nutmeg to taste
- Seasoning
- 275 ml/10 fl oz coconut cream
- Tomatoes, sliced to top

Pre-heat your oven to 180°C/350°F/GM 4.

Make the pastry and bake for 10 to 15 minutes, then remove.

To make the filling

Sauté the chopped onion, pepper and garlic in butter or ghee.

Mix the beaten eggs, onion powder, nutritional yeast flakes, tamari, nutmeg and seasoning into the coconut cream.

Stir the onions, pepper and garlic into the egg and coconut cream mix and season well.

Pour over the pastry.

Top with sliced tomatoes and a pinch of nutmeg.

Transfer to the oven and bake for about 25 minutes until the top looks golden and the quiche set.

Lamb

Greek-style marinated lamb cutlets

Ingredients:
Serves 4
- 4 lamb cutlets

Ingredients for marinade:
- Bunch fresh mint
- 4 cloves garlic, crushed
- 1 tbs flatleaf parsley, chopped
- Juice ½ lemon
- Olive oil
- 150 ml/5 fl oz Urban Caveman coconut yoghurt (see page 39)

Purée all ingredients, except the lamb, in a food processor making sure you have enough of the mixture to coat all the meat.

Marinade the lamb for at least three hours, or preferably overnight.

Barbecue, fry, roast or grill the lamb.

Lamb marinated in mustard

Ingredients:
Serves 4
- 4 lamb cutlets

Ingredients for marinade:
- 1 tbs white wine vinegar
- 2 tbs olive oil
- 2 tbs mustard

- **1–2 tbs freshly chopped parsley**
- **Seasoning**

In a large shallow bowl combine the marinade ingredients.

Steep the cutlets in the marinade, coating on both sides.

Cover and refrigerate for two hours.

Cook under a moderate grill for about 12 minutes, turning once.

Greek-style lamb kebabs

Ingredients:
Makes 8 kebabs
- **2 onions, cut into eighths**
- **2 peppers, cut into large chunks**
- **8 mushrooms, cut into large chunks**
- **700 g/1½ lb lamb, cut into large chunks**

Ingredients for the marinade:
- **4 cloves garlic, crushed**
- **1 tbs flatleaf parsley, chopped**
- **Juice of ½ lemon**
- **Olive oil**
- **150 ml/5 fl oz Urban Caveman coconut yoghurt (see page 39)**
- **Bunch of fresh mint, stalks removed**
- **Seasoning**

Place the vegetables and meat on skewers.

Combine the marinade ingredients in a food processor.

Steep kebabs in the marinade and refrigerate for at least three hours.

Cook over a barbecue.

Barbecued lamb kebabs with minty yoghurt sauce

Ingredients for the kebabs:
Makes 4 kebabs
- 25 g/1 oz breadcrumbs made from Urban Caveman loaf (see page 64)
- 450 g/1 lb minced lamb
- 1 onion, finely chopped
- 1 dessert apple, peeled and grated
- 1 tbs ground cumin
- Seasoning

Ingredients for the baste:
- 3 tbs olive oil
- 1 tbs lemon juice

Ingredients for the yoghurt and herb sauce:
- 4 tbs olive oil
- 350 ml/12 fl oz Urban Caveman coconut yoghurt (see page 39)
- Zest of 1 lemon
- 4 tbs chopped fresh mint leaves

Mix the breadcrumbs into the minced pork in a large bowl.

Add onion, grated apple, cumin and seasoning.

Refrigerate for one hour.

Meanwhile prepare the yoghurt sauce by whisking all the ingredients together in a food processor. Refrigerate.

Form the mince mixture into balls and place on skewers.

Mix the oil and lemon juice together and brush over the kebabs.

Barbecue for about 12 minutes, turning until golden brown all over.

Serve with the yoghurt sauce.

Barbecued sliced lamb

Ingredients:
Serves 4–6

- 1 boned leg of lamb (your butcher will do this)
- Olive oil
- 3 large onions, cut into rings

Ingredients for the marinade:

- 110 ml/4 fl oz olive oil
- 3 cloves garlic, crushed
- 4 tbs sun-dried tomato paste
- 1 tbs dried oregano
- 5 tbs balsamic vinegar
- 1 tsp Himalayan salt

Open flat the boned leg of lamb in a large dish.

Mix the marinade ingredients together and pour over the lamb, turning it so it is covered all over.

Cover and refrigerate overnight.

Remove from the fridge and leave to reach room temperature.

Brush oil on both sides of the onions.

Place the lamb on a medium/hot barbecue and cook for 20 minutes each side.

Transfer to a carving board, cover and allow to stand for 15 minutes before carving into slices.

Meanwhile cook the onion rings on the barbecue and serve with the lamb.

Fried lamb chops with red onion and braised celery

Ingredients:
Serves 4

- 2 bunches celery stalks, cut in half lengthways
- 50 g/2 oz ghee or butter
- 275 ml/½ pint meat stock
- 2 sprigs thyme, chopped
- 8 lamb chops
- Seasoning
- 1 tbs coconut oil
- 1 large red onion, peeled and finely sliced

Place the celery in a shallow pan with the butter, stock and thyme.

Bring to the boil.

Reduce the heat, cover and simmer for 15 minutes, until most of the stock is absorbed.

Meanwhile place the chops on a chopping board and season on both sides.

Heat the oil in a large frying pan and cook the chops for 10 minutes, turning once.

Add the onion and cook for a further four minutes.

Transfer the lamb and onions to a warm plate.

Drizzle over any juices left in the pan.

Serve with the braised celery. Goes well with mashed sweet potatoes or mashed cauliflower.

Grilled lamb chops with damson glaze

Ingredients:
Serves 4

- 8 lamb chops
- Seasoning
- 2 sprigs rosemary, chopped

Ingredients for glaze:
- 1 jar damson jam (sugar-free)
- 1 tbs balsamic vinegar
- Dash Worcester sauce (gluten- and sugar-free, from health-food shops)

Place lamb on a chopping board, season and sprinkle rosemary on both sides.

Mix the glaze ingredients together and brush over the lamb.

Grill under a moderate grill for 12 to 16 minutes, turning and basting occasionally.

Slow-cooked lamb

Ingredients:
- 2 onions, sliced
- 2 cloves garlic, crushed
- Oil for sautéing
- 225 g/8 oz lamb per person, diced
- 1 tbs kuzu
- Water or stock to just cover the lamb
- Tamari, coconut soy-sauce -substitute or yeast extract for flavouring
- Seasoning
- Rosemary sprigs

Set your slow cooker to Low whilst preparing the meat.

Sauté the onions and garlic in a little oil and transfer to the slow cooker.

Sauté the lamb in the oil and transfer to the slow cooker.

Mix the kuzu with a little water or stock to dissolve it.

Warm the rest of the water or stock in the frying pan and, when almost boiling, stir in the kuzu mixture, stirring until thickened.

Add tamari and seasoning.

Arrange the rosemary in the slow cooker and pour the thickened gravy on.

Leave to cook for four to five hours.

Check occasionally whether any more water or stock is needed.

Serve with mint sauce (see page 297).

Slow-cooked lamb shanks

Ingredients:
- 1 lamb shank per person
- Oil for sautéing
- 1–2 onions per person, sliced onions, sliced
- 4 garlic cloves, crushed
- 1 tbs kuzu
- Stock or water to just cover shanks
- 2 tbs tamari or coconut soy-sauce substitute
- 2 tbs balsamic vinegar
- 1 tbs yeast extract
- Seasoning
- 2 bay leaves, broken in half to release the flavour

Set your slow cooker to Low.

Sauté the lamb shanks in oil, until browned.

Transfer to the slow cooker.

Sauté the onions and garlic in the oil and transfer to the slow cooker.

Mix the kuzu with a little water or stock to dissolve it.

Place the rest of the water or stock in the frying pan and add the tamari, balsamic vinegar and yeast extract.

Once the sauce is almost boiling stir in the dissolved kuzu water and season. Stir until thickened, then pour over the meat and onions in the slow cooker. Add bay leaves.

Leave to cook for eight to ten hours, checking occasionally whether any more water or stock is needed.

Slow-cooked spicy lamb

Ingredients

- 1 lamb shank per person
- 3 tbs coconut oil, goose fat, butter or ghee
- 1–2 onions, chopped
- 2 stalks celery, chopped
- Fresh coriander, chopped
- 2 cloves garlic, crushed
- 1 tsp ground coriander
- 1 tsp ground cumin
- 1 tsp harissa
- 425 ml/¾ pint meat stock
- Juice of ½ orange or 1 lime
- 50 g/2 oz dried apricots
- 1 x 400 g tin sour cherries
- Seasoning
- Urban Caveman coconut yoghurt, to serve (see page 39)

Set your slow cooker to High.

Brown the lamb shanks in half the oil and place in the slow cooker.

Add the remaining oil and sauté the onion and celery.

Chop coriander with the garlic and add to the pan with the ground coriander and cumin.

After a few minutes, add the harissa and stock.

Pour the sauce over the lamb shanks and season well.

Pour the orange or lime juice over the top.

Cook on Medium for one hour then turn down to Low and cook for eight hours.

Stir in the apricots and cherries in their juice and cook for a further one to two hours, until the meat is falling off the bone.

Serve with coconut yoghurt.

Slow-cooked lamb in plum sauce

Ingredients:

- 2 tbs coconut oil, goose fat, butter or ghee
- 575 g/1¼ lb lamb fillets
- 2 tbs Ume Plum Seasoning (similar to vinegar and made from fermented plums. Used in Japanese cooking)
- 1 jar Mirabelle or Meridian plum jam (sugar-free)
- 1 tbs tamari or coconut soy-sauce substitute
- 275 ml/½ pint lime juice and zest of 1 lime
- 1 tbs balsamic vinegar
- 1 tbs kuzu or arrowroot
- Flatleaf parsley and chopped fresh plums, to serve

Set your slow cooker to High.

Heat the oil and sauté the lamb fillets. Set aside.

Combine the plum seasoning, jam, tamari, lime juice, lime zest and vinegar, and heat gently.

Brush over the fillets and place them in the slow cooker, pouring any remaining sauce over the top.

Cook for six to eight hours, until tender.

Keep the fillets warm and transfer the sauce to a saucepan.

Heat and reduce the sauce.

Dissolve arrowroot or kuzu in a little water and stir into the sauce until thickened.

Slice the fillets, drizzle the sauce over them and decorate with sliced fresh plums and flatleaf parsley.

Can be served on a bed of cauliflower or mashed sweet potato.

Slow-cooked ragout of lamb

Ingredients:
Serves 4-6

- 1 kg/2.2 lb lamb, diced
- Seasoning
- 1 tbs coconut oil, goose fat, ghee or butter
- 2 onions, chopped
- 4 cloves garlic, crushed
- 1 tbs kuzu or arrowroot
- 200 ml/7 fl oz water
- 4 tomatoes, peeled
- 2 bay leaves
- 1 sprig fresh thyme or ½ tsp dried
- Either 400 g small, new potatoes or swede, or 4 carrots, cut into chunks

Set your slow cooker to High.

Roll the diced lamb into the seasoning.

Sear the meat in the oil in a frying pan, a few pieces at a time, and place in the slow cooker.

Next, sauté the onions and garlic.

Dissolve the kuzu or arrowroot in a little water.

Pour the remaining water into the onions and garlic and bring almost to boiling point.

Add the kuzu to the water, stirring until thickened.

Place the tomatoes in the slow cooker and pour the sauce over the top.

Break the bay leaves in half and add to the pot.

Add the thyme, and season well.

Cook for one hour then turn the temperature down to Low and cook for a further three hours.

Add the potatoes, swede or carrots, and cook for two hours.

Check the seasoning and serve.

Stewed lamb

Ingredients:
Serves 8
- Leg of lamb
- Goose fat, coconut oil or butter or ghee, for sautéing
- 2 onions, chopped
- 2 leeks, chopped
- 275 ml/½ pint meat stock
- 2 bay leaves
- Vinegar or lemon juice (dash)
- 2 carrots, diced
- 1 swede, diced
- 1 celeriac, diced
- Several cloves garlic, roughly chopped
- Tamari, for flavour
- Large bunch fresh mint

Sear the lamb in the fat in a large roasting tin or stainless steel tureen.

Add the onions and leeks.

Cover with water and stock.

Drop in the bay leaves and add a dash of vinegar or lemon juice to release the minerals from the bone.

Simmer on the hob for three hours.

After three hours, add the rest of the vegetables, tamari and the mint and continue cooking for two more hours. Once cooked, the meat should have fallen off the bone. (Cooking on the bone ensures a high mineral content to the meal.)

Lamb moussaka

Ingredients:
(Serves 4)

- Seasoning
- 450 g/1 lb aubergines, sliced lengthways
- Coconut oil, butter, ghee or goose fat, for frying
- 1 onion, finely chopped
- 2 cloves garlic, crushed
- ¼ tsp ground cumin
- 575 g/1¼ lb minced lamb
- 1 tbs tomato purée
- 1 x 400 g tin tomatoes
- 2 tbs chopped parsley
- 200 g/7 oz Urban Caveman coconut yoghurt (see page 39)
- 1 egg, beaten
- 2 tsp xanthan gum
- 2 tbs nutritional yeast flakes

Pre-heat your oven to 180°C/350°F/GM 4.

Sprinkle salt over the aubergines and leave for about 15 minutes.

Rinse the salt off and pat dry.

Melt the fat and sauté the onion and garlic for a few minutes.

Add the cumin and mince and cook for about 10 minutes.

Stir in the tomato purée and tinned tomatoes, and season well.

Bring to the boil, reduce the heat, cover and simmer for 10 to 15 minutes.

Add the parsley.

Arrange half the aubergines on the bottom of an ovenproof dish and spoon over half the mince mixture. Repeat.

Blend together the yoghurt, egg, xanthan gum and nutritional yeast flakes.

Warm gently in a saucepan until the mixture thickens.

Pour over the mince and aubergines in the ovenproof dish.

Bake for 40 minutes, or until the top is brown.

Scandinavian stuffed lamb with apricots

Ingredients for stuffing:

Serves 6

- **Rack of lamb, boned**

Ingredients for stuffing:

- **2 stalks celery, finely chopped**
- **75 g/3 oz dried apricots**
- **30 mint leaves**
- **2 cloves garlic, chopped**
- **Seasoning**

Ingredients for spinach:

- **50 g/2 oz butter or ghee**
- **½ tsp nutmeg**
- **3 kg/9 lb spinach leaves**

Ingredients for potatoes:

- **1 kg/2.2 lb new potatoes, sliced**
- **3 sprigs mint**
- **Butter, ghee, goose fat or coconut oil, for frying**

Pre-heat your oven to 200°C/400°F/GM 6.

Mix the celery, apricots, mint, garlic and seasoning together.

Lay the lamb out on a chopping board, spread the stuffing mixture over it and fold so that the two sides meet. Tie with string.

Transfer to a roasting tin and season.

Roast for one hour and 20 minutes.

Boil the potatoes with one mint sprig in salted water until tender. Drain well.

Pick the leaves from the remaining mint sprigs and fry potatoes and mint in the butter. Season.

Melt more butter and add the nutmeg.

Sauté the spinach lightly, and season. Do not over-cook.

To serve, carve the lamb into slices and arrange over the spinach, and arrange the potatoes.

Roast lamb

Ingredients:

Serves 6

- **Leg or shoulder of lamb**
- **2 small onions**
- **1 large carrot**
- **2 stalks celery**
- **8 whole cloves garlic**
- **Seasoning**

Pre-heat your oven to 230°C/450°F/GM 8.

Roast lamb for half an hour covered with a Roastcosy or tin foil.

Turn the heat down to 180°C/350°F/GM 4, remove the Roastcosy and cook for an additional half an hour per 450 g/lb.

After about one hour, remove the joint from the oven and place it on a plate. Arrange the onions, carrot, celery and garlic on the roasting tray and place the joint on top.

Return to the oven and complete roasting, for 10 minutes for rare, 20 minutes for medium, 25-30 for well done.

(See page xxx for my gravy recipe using the roasted vegetables.)

Stuffed breast of lamb

Ingredients:
Serves 4

- 50 g/2 oz breadcrumbs from the Urban Caveman loaf
- 1 onion, chopped
- 1 tbs fresh parsley, chopped
- 1 tbs fresh mint leaves, chopped
- ½ tsp ground nutmeg
- 1 tsp rosemary, dried
- Zest of ½ lemon
- Seasoning
- 1 egg, beaten
- 1 large breast of lamb
- Sugar-free redcurrant jelly, to serve

Pre-heat your oven to 180°C/350°F/GM 4.

Place the breadcrumbs, onion, parsley, mint, nutmeg, rosemary and lemon zest in a bowl and mix them together.

Season well and stir in the egg.

Spread the stuffing mix over the breast of lamb.

Roll it up and secure with three pieces of string, tucking the ends over.

Place the stuffed lamb in a roasting tin and cover loosely with baking parchment, topped with foil.

Cook for one-and-a-half hours, then remove the covering and baste.

Return to the oven for a further half hour to brown.

Serve cut into slices with mint sauce or redcurrant jelly.

Chicken

The chicken you cook should not only be free-range and organic, but also pasture-fed to ensure it contains all the vitamins you need. Factory-reared chickens often contain water to make them look bigger, but shrink when cooked. This is a method of selling younger chickens which are cheaper to produce but lower in nutrients.

Chicken in satay sauce

This recipe contains nuts.

Ingredients:
- 1 chicken breast per person, cut into strips or diced
- Coconut oil, butter or ghee, for frying
- 1 jar almond or cashew butter
- 1 tsp curry paste
- 1 tsp paprika
- 2–3 cloves garlic, crushed
- 1 x 400 ml tin coconut cream

Fry the chicken in the coconut oil.

Skewer the chicken and keep warm on a low oven.

Warm the nut butter, curry paste, paprika, garlic and coconut cream in a saucepan, reduce and simmer for about 10 minutes.

Serve over chicken.

Stir-fried chicken or beef

Ingredients:

- 1 onion per person, sliced
- 1 tsp ground ginger or small piece fresh ginger, grated
- 6 cloves garlic, sliced
- Coconut oil, butter or ghee for frying
- Strips of beef or chicken (about one chicken breast or small steak per person)
- 1 carrot per person, sliced into sticks
- 2 stalks celery per person, sliced into sticks
- Broccoli, cut into florets
- 1–2 peppers, sliced
- 3 mushrooms per person, sliced
- Tamari or coconut soy-sauce substitute
- 2–3 bok choi or 1 cabbage, shredded
- Konjac rice or grated cauliflower (see page 268), to serve

Sauté the onion, ginger and garlic in the coconut oil.

Stir fry the meat until cooked. Transfer it to a plate and keep it warm.

Next fry all the vegetables apart from the bok choi or cabbage, adding a little water if necessary.

Add the tamari or coconut soy-sauce substitute to flavour, return the meat to the wok and mix in well.

Just before serving, stir in the bok choi or cabbage.

Serve hot over rice.

Fried chicken with lemon and coconut cream

Ingredients:

- Seasoning
- Garlic salt to taste
- 1 chicken breast per person
- Coconut oil
- 6–8 cloves garlic, roughly chopped
- 1–2 onions, chopped
- Juice and zest of 1 lemon
- 1 tsp Madras curry powder
- 1–2 x 400 ml tins coconut cream
- 2 bay leaves
- Fresh coriander

Set your slow cooker to Low.

Mix salt, pepper and garlic salt together in a bowl.

Dip the chicken breasts in and cover each with seasoning.

Fry them in the coconut oil and transfer to the slow cooker.

Add the garlic cloves to the chicken.

Fry the onions in the coconut oil.

Add the lemon juice, zest and curry powder to the onions and cook together until the onion is tender.

Add the coconut cream and bay leaves and bring almost to the boil.

Transfer the mixture to the slow cooker and cook for about three hours. Serve sprinkled with chopped coriander.

Chicken (or veal) schnitzel

Ingredients:

- Paprika or other seasoning, like Cajun or similar
- Ground onion powder to taste
- Garlic powder to taste
- Desiccated coconut as a breadcrumb substitute
- Seasoning
- 1 chicken breast or veal steak per person, cut into strips
- 1 beaten egg for 2–3 chicken breasts
- Coconut oil for frying
- Approx 1 tsp wholegrain mustard (wheat-free, sugar-free)

Mix the paprika, onion powder and garlic powder into the desiccated coconut and season generously.

Dip strips of chicken breast in the beaten egg and then into the seasoned desiccated coconut.

Sauté in coconut oil until cooked through.

Stir the mustard into a *little* water and warm over a gentle heat. For more nutrition, you could use the water under which you steamed any accompanying vegetables.

Serve the schnitzels with the hot mustard sauce.

Sweet and sour chicken

Ingredients:

- 1 chicken breast per person, diced
- Coconut oil
- 2 onions, sliced
- 2 peppers, sliced

Ingredients for the sauce:

- 3 tbs balsamic vinegar
- 1-2 tbs maple syrup
- 1 tbs tomato purée
- 2 tbs tamari or coconut soy-sauce substitute
- 450 g/1 lb tinned crushed pineapple
- 2 dsp kuzu to thicken

Sauté the chicken in coconut oil until browned.

Place in a saucepan or your slow cooker set to Low.

Sauté the onions and add them to the chicken.

Add the sliced peppers.

Whisk all the sauce ingredients together, except the kuzu.

Dissolve the kuzu in a little cold water.

Heat the sauce until nearly boiling and add the kuzu mixture, stirring continuously until the mix has thickened and darkened.

Pour the sauce over the chicken and vegetables and leave in the slow cooker for three to five hours.

If you don't have a slow cooker, simmer on a low heat for about an hour.

This sweet and sour chicken is great served with stir-fried vegetables and konjac rice.

Slow-cooked chicken hot pot

Ingredients:
Serves 4

- 500 g/1¼ lb chicken thighs, skinned
- Coconut or goose fat for frying
- Butter or ghee for topping
- 2 onions, chopped
- 4 cloves garlic, crushed
- 1 tsp dried mixed herbs
- 450 g/1 lb potatoes or sweet potatoes, sliced thinly
- 2 carrots, sliced
- 2 parsnips, sliced
- 4 stalks celery, sliced
- Seasoning
- 570 ml/1 pt chicken stock
- Parsley, to garnish

Set your slow cooker to High.

Sauté the chicken in some of the fat.

Transfer to a plate and keep warm.

Next, sauté the onion, garlic and herbs in the fat in which you cooked the chicken.

Arrange a layer of potato in the bottom of the slow cooker's crock pot, top with a layer of carrot, parsnip and celery and season.

Place the chicken thighs on top.

Repeat the layering, finishing with sliced potatoes on top.

Bring the stock to the boil and pour over the chicken and vegetables.

Cook for three hours on high.

Reduce the setting to Low and cook for a further three to six hours.

Remove the lid and top with melted butter and grill until golden.

Slow-cooked garlic chicken

Ingredients:
Serves 4-6
- **1 chicken**
- **50 cloves of garlic**
- **Butter or ghee**
- **3-5 sage leaves, finely sliced**
- **Seasoning**

Set your slow cooker to High and spread its crock pot with butter or ghee.

Wash the chicken and insert 20 garlic cloves under the skin of the breasts.

Heat the ghee in a large frying pan and brown the chicken on both sides.

Transfer to the slow cooker and pour the fat from the frying pan over the top, adding more butter or ghee so the bird cooks in fat.

Place the chopped sage leaves and remaining garlic cloves on and around the chicken.

Season well.

Leave to cook for four to five hours, depending on the size of the chicken.

Slow-cooked chicken in tangy tomato sauce

Ingredients:
Serves 4-6

- 4–6 chicken breasts, cut into large chunks
- Oil for frying
- 2 onions, chopped
- Sun-dried tomatoes – amount to taste - chopped
- 1 x 400 g tin chopped tomatoes
- 4–6 cloves garlic, chopped
- 1 bouquet garni
- Chopped fresh basil leaves
- Chopped coriander
- Seasoning

Set your slow cooker to High.

Sauté the chicken in the oil and, when browned, transfer to the slow cooker.

Sauté the onions, adding more oil if necessary.

Add the chopped sun-dried tomatoes and tinned tomatoes to the onions and bring to the boil.

Place the chopped garlic, bouquet garni and herbs in the slow cooker with the chicken.

Season the tomato sauce and pour over the chicken in the slow cooker.

Cook for one hour and then turn down to Low and leave for around four hours.

You can add boiling water if necessary during cooking to ensure a good stock.

Serve with extra chopped fresh basil or coriander.

Chicken in lemon sauce

Ingredients:

- 75 g/3 oz butter or ghee, or coconut oil for a less creamy flavour
- 2 cloves garlic, crushed
- Seasoning

- Juice of ½ lemon
- 1 chicken, preferably with giblets for the stock
- 2 whole lemons

Ingredients for the sauce:
- 50 g/2 oz ghee or butter
- 175 ml/⅓ pint chicken stock, made with the giblets (see recipe or can be bought ready-made from some supermarkets, but don't use cubes!)
- 1 tbs kuzu
- Juice and zest of 1 lemon
- ½ x 400 ml tin coconut cream
- 2 stalks lemongrass
- Shredded cabbage or courgette spaghetti or cauliflower rice (see page 268), to serve

Pre-heat your oven to 200°C/400°F/GM 6.

Mix the butter or ghee with garlic, salt, pepper and the lemon juice.

Spread over the chicken.

Quarter the lemons and place inside the chicken.

Cover with Roastcosy or baking parchment and foil.

Roast for about half an hour, and then remove the Roastcosy/parchment and foil.

Return to the oven and cook for a further hour or so, basting regularly, until juices run clear.

Leave aside so the juices can settle.

Melt the ghee or butter to make the sauce.

Add the stock, reserving a little in which to dissolve the kuzu, lemon juice and zest.

Whilst the sauce is coming to the boil, dissolve the kuzu, lemon juice and zest in the remaining stock.

Add to the pan, stirring continuously until the sauce thickens.

Simmer for a couple of minutes then stir in the coconut cream and any juices from the roasting tin, together with the lemongrass.

Serve the chicken on a bed of shredded cabbage, courgette spaghetti or cauliflower rice and pour the sauce over the top.

Roast chicken with stuffing and gravy

Ingredients:

Serves 4–6

- Ghee, butter or coconut oil
- 1–2 sweet potatoes
- 1 carrot
- 2 stalks celery
- 1 onion, cut roughly
- 8 cloves garlic, in their skins
- Seasoning
- 1 chicken, preferably with giblets
- *Optional:* Streaky bacon strips
- *Optional:* Sweet potatoes and parsnips for roasting

Ingredients for the stuffing (can be made in advance):

- 300 g/11 oz pork sausage meat (gluten-free). (A good butcher will make this for you – you can even provide the Himalayan salt.)
- 1 large onion, finely chopped
- Either 50 g/2 oz breadcrumbs made from an Urban Caveman loaf, or 50 g/2 oz ground hazelnuts
- Bunch fresh sage leaves, chopped finely or 1 dsp dried sage
- Seasoning

Pre-heat your oven to 200°C/400°F/GM 6.

Place the roasting tin in the oven with the ghee, butter or coconut oil in it, to melt.

Once melted, arrange the sweet potatoes, carrot, celery, onion and garlic in the roasting tin to sit under the chicken.

Place the chicken on the vegetables and, if using bacon, lay strips over the chicken.

Place in the oven and turn oven down immediately to 180°C/350°F/GM 4 and roast for about 30 to 50 minutes, basting occasionally.

Meanwhile, if roasting potatoes, scrub them well and par-boil them in salted water for 10 minutes (not necessary if using sweet potatoes). Then strain through a sieve and shake well to fluff them up.

About one hour before the chicken is due to be ready, arrange the potatoes around it, making sure they are covered in fat. Return the roasting tin to the oven.

Turn the oven down to 150ºC/300ºF/GM 2 and roast for about one hour and 15 minutes, basting until the skin is brown and crispy. To test whether the chicken is cooked, insert a skewer. Juices should run clear.

Once cooked, place the chicken on a serving dish and allow the juices to settle for about 10 minutes whilst you make the gravy. This is the time to steam any accompanying vegetables.

If the potatoes are not crispy, leave them in the roasting tin and return it to the oven, turning the temperature up to 180ºC/350ºF/GM 4, and brown them for about 10 minutes.

To make the gravy:

Remove the vegetables (apart from the potatoes) from the roasting tin and transfer to a large saucepan with some of the juices from the roasting tin.

Warm the vegetables in the cooking juices with the giblets.

Dissolve 1 tbs kuzu in a little water.

Add the water from any green vegetables you have steamed to accompany the meat to the vegetables and giblets and bring to the boil, stirring occasionally.

Simmer for about 15 minutes, until the giblets are cooked.

Add the kuzu water and stir until thickened.

Purée in a food processor.

Check the seasoning and transfer to a gravy boat to serve with the chicken.

Stuffing:

The stuffing can be made in advance and refrigerated.

In a large bowl, mix all the stuffing ingredients together.

Take some fat from the roasting chicken, adding more if needed, and place this in a small rectangular or square roasting tin.

About half an hour before the end of cooking time for the chicken, place the tin in the oven to get the fat nice and hot. Then flatten the stuffing mix down in the roasting tin and return to the oven. It is ready when it has a crispy, brown topping.

Divide into portions.

Serve slices of chicken with stuffing, roast potatoes and gravy.

Roast chicken with coriander dipping sauce

Ingredients:
Serves 4–6

- Ghee, butter or coconut oil
- 1 chicken
- Ground cumin and paprika to taste
- Seasoning
- Coriander sauce (see page 294)

Pre-heat your oven to 200°C/400°F/GM 6.

Rub the fat on the chicken and sprinkle with ground cumin and paprika and season.

Place in the oven and turn down immediately to 180°C/350°F/GM 4 and roast, basting occasionally, for about 20 minutes.

Turn the oven down further to 150°C/300°F/GM 2 and roast for about one hour and 10 minutes, until the skin is brown and crispy and the chicken is well cooked.

Remove from the oven and let the juices settle for about 10 minutes before carving.

Serve hot with cold coriander sauce.

Braised Thai chicken curry in coconut cream

Ingredients:
Serves 4–6

- Coconut oil for frying
- 2 onions, chopped
- Freshly grated ginger – about 1 dsp, according to taste
- 6–8 cloves garlic, crushed
- 2 peppers, chopped
- 2–3 red chilli peppers, chopped small
- 3 carrots, sliced into thin sticks
- 2 stalks celery, sliced into thin sticks

- 1 tsp Thai curry paste (sugar- and additive-free)
- Zest and juice of 1 lime
- 2 x 400 ml tins coconut cream
- 4–6 chicken breasts, diced into large chunks
- Seasoning
- Coriander, freshly chopped to serve
- *Optional rice substitutes*: konjac rice or cauliflower rice, ground raw in a food processor and lightly steamed or sautéed in butter and seasoning, to serve

Melt the coconut oil and add the chopped onion, grated ginger and garlic. Sauté for about five minutes.

Add the rest of the vegetables and stir fry.

Stir in the Thai paste and the lime zest and juice.

Add the coconut cream and the diced chicken.

Cover and cook for about 20 minutes, until the chicken is tender.

Season and serve with coriander leaves and the rice substitute.

Roasted chicken rolls with creamy sauce

Ingredients:
Serves 4–6

- Bacon or goose fat for roasting
- 1 chicken breast per person
- Tomato pesto (see page 304)
- 1 slice Parma ham (from good butcher or organic charcuterie) for each chicken breast

Ingredients for the sauce:
- 1 tsp bacon or goose fat
- 1 onion, finely chopped
- 1 jar hazelnut butter
- Juice of ½ lime
- 1 x 400 ml tin coconut cream
- 2 tsp tamari or coconut soy-sauce substitute

Pre-heat your oven to 150°C / 300°F / GM 2.

Warm the bacon or goose fat in a roasting tin.

Slice the chicken breasts through the middle so that they open up and spread the pesto on them.

Roll them up and wrap a slice of parma ham round the outside then skewer to hold in place.

Bake for about 50 minutes.

To make the sauce.

Meanwhile melt the fat and sauté the onion.

Drain the oil out of the hazelnut butter and stir the butter into the onion together with the lime juice and coconut cream.

Heat gently, stirring, and add the tamari or coconut soy-sauce substitute.

Serve warm alongside the chicken rolls.

Chicken strips

These are good for lunchboxes.

Ingredients:
- Seasoning
- Bacon fat from cooking bacon, melted
- 1 chicken breast per person, cut into strips

Pre-heat your oven to 150°C/300°F/GM 2.

Generously season the melted bacon fat.

Steep the chicken strips in melted bacon fat and add more seasoning if necessary.

Roast in the oven for 30 to 40 minutes.

Cool in the fridge and serve over salad.

Chicken Caesar salad

Ingredients:
Serves 6

- 1 whole chicken, cooked and now cold
- 1 whole lettuce, preferably cos or similar, chopped
- 2 avocados, diced
- 2 sticks of celery, sliced
- Any other fresh leaves if desired

Ingredients for the dressing:

- Approximately 300–400 ml extra virgin olive oil (as coconut oil hardens) depending on how runny you want the mayonnaise
- Fresh garlic, chopped
- Fresh basil leaves (lots!)
- 2 tbs coconut oil
- Lemon juice, freshly squeezed
- 1 tsp home-made mayonnaise (see page 296)
- 1 heaped tsp puréed anchovies from either a jar or tube
- 250 g/9 oz pine nuts, ground to fine powder in a coffee grinder
- Black pepper
- Curly-leaf parsley, chopped, to serve

Purée the pesto ingredients in a food processor until a creamy consistency is formed.

Break the meat off the chicken and arrange in a bowl with the lettuce, avocado and celery.

Stir in the pesto dressing and serve with lashings of black pepper and parsley.

Duck

Roast duck

Ingredients:
Serves 2–3
- 1 duck, with giblets
- Seasoning
- Bunch watercress to serve

Ingredients for the sauce:
- 2 small Seville oranges
- 1 dsp kuzu
- 275 ml/10 fl oz duck stock made from the giblets (see recipe for chicken stock page 147)
- Sweetener of choice
- 4 tbs red wine vinegar
- Seasoning

Pre-heat your oven to 220°C/425°F/GM 7.

Place the duck in a roasting tin and prick to allow fat to escape during cooking.

Season well and place in the oven for 20 minutes.

Reduce the heat to 180°C/350°F/GM 4 and leave to cook for three hours, periodically getting rid of the fat.

Reserve some of the fat for any potatoes you may be roasting to accompany the duck.

Remove from the oven and open the skin to allow more fat to drain away.

Place on a wire rack over a baking tin and after five minutes, carve into portions.

Pour the fat out of the roasting tin so that the tin can be used to make the sauce.

To make the sauce:

Using a peeler or fine grater, remove the zest from the oranges.

Blanch the zest for five minutes in boiling water and strain.

Squeeze the juice from the oranges.

Dissolve the kuzu in a little of the orange juice.

Pour the stock into the roasting tin over a low heat.

As it comes to the boil, stir in the kuzu juice and the sweetener.

After it has thickened, stir in the remaining orange juice, red wine vinegar and zest.

Season and serve hot with the duck, garnished with watercress.

Slow-cooked duck with cherries

Ingredients:
Serves 2–3

- 1 oven-ready duck
- 1 onion, cut into wedges
- 1 apple, cut into wedges
- Ghee, butter, goose fat or coconut oil for frying
- 1 x 400 ml tin sour cherries (from health-food shops)
- 1 tbs balsamic vinegar
- 1 tbs kuzu or arrowroot
- Seasoning
- Fresh cherries and rocket or watercress, to serve

Set the slow cooker to High and allow to warm.

Prick the skin of the duck with a fork.

Rinse and pat dry with kitchen roll.

Place the onion and apple wedges inside the duck.

Brown in the melted ghee, butter, goose fat or coconut oil.

Transfer to the slow cooker, cover and cook for three hours.

Drain off the fat.

Drain the cherries, reserving the juice.

Add enough water to the juice to make up to 300 ml / 11 fl oz.

Stir in the vinegar and bring the juice to the boil.

Dissolve the kuzu or arrowroot in a little water and stir into the boiling juice.

Stir until the sauce thickens, season, and add the cherries.

Pour over the duck and cook for a further one to two hours turning the setting down to Low.

Serve garnished with the rocket or watercress and fresh cherries.

Beef

Home-made meatballs

Ingredients:
Makes about 16
- 700 g/1½ lb minced beef
- 2 eggs, beaten
- 2 onions, finely chopped
- 4 cloves garlic, crushed
- 1 dsp dried oregano
- 1 tsp ground cumin
- ½ tsp ground nutmeg
- 1 tbs fresh parsley, chopped
- 1 tbs tomato purée
- Seasoning
- Coconut flour for coating meatballs

Mix all the ingredients except the coconut flour together in a large bowl.

Take about 1 tbs of the mixture at a time and form into balls with your freshly-washed hands.

Place some of the coconut flour in a bowl and roll the meatballs around until they are coated.

Brown them in a frying pan until cooked.

Alternatively, after browning they could be baked in the oven (190°C / 375°F / GM 5) for about 30 to 40 minutes and served with onion gravy (see page 289).

You can serve them either with bolognese sauce (see page 228) or with white sauce (see page 290).

Meatballs in creamy sauce

Ingredients:
Serves 4

- Home-made meatballs (see above)
- Coconut oil or butter for sautéing
- Fresh or dried thyme
- 1-2 large onions, chopped
- 250 g/9 oz mushrooms, sliced
- 4–6 cloves garlic, crushed
- 1 dsp mustard
- 1 tsp ground nutmeg
- 1 x 400 ml tin coconut cream
- 4–6 tbs nutritional yeast flakes
- Seasoning
- Chopped parsley to serve
- Konjac noodles or shredded lightly steamed cabbage or courgette spaghetti to serve

Sauté the meatballs in the coconut oil and thyme and leave on a plate to keep warm.

Sauté the onions and mushrooms with the crushed garlic.

Stir in the mustard and nutmeg and add the cream, stirring.

Simmer, and dissolve the nutritional yeast flakes in the sauce.

Return the meatballs to the pan and season.

Sprinkle chopped parsley and black pepper on top and serve on a bed of either konjac noodles, shredded cabbage or courgette spaghetti.

Slow-cooked braised beef

Ingredients:
Serves 4–6
- 4 onions, sliced
- 2 cloves garlic, crushed
- Coconut oil for sautéing
- 700 g/1½ lb beef, diced – about 250 g per person
- 1 tbs kuzu
- 1 tbs tomato purée
- Enough beef stock to just cover (see page 148)
- 1 tbs paprika
- Nutmeg to taste
- Seasoning
- 4 large tomatoes, chopped
- Mushrooms, chopped

Set your slow cooker to High and allow to warm.

Sauté the onions and garlic in the coconut oil for a few minutes and add the beef to brown.

Transfer to the slow cooker.

Mix the kuzu with a little water.

Warm the tomato purée, kuzu mixture and stock in the pan in which the beef was sautéed, flavouring with paprika and a pinch of nutmeg.

Season.

Add to the slow cooker and cook for two hours.

Add the chopped tomatoes and mushrooms and cook on Medium for a further two hours.

Serve hot with vegetables.

Slow-cooked chilli con carne

Ingredients:
Serves 4

- 500 g/1¼ lb minced beef
- 1 tbs coconut oil or goose fat
- 1 large onion, chopped
- 2–3 red chilli peppers, de-seeded and chopped
- 4 cloves garlic, crushed
- 2 stalks celery, chopped
- 2 x 400 g tins chopped tomatoes
- 200 ml/7 fl oz tomato purée
- 1 dsp kuzu
- 2 tbs fresh coriander, chopped
- Seasoning
- Konjac rice or grated cauliflower (see page 268), to serve
- Urban Caveman coconut yoghurt or soured cream (see pages 39 and 41)

Set your slow cooker to High.

Sear the beef in the fat and keep warm.

Sauté the onion, chilli peppers, garlic and celery for a few minutes.

Return the mince to the frying pan and stir in the tinned tomatoes.

Whizz the tomato purée with 300 ml / 12 fl oz water and stir in the kuzu or arrowroot.

Stir into the beef and vegetable mixture, until thickened.

Stir in about half the chopped coriander and season.

Transfer to the slow cooker, turn down to Low and cook for seven to nine hours.

Serve with rice, chopped coriander leaves and Urban Caveman coconut yoghurt or Urban Caveman sour cream.

Slow-cooked beef casserole with thyme

Ingredients:
Serves 4–6
- 700 g/1½ lb braising steak, diced
- 2 tbs red wine vinegar
- 2 tbs coconut or goose fat or ghee or butter
- 12 onions, peeled
- 6 cloves garlic, crushed
- 200 ml/7 fl oz beef stock
- 1 tbs kuzu or arrowroot
- Seasoning
- Fresh thyme
- Puréed cauliflower mash and spring onions, to serve

Set your slow cooker to High.

Marinate the beef in the vinegar for half an hour.

Heat the fat and sear the beef.

Add the onions and garlic and sauté for a few minutes.

Gradually stir in the marinade and stock.

Dissolve the kuzu or arrowroot in a little water and stir into the almost boiling stock.

Stir until thickened and season.

Transfer to the slow cooker, adding some of the thyme.

Cook for five to seven hours.

Serve over a bed of mashed cauliflower to which lots of black pepper and finely chopped spring onions have been added.

Garnish with sprigs of thyme.

Slow-cooked beef casserole with tamari

Ingredients:
Serves 4–6

- **4 onions, chopped**
- **Coconut oil or goose fat for sautéing**
- **1–2 dsp mixed herbs**
- **700 g/1½ lb stewing beef, diced**
- **1 dsp kuzu**
- **Dash tamari, coconut soy-sauce substitute or yeast extract**
- **1 bay leaf**
- **Seasoning**
- ***Optional*: Mushrooms**

Set your slow cooker to High.

Sauté the onions in the fat and herbs.

Transfer to the slow cooker.

Brown the beef in the fat and add to the onions in the slow cooker.

Stir the kuzu into a little water, add the flavouring and pour over the onions and beef, adding the bay leaf and seasoning.

Cook for one hour and then turn down to Medium for a further three to four hours, *or* cook for seven hours on Low.

If using mushrooms, these should be added for the last hour of cooking.

Slow-cooked winter warmer

Ingredients:
Serves 6–8

- 1.3 kg/3 lb brisket or silverside joint
- Himalayan salt
- 1½ tsp cayenne pepper
- 2 tbs coconut oil or goose fat
- 50 g/2 oz streaky bacon, diced
- 2 cloves garlic, finely chopped
- 2 onions, chopped
- 2 large carrots, chopped
- 1 stalk celery, chopped
- 1 small celeriac, peeled and diced
- 275 ml/½ pint hot beef stock
- 1 x 400 g tin chopped tomatoes
- 2 bay leaves
- 2 tbs freshly chopped parsley

Pre-heat your slow cooker to High.

Place the beef on a chopping board and make several slashes over the surface, but don't cut the butcher's string.

Season with salt and dust with cayenne pepper on both sides.

Heat the oil and brown the beef with the bacon.

Transfer to the slow cooker, turning to Low.

Next, fry the garlic, onion, carrot, celery and celeriac in the same pan for a few minutes.

Add the stock, chopped tomatoes and bay leaves.

Bring to the boil and reduce the stock by about a third.

Transfer to the slow cooker and cook on Low for six to seven hours.

Cut the meat into slices to serve.

Garnish with parsley and serve with cauliflower cheese (see page 270).

Slow-cooked oxtail stew

It is important to use a good home-made stock for this stew as it gives it a wonderful flavour.

Ingredients:
Serves a family for days
- **Ghee, butter or coconut oil for sautéing**
- **4 kg/9 lb oxtails**
- **6 onions, sliced**
- **6 stalks celery, chopped**
- **4 leeks, finely chopped**
- **Approx 725 ml/1¼ pt home-made beef stock**
- **2 bay leaves**
- **4 sprigs fresh thyme**
- **1 dsp balsamic vinegar**
- **Seasoning**
- **6–8 cloves garlic, crushed**
- **Fresh parsley, chopped**

Set your slow cooker to High.

Melt the fat in a frying pan and brown the oxtails, then add them to the slow cooker.

Sauté the onions for a few minutes.

Add the celery and leeks.

Pour the beef stock over the vegetables and add the bay leaves, thyme, balsamic vinegar and seasoning and bring to the boil.

Place garlic cloves in the slow cooker and pour the stock and vegetables in.

Cook for two hours, then reduce the temperature to Low and cook for a further three to four hours.

Serve with chopped parsley and black pepper.

Spaghetti Bolognese

Ingredients for sauce:
Serves 4

- 1 large onion, chopped
- 2 peppers, chopped
- 10 mushrooms, chopped
- 2 stalks celery, sliced
- 2 carrots, diced small
- Fresh garlic, chopped or crushed to taste
- Coconut oil or goose fat, for frying
- Dried or fresh basil, to taste
- Dried or fresh oregano, to taste
- 1 kg/2 lb minced beef
- 200 g/7 oz tomato purée
- 3 x 400 ml tins chopped tomatoes
- Seasoning
- *Optional*: grated Urban Caveman parmesan or Cheddar cheese and chopped fresh basil leaves, to serve

Pasta substitutes:

1. Courgette, sliced using julienne grater into spaghetti strips, lightly tossed in olive oil or butter and seasoned

2. Finely shredded cabbage with black pepper and melted butter

3. Kelp noodles

4. If you are wanting to lose weight, konjac noodles

Sauté the vegetables and garlic in coconut oil in a large wok.

Add the herbs and meat and cook, stirring, until browned.

Stir in the tomato purée and tinned tomatoes.

Cook with the lid on for about 10 minutes, then season to taste.

Serve with the pasta substitute and arrange the fresh basil leaves on top.

Meat loaf

This dish is delicious cold, with a salad, and great for lunch boxes. It is also good hot with onion gravy (see page 289).

Ingredients:
Serves 6

- 800 g/1 ¾ lb lean minced beef
- 1 onion, finely chopped
- 2 stalks celery, finely chopped
- 1–2 tbs tamari or coconut soy-sauce substitute
- 3–4 cloves garlic, crushed
- Seasoning
- 1 dsp mixed herbs
- 1 egg, beaten

Pre-heat your oven to 170°C/325°F/GM 3.

Mix all the raw ingredients together and form into a roll.

Transfer to a greased loaf tin.

Bake in the oven for about one hour and cut into slices.

Tomato meat loaf

Ingredients:
Serves 6

- 800 g/1¾ lb minced beef
- 1 onion, finely chopped
- 2 stalks celery, finely chopped
- 200 g/7 oz tomato purée
- 2–3 cloves garlic, crushed
- Seasoning
- 1 tsp dried basil
- 1 egg, beaten

Pre-heat your oven to 170°C/325°F/GM 3.

Mix all the raw ingredients together and form into a roll.

Transfer to a greased loaf tin.

Bake in the oven for about one hour.

Beefburger

Ingredients:
Makes 6

- **1 onion, finely chopped**
- **Coconut oil, butter, goose fat or ghee for sautéing**
- **800 g/1¾ lb minced beef**
- **1 tbs Worcester sauce (gluten-free, sugar-free, from health-food shops)**
- **1 tsp tomato purée**
- **1 tbs mixed herbs**
- **1 tsp onion powder**
- **Seasoning**
- **2 onions, cut into rings**

Lightly sauté the onion in the oil.

Add the minced beef to the pan and mix.

Stir in the Worcester sauce, tomato purée, mixed herbs, onion powder and seasoning.

Mix well and form into six balls.

Flatten each ball into a burger shape.

Fry in the coconut oil.

Set aside to keep warm.

Fry the onion rings in the remaining fat and serve on top of the burgers.

Beef roulade

Ingredients:

- **Wholegrain mustard to taste**
- **Thin slices of raw beef (butcher will cut this) – 1–2 per person**
- **1 rasher unsmoked bacon per person, diced**
- **½ small onion per person, finely chopped**
- **Garlic, crushed, to taste**
- **Cucumber or celery, finely diced**
- **Coconut, goose fat, ghee or butter, for frying**
- **Tamari or coconut soy-sauce substitute to taste**
- **Seasoning**

Spread the mustard on to one side of the sliced beef.

Sprinkle each slice of beef with the diced bacon, onion, garlic, cucumber or celery.

Roll up, securing with a short metal skewer.

Brown in a little fat in a lidded pan.

Then add enough water to almost reach the top but don't cover, and simmer with the lid on for one hour and 20 minutes.

Remove the roulade(s) from the pan and purée the pan contents, adding tamari or soy-sauce substitute to make a gravy.

Season to taste.

Serve the roulade(s) with the gravy in which they have been cooked.

Minced beef cooked on the hob

Ingredients:

- **1 onion per person, chopped**
- **1 tbs dried mixed herbs**
- **1 clove garlic per person, crushed**
- **Coconut or goose fat, ghee or butter, for frying**

- 3 large carrots, diced
- 3 stalks celery, chopped
- 250 g/9 oz minced beef per person
- 425 ml/¾ pt beef stock
- 1 tbs yeast extract
- Seasoning
- 1 tbs kuzu
- Chopped parsley to serve

Sauté the onion, mixed herbs and garlic in the fat for a few minutes.

Add the carrots and celery and cook for a few more minutes.

Stir in the minced meat and cook vigorously until browned.

Stir in the beef stock and yeast extract. Season.

Dissolve the kuzu in a little water and stir into the stock, until thickened. Cover and leave to simmer for half an hour, stirring occasionally.

If you need more gravy, add a little more stock or water.

Stuffed peppers

Ingredients:
- 1 pepper per person, de-seeded
- 1 clove garlic per person
- Dried oregano
- 1 onion per person, finely chopped
- Butter, ghee, goose fat or coconut oil, for frying
- ½ stalk celery per person, finely chopped
- 2 mushrooms per person, finely chopped
- 110 g/4 oz minced beef, per person
- Tomato purée – about 2–3 tbs person
- Seasoning
- Urban Caveman cheese, either mozzarella or Cheddar-style, grated
- Parsley, chopped

Pre-heat your oven to 150°C/300°F/GM 2.

Cut the stalk ends off the peppers and put to one side.

Place the peppers in boiling water for five minutes. Drain.

Sauté the garlic, oregano and onions in fat for a few minutes.

Dice the tops of the peppers.

Add the rest of the vegetables, including the diced pepper tops, to the pan and sauté for a few minutes.

Stir in the mince and cook until browned.

Work in the tomato purée and season.

Stand the peppers on a baking tray. It may be necessary to cut the bottoms to enable them to stand up. If they are in danger of falling, place a hollow cake tin around them.

Stuff the mince and vegetable mixture into the peppers.

Top with grated Urban Caveman cheese and bake in the oven for about 25 minutes, until the cheese is melted and golden.

Serve with chopped parsley.

Marinated steak

Ingredients:
Serves 4

- **110 ml/4 fl oz olive oil**
- **4 spring onions, finely chopped**
- **1 tsp mixed herbs**
- **2 cloves garlic, crushed**
- **1 tsp Thai green curry paste (sugar- and additive-free)**
- **2 tbs water**
- **Juice of ½ lime**
- **Sweetener of choice to taste**
- **Seasoning**
- **4 steaks**

Add all the marinade ingredients to a jug and whisk with a stick blender.

Place the steaks in a bowl, cover with the marinade and leave for at least two hours, or even better, overnight.

Barbecue.

Roast beef with Yorkshire pudding and gravy

Ingredients:
- Joint of beef, grass-fed and properly hung
- Pepper
- Mustard powder

Ingredients for the gravy:
- 2 onions, chopped
- *Optional*: Sliced mushrooms
- Juices from the roast beef
- 1 tbs kuzu
- About 700 ml/1¼ pt beef stock or water
- Dash tamari or coconut soy-sauce substitute
- 1–2 tsp yeast extract
- Seasoning

Ingredients for the Yorkshire puddings:
- 3 eggs
- 3 tbs melted butter or ghee plus extra for the tin
- 300 ml/11 fl oz coconut milk
- 110 ml/4 fl oz beef stock
- 1 tbs tamari or coconut soy-sauce substitute
- 1 dsp gluten-free baking powder
- Seasoning
- 1 tsp xanthan gum
- 10 g/½ oz coconut flour, sifted

- **20 g/¾ oz coconut powder**
- **20 g/¾ oz egg-white protein powder**

Yorkshire puddings:

The mixture for the Yorkshire puddings can be made in advance.

Blend the eggs, ghee or butter, coconut milk, stock and tamari in a food processor.

Mix the baking powder, seasoning, and xanthan gum into the coconut flour, coconut powder, and egg-white protein powder and add to the food processor, blending well.

Keep until ready to cook. If making the day before keep overnight in the fridge.

To cook the beef:

Pre-heat your oven to 240°C/475°F/GM 9.

Add pepper (but not salt) and a dusting of dried mustard to the beef. Roast for 20 minutes.

Turn the oven down to 190°C/375°F/GM 5 and roast for a further 15 minutes per 450 g/1 lb for medium rare, or if you like your beef well done, for a further 30 minutes, remembering to baste.

About 10 minutes before the beef is ready to come out, turn the oven up to 220°C/425°F/GM 7 to warm the oil for the Yorkshire puddings.

Remove the beef, and keep warm whilst allowing it to 'rest'.

To cook the Yorkshire pudding:

Put the extra fat in a square or rectangular roasting tin and place in the oven to get hot.

Once sizzling hot, pour the batter in and return to the oven for about 25 minutes, turning the temperature down to 170°C/325°F/GM 3 after 10 minutes.

Cook until browned (about 15 minutes).

To make the gravy:

Whilst the beef is resting and the Yorkshire pudding is cooking, sauté the chopped onions (and mushrooms if using) in the juices from the beef.

Dissolve the kuzu in a little cold water.

Add the remaining gravy ingredients and stir until thickened.

Pork

Carbonara

Ingredients for sauce:

Serves one – just multiply the ingredients when making this for more people

- 4 rashers streaky bacon or ham, diced
- 2 cloves garlic, crushed
- Coconut oil/butter or ghee for frying
- 2 egg yolks
- 1 x 400 ml tin coconut cream
- 40 g/1½ oz nutritional yeast flakes
- Fresh basil leaves, chopped
- Seasoning

Pasta substitutes:

1. Courgette, sliced using julienne grater into spaghetti strips

2. Finely shredded cabbage

3. Kelp noodles

4. If you are wanting to lose weight, konjac noodles, drained

Fry the bacon and crushed garlic in the fat.

Using an electric stick blender, whisk the egg yolks into the coconut cream.

Pour over the bacon once it is cooked and stir in the nutritional yeast flakes.

Stir until gently boiling.

Mix the 'pasta' into the egg and coconut cream, and warm.

Transfer to a pasta dish and serve with chopped fresh basil and black pepper.

Toad in the hole

Ingredients:
Serves 6

- 12 gluten-free (100% meat) organic, free-range sausages (ask a good butcher to make them for you)

Ingredients for the batter:
- 3 eggs
- 3 tbs melted butter or ghee
- 4-5 tbs coconut milk
- 1 tbs tamari or coconut soy-sauce substitute
- Himalayan salt
- 1 dsp gluten-free baking powder
- 1 tsp xanthan gum
- 30 g/1¼ oz coconut flour, sifted
- 10 g/½ oz egg-white protein powder
- 10 g /½ oz coconut milk powder

Ingredients for the gravy:
- 2 onions, sliced into rings
- Coconut oil, goose fat or butter or ghee for frying
- 1 tbs kuzu
- 1 tsp wholegrain mustard
- 1 tbs tamari or coconut soy-sauce substitute
- Seasoning

Pre-heat your oven to 200°C/400°F/GM 6.

Place the onion rings (for the gravy) in enough fat to coat the base of your roasting tin, and place the roasting tin on the highest shelf in the oven.

Place the sausages on a lower shelf in the oven in another roasting tin.

After 10 minutes, take the sausages out of the oven but leave them in their roasting tin.

Leave the onions to continue cooking for another five minutes. Then remove them and set them to one side.

Blend the eggs, ghee or butter, coconut milk, tamari and salt in a food processor.

Mix the baking powder and xanthan gum into the coconut flour, egg-white protein powder and coconut milk powder and add to the food processor, blending well.

Place the sausages, in their roasting tin, on the hob, adding a little fat if necessary, and cook for a few minutes.

Once the oil is really hot, pour in the batter mix, partially covering the sausages.

Return to the oven and cook for about 20 to 30 minutes, until the batter and sausages are browned.

To make the gravy:

Stir the kuzu into a litte water and add the mustard and tamari.

Season well.

Place the onions in their roasting tin on the hob over a gentle heat and stir in the gravy mix, until thickened, stirring continuously.

Season to taste.

Serve with the sausages in their batter.

Pork belly

Ingredients:
Serves 4
- 1 kg/2.2 lb boneless pork belly, skin scored (ask your butcher to do this for you)
- 1 tbs Himalayan salt
- 1 large onion, cut into wedges
- 3 celery stalks, cut into chunks

Pre-heat your oven to 190°C/375°F/GM 5.

Rub the salt all over the skin of the pork belly, especially in the scores.

Place the onion wedges and celery in a roasting tin with the pork belly on top.

Roast for one hour.

Turn the temperature up to 220°C/425°F/GM 7 and roast until the crackling is crisp – about 20 minutes.

Place on a serving tray to allow the juices to settle for 15 minutes before carving.

Pork chops with cream sauce

Ingredients:

- 2 tbs sage leaves, chopped, or 1 dsp dried
- Either crumbs from an Urban Caveman loaf or desiccated coconut – enough to coat the chops
- Seasoning
- 1–2 pork chops per person
- 1–2 eggs, beaten
- Coconut oil, goose fat, ghee or butter for frying
- 2–3 eating apples, cut into rings
- 1–2 onions, cut into rings
- 1 portion white sauce per person (see page 290), to serve

Mix the sage into the breadcrumbs or desiccated coconut and season well.

Dip the chops into the beaten egg and then into the dry mixture to coat.

Heat the fat and fry the chops on high to brown, and then reduce the heat and cover so they cook through, which could take half an hour.

In a second pan, melt some fat and fry the apple and onion rings.

Serve with Urban Caveman white sauce.

Warming German-sausage stew

This dish stands or falls on the quality of the sausages. These should be 100 per cent meat. You should ask your butcher to make them for you.

Ingredients:

- Potatoes or sweet potatoes, roughly diced, about 2 per person
- Ghee or butter, for frying
- Mixture of home-made chicken or beef stock and water to cover the ingredients
- 4 best quality sausages (100% meat) per person
- 2 large packets curly kale
- Herbamere (a brand of sea salt with herbs added) salt or Marigold vegetable bouillon, to taste
- 1 dsp tamari or coconut soy-sauce substitute
- Black pepper

Toss the potatoes in the fat for a few minutes.

Add the stock and the sausages and cover and bring to the boil.

Meanwhile chop the kale and add it to the pan.

Simmer for about 30 to 40 minutes, until the sausages are cooked. They will leak fat into the stock, giving this stew a lovely flavour. Add Herbamere or bouillon.

Add the tamari and black pepper (it isn't usually necessary to add salt) and serve in bowls with Urban Caveman bread.

Slow-cooked spare ribs

Ingredients:
Serves 4–6

- 1 onion, chopped
- 4 cloves garlic, crushed
- 2 tbs maple syrup
- 2 tbs Urban Caveman tomato ketchup (see page 327)

- **1 tsp mustard or mustard powder**
- **1 dsp powdered horseradish**
- **Juice of ½ lemon**
- **2 tbs cider vinegar**
- **4 tbs apple juice, unpasteurised, unsweetened**
- **1 tbs tamari or coconut soy-sauce substitute**
- **Seasoning**
- **1 kg/2.2 lb pork ribs**
- **1 tbs kuzu or arrowroot**
- **Chopped parsley to garnish**

Set your slow cooker to High.

Using a stick blender, whizz all the ingredients together except for the ribs and kuzu.

Place the ribs in the slow cooker.

Warm the sauce and pour it over the ribs.

Cook for one hour.

Turn the temperature down to Low and cook for a further three to four hours.

Arrange the ribs on a serving dish.

Dissolve the kuzu or arrowroot in a little water.

Return the sauce to a pan, and bring to the boil.

Stir in the kuzu or arrowroot water and boil to reduce by about a half.

Serve over konjac rice, shredded cabbage, cauliflower rice (see page 268) or cauliflower mash (see page 268), and garnish with chopped parsley.

Pork goulash

Ingredients:
Serves 6–8

- 1 onion, cut into wedges
- 4 cloves garlic, crushed
- 2 tbs coconut oil
- 700 g/1½ lb pork, diced
- 1 tbs ground paprika
- 1 tbs kuzu or arrowroot
- 300 ml/11 fl oz chicken stock
- 200 ml/7 fl oz tomato purée
- 1 x 400 g tin chopped tomatoes
- 2 tbs red wine vinegar
- Seasoning
- 1 pepper, sliced
- 110 g/4 oz mushrooms, sliced
- To serve, Urban Caveman yoghurt or sour cream into which you have chopped fresh chives

Set your slow cooker to High.

Sauté the onion and garlic in the oil for a few minutes and transfer to the slow cooker.

Sear the pork in the oil and paprika, adding more oil if necessary.

Transfer the pork to the slow cooker.

Dissolve the kuzu or arrowroot in a little water.

Pour the stock, tomato purée, tinned tomatoes and red wine vinegar into the pan and bring to the boil.

Stir in the kuzu or arrowroot water.

Season and pour into the slow cooker.

Reduce the temperature to Low and cook for four to five hours.

Add the sliced pepper and mushrooms to the pot and cook for a further hour.

Serve decorated with Urban Caveman yoghurt or soured cream with chives. Goes well with konjac rice, cauliflower rice or shredded cabbage.

Pork chops with spring onion butter

Ingredients:
Serves 4

- 2 cloves garlic, crushed
- 6 spring onions, chopped
- Black pepper, coarsely ground
- 1 bunch fresh chives, chopped very small
- 150 g/5 oz butter or ghee, room temperature
- 4 pork chops

Mix the garlic, onions, pepper and chives into the softened butter with a fork.

Grill the chops.

Serve the chops with a dollop of the herb butter on top.

Barbecued pork kebabs

Ingredients for the kebabs:
Serves 4-6

- 25 g/1 oz breadcrumbs made from Urban Caveman loaf
- 450 g/1 lb minced pork
- 1 onion, finely chopped
- 1 dessert apple, peeled and grated
- 1 tbs fresh rosemary, chopped
- Seasoning

Ingredients for the baste:

- 3 tbs olive oil
- 1 tbs lemon juice

Ingredients for the yoghurt and herb sauce:

- 4 tbs olive oil
- 350 ml/12 fl oz Urban Caveman coconut yoghurt (page 39)
- Grated zest of 1 lemon
- 4 tbs flatleaf parsley, chopped

Mix the breadcrumbs into the minced pork in a large bowl.

Add the onions, grated apple, rosemary and seasoning.

Refrigerate for one hour.

Meanwhile prepare the yoghurt sauce by whisking all the ingredients together with an electric stick blender. Refrigerate.

Form the mince mixture into balls and place these on skewers.

To baste mix the oil and lemon juice together and brush over the kebabs.

Barbecue for about 12 minutes, turning until golden brown all over.

Serve with the yoghurt sauce.

Chicken liver

Slow-cooked chicken liver and bacon casserole

Ingredients:
Serves 4

- 2 onions, chopped
- 8 whole cloves garlic, chopped
- About 10 rashers organic bacon, diced
- 1 dsp mixed herbs

- **2 sticks celery, chopped**
- **Coconut oil, goose fat, butter or ghee, for frying**
- **800 g/1¾ lb chicken or calf livers**
- **1 dsp kuzu**
- **1 tbs balsamic vinegar**
- **1 dsp tamari, coconut soy-sauce substitute or yeast extract**
- **500 ml/1 pint beef stock**
- **Seasoning**
- **2 carrots, diced**

Set your slow cooker to high.

Lightly sauté the onions, garlic, bacon, mixed herbs and celery in the oil and transfer to the slow cooker.

Lightly sauté the chicken livers in the oil and transfer to the slow cooker.

Dissolve the kuzu in a little water and add the vinegar and tamari. Add to the stock.

Warm in the pan, stirring until thickened.

Season well and pour over the liver.

Turn the heat down to medium and cook for about four hours. Add carrots one hour before the end of cooking time.

Goes well over a bed of mashed cauliflower or sweet potato with chopped chives.

Fried chicken livers with onion gravy

Ingredients:
Serves 4

- Black pepper and salt, coarsely ground
- 400 g/14 oz chicken livers, cut into large strips
- Ghee, butter, coconut oil or goose fat, for frying
- 2 onions, cut into rings
- 2 cloves garlic, crushed
- 725 ml/1¼ pt chicken stock
- 1 tbs kuzu
- 1 dsp yeast extract
- Mashed sweet potatoes or mashed cauliflower (see page 268) with chopped chives and black pepper, to serve
- Flatleaf parsley, chopped

Grind the pepper and salt into a bowl and press into the liver.

Fry the liver in the fat.

Once the liver is cooked (a few minutes – don't overcook or it will become tough), transfer it to a plate and keep it warm.

Fry the onion rings and garlic in the pan, adding more fat if necessary.

Once browned, pour in the stock. Dissolve the kuzu in a little water and add when the stock is almost boiling, stirring constantly until thickened to form the gravy.

Stir in the yeast extract and season.

Arrange the liver over a bed of either mashed sweet potatoes or mashed cauliflower with chopped chives and pepper and pour the onion gravy over the top.

Scatter chopped flatleaf parsley over the top.

Spicy fried chicken livers with Urban Caveman soured cream sauce

Ingredients:
Serves 4

- 1 onion, finely chopped
- 1 green pepper, de-seeded and chopped into thin strips
- 75 g/3 oz ghee, butter, coconut oil or goose fat, for frying
- 450 g/1 lb chicken livers, cut into narrow strips
- Seasoning
- 1 tbs paprika
- 1 tbs red wine vinegar
- 150 ml/¼ pint Urban Caveman soured cream (see page 41)
- To serve, either mashed sweet potatoes or mashed cauliflower with chives
- Flatleaf parsley to garnish

Sauté the onion and green pepper in a little of the fat in a large frying pan and set aside after about 10 minutes.

Melt more butter and fry the chicken livers until browning – don't overcook them or they will be tough.

Add the seasoning, paprika and the fried vegetables.

Add the vinegar, and heat.

Remove from the heat and and stir in the soured cream to make a sauce.

Arrange the liver over the mash, and pour the sauce on top.

Garnish with chopped flatleaf parsley.

Jerky

Jerky makes a great protein snack but ideally requires a dehydrator. (If you don't have a dehydrator cook in the oven on the lowest setting, for a similar length of time. Originally made by American Indians, the meat was cut into strips and left out to dry in the sun. Unlike other Urban Caveman meats, meat for jerky needs to be low in fat as fat reduces the storage life. Lean jerky can last about a month without refrigeration so is a great Paleo snack when travelling and away from fridges.

Jerky is steeped in either a dry or brine cure before dehydrating. A dry cure could be something like seasoning and herbs, and a brine cure would be made from water with salt and seasoning. The meat is soaked in the brine until the salt has been absorbed.

Dry-cure chicken jerky

Ingredients:
- **Raw chicken breasts, cut into strips about 1 cm thick**
- **1 tbs dried sage**
- **Seasoning**

Spread the slices of meat on a chopping board.

Mix the sage into the seasoning and press into the strips of meat.

Transfer the seasoned meat into a glass bowl and apply pressure by placing a weight on top. Make sure it is well sealed.

Refrigerate overnight.

Spread the meat strips on the dehydrator tray in a single layer.

Dehydrate on the meat setting 155 for four to six hours, turning over halfway through.

When ready the meat should crack but not break.

Store in an airtight container.

Chicken jerky in sage-and-onion brine

Ingredients:

- 4-6 chicken breasts, cut into strips about 1 cm wide

Ingredients for the brine:

- 1 dsp onion powder
- 1 dsp garlic powder
- 1 dsp dried sage
- Seasoning
- Enough water to cover the chicken
- Dash tamari or coconut soy-sauce substitute

Mix the brine ingredients together.

Place the strips of meat in a glass bowl and pour the brine over them to cover.

Place a weight on the top and seal well.

Refrigerate overnight.

Spread the meat strips on the dehydrator tray in a single layer.

Turn your dehydrator to meat setting 155 and dehydrate for four to six hours, turning halfway through.

When ready the dried meat should crack but not break.

Store in an airtight container.

Dry-cure beef jerky

Ingredients:

- Seasoning
- 1 level dsp mixed herbs
- 1 level dsp garlic powder
- Approximately ¾ kg/2 lb raw beef, cut into strips about 1 cm thick

Mix the dry ingredients together.

Arrange the strips of meat on a chopping board and sprinkle the dry cure over them.

Transfer to a glass bowl and push them down tightly.

Place a weight on the top and seal well.

Refrigerate overnight.

Spread the meat strips on the dehydrator tray in a single layer.

Set your dehydrator to the meat setting 155 and dehydrate the meat for four to six hours, turning over halfway through.

When ready, the dried meat should crack but not break.

Store in an airtight container.

Beef jerky in tamari brine

Ingredients:
- **Raw beef, cut into strips about 1 cm thick**

Ingredients for the brine:
- **Enough water to cover the beef**
- **Seasoning**
- **1 tsp mixed herbs**
- **1 dsp garlic powder**
- **1 dsp tamari or coconut soy-sauce substitute**

Mix the brine ingredients together.

Place the strips of meat in a glass bowl and pour the brine over them.

Place a weight on the top and seal well.

Refrigerate overnight.

Spread the meat strips on the dehydrator tray in a single layer.

Set your dehydrator to the meat setting 155 and dehydrate the meat for four to six hours, turning over halfway through.

The dried meat should crack but not break.

Store in an airtight container.

Beef jerky in tomato sauce

Ingredients:
- **Approximately 1 kg/2.2 lb raw beef, cut into strips about 1 cm wide**
- **200 ml/7 fl oz tomato purée**
- **1 tsp garlic powder**
- **1 tsp onion powder**
- **Enough water to cover the meat**
- **Seasoning**
- **1 tsp dried basil**

Mix the sauce ingredients together.

Place the strips of meat in a glass bowl and pour the sauce over them.

Place a weight on top and seal well.

Refrigerate overnight.

Spread the meat strips on the dehydrator tray in a single layer.

Set your dehydrator to the meat setting 155 and dehydrate the meat for four to six hours, turning over halfway through.

The dried meat should crack but not break.

Store in an airtight container.

Beef jerky in barbecue sauce

Ingredients:
- Approximately 1 kg/2.2 lb raw beef, cut into strips about 1 cm wide

Ingredients for the sauce:
- 1 tbs olive oil
- 1 dsp lemon juice
- 1 tbs tamari or coconut soy-sauce substitute
- 1 tbs balsamic vinegar
- 2 cloves garlic, crushed
- 1 tsp mustard
- 1 dsp tomato purée
- Seasoning

Mix the sauce ingredients together.

Place the strips of meat in a glass bowl and pour the sauce over them.

Blend all the ingredients together and pour the barbecue brine over the beef.

Place a weight on the top and seal well.

Refrigerate overnight.

Spread the meat strips on the dehydrator tray in a single layer.

If you don't have a dehydrator you can place in the oven on the lowest setting for four to six hours, turning over halfway through.

The dried meat should crack but not break.

Store in an airtight container.

Scandinavian fish jerky

Ingredients:

- Approximately 800 g–1 kg/1¾–2.2 lb any white fish, completely fresh, cut into strips about 1 cm wide (Oily fish is not suitable for this recipe as it could go rancid)
- 125 g/4½ oz salt to 1 l/1¾ pt cold water
- 1 dsp dried dill
- Seasoning

Marinate the fish in enough salt water to cover, for half an hour.

Mix together the dill and seasoning to make the dry cure.

Rinse the fish thoroughly to remove the brine and arrange on a chopping board.

Coat with the dry-cure ingredients.

Transfer to a glass bowl and press down firmly.

Place a weight on the top and seal well.

Refrigerate for six to 10 hours.

Set your dehydrator to the meat setting 155.

Spread the strips of fish singly over the dehydrator tray and dehydrate for 12 to 14 hours.

The fish should not be crumbly or crunchy. It should have a mild fish flavour, slightly soft with no visible surface moisture.

Store in an airtight container.

Fish

Salmon with spicy sauce

Ingredients:
- 1 salmon fillet, wild, per person
- 1–2 tsp harissa sauce per fillet (see page 295)

Spread the harissa sauce over the salmon and grill.

White fish in coconut cream sauce

Ingredients:
Serves 4
- Ghee or butter for frying
- 2 onions, finely chopped
- 1 small potato per person
- 350 g/12 oz leeks, finely sliced
- 400 ml/14 fl oz fish stock
- 1 bouquet garni
- 8 tbs coconut cream
- Seasoning
- 4 white fish fillets (not farmed)
- Freshly chopped chives, to serve

Melt the fat and sauté the onion and potato in a saucepan for about 10 minutes.

Add the leeks and cook for a further five minutes.

Pour in the stock and bouquet garni and simmer until the potato is cooked.

Add the coconut cream.

Remove the bouquet garni, and, using a stick blender, liquidise the sauce.

Season and keep warm.

Meanwhile, melt more fat in a frying pan and sear the fish fillets on both sides. Then reduce the heat and fry for a few more minutes until cooked.

Serve the fillets on a warm plate with the sauce poured over them and the chives sprinkled on top.

Sicilian-style barbecued salmon or trout with salsa verde

Ingredients:
Serves 4

- 150 ml/¼ pint olive oil
- 3 tbs lemon juice
- 2 tbs chopped parsley
- Seasoning
- 4 wild salmon or trout fillets
- 2 tbs capers
- 2 cloves garlic, crushed
- Zest of 1 lemon
- 2 tsp pure anchovy paste

In a shallow dish mix 3 tbs of the olive oil with half the lemon juice and 1 tbs of the chopped parsley.

Season.

Place the fish fillets in the mixture and make sure they are coated on both sides.

Cover and refrigerate for at least half an hour, turning once.

Place the capers in a food processor with the remaining oil, parsley and lemon juice plus the garlic, lemon zest and anchovy paste. Purée to make a salsa.

Transfer to a serving bowl and refrigerate.

Barbecue the salmon for a few minutes each side on a hot grill.

Serve the fish topped with the salsa.

Barbecued sea bass in lemon and dill

Ingredients:
Serves 2

- 90 ml/3½ fl oz olive oil
- Juice of ½ lemon
- 2 tbs fresh dill, chopped
- 2 medium sea bass, cleaned and de-scaled
- ½ lemon, sliced

Mix the oil, lemon juice and half the dill together in a glass dish to make the marinade.

Cut slashes in the fish skin.

Push the lemon slices and remaining dill into the fish cavity.

Steep the fish in the marinade and spoon the juices all over the fish.

Cover and marinate for half an hour in the fridge, turning once.

Wrap the fish in a Roastcosy or greaseproof paper and then cover with foil.

Cook over a hot barbecue for 15 to 20 minutes, turning once.

Serve with Urban Caveman tartare sauce (see page 300).

Pan-fried sprats

Ingredients:
- Whole sprats from fishmonger, 6–8 per person
- Beaten eggs – enough to dip the sprats in
- Coconut oil, butter or ghee for frying

Ingredients for the breadcrumb coating:
- Half-and-half mixture of breadcrumbs from an Urban Caveman loaf (see page 64) and desiccated coconut – enough to coat the sprats

- **1 dsp paprika**
- **1 tsp onion powder**
- **1 tsp garlic powder**
- **Seasoning**

Mix the ingredients for the breadcrumb coating together in a medium-sized bowl.

Dip the sprats in the beaten egg and then coat them in the breadcrumb mix.

Heat the coconut oil and fry the sprats, setting them aside on kitchen paper as they become ready.

Serve with Urban Caveman tartare sauce (see page 300).

Salmon stir-fry

Ingredients:

- **Ground ginger**
- **4 cloves garlic, sliced**
- **Coconut oil for frying**
- **I fillet of wild salmon per person**
- **Onions, cut into slices**
- **Carrots, sliced into sticks**
- **Celery, sliced into sticks**
- **Broccoli, cut into florets**
- **Peppers, sliced**
- **Mushrooms, sliced**
- **Tamari or coconut soy-sauce substitute**
- **Bok choi or cabbage, shredded**
- **Konjac or kelp rice or ground raw cauliflower rice (see page 268), lightly steamed**

Sauté the ginger and garlic in the coconut oil.

Stir fry the fish until cooked – about 10 minutes. Transfer to a plate and keep warm.

Next fry all the vegetables, apart from the bok choi or cabbage, adding more fat if necessary.

Add the tamari or coconut soy-sauce substitute, to flavour, return the meat to the wok and mix in well. Add water if too dry.

Just before serving, stir in the bok choi or cabbage.

Serve hot over rice.

Fishfingers

Ingredients:
Serves 4

- **300 g/11 oz fish – salmon, halibut – filleted and skinned**
- **1 large egg, beaten**
- **40 g/1½ oz coconut flour**
- **½ tsp paprika**
- **Seasoning**
- **1 tbs nutritional yeast flakes, ground in a coffee grinder or food processor**
- **75 g/3 oz Urban Caveman loaf breadcrumbs**
- **Coconut oil, butter or ghee, for frying**

Using a carving knife, cut the fish into finger shapes.

Place the beaten egg in one bowl.

Mix the flour, paprika, seasoning and ground nutritional yeast flakes in a second bowl.

Place the Urban Caveman breadcrumbs in a third bowl.

Coat the fish in the flour mixture, then the egg, and finally the breadcrumbs.

Fry in the oil and drain on kitchen paper.

Serve with Urban Caveman tartare sauce or ketchup.

Scandinavian soused herrings

Ingredients:
Serves 8
- 1½ tbs Himalayan salt
- 8 herrings, filleted
- 2 cornichons (similar to gherkins - sugar-free, from health-food shops)
- 1 dsp mustard powder
- 1 onion, sliced

Ingredients for the marinade:
- 570 ml/1 pt white wine vinegar
- 1 tsp allspice berries, from health-food shops
- 1 tsp coriander seeds
- ½ tsp mustard seeds
- 1 dried chilli pepper
- 2 bay leaves
- 2 tsp maple syrup
- 150 ml/¼ pt cold water

Special equipment:
- 8 cocktail sticks

Make the marinade. Mix the vinegar, spices, bay leaves and maple syrup in a saucepan with the water.

Boil and then simmer for five minutes.

Leave to cool.

Sprinkle the salt on the herrings and leave draining for about three hours in a colander.

Rinse the salt off and dry on kitchen paper.

Cut the cornichons lengthways into three pieces.

Spinkle the inside of each piece of fish with mustard.

Place one cornichon and some sliced onion at the head end of each fish piece and roll the fish up (skin outermost), securing with a cocktail stick.

Pack into a rectangular dish, sprinkling the remaining onion on top.

Once cold, pour the marinade over the top.

Cover securely and refrigerate for at least 48 hours before serving.

They will keep for a week.

Oven-baked trout with rosemary

Ingredients:
Serves 2
- **1 large filleted trout**
- **6–8 cloves garlic, sliced**
- **4–6 sweet potatoes, chopped into large chunks**
- **Ghee or butter**
- **Sprigs of fresh rosemary**
- **Seasoning**

Pre-heat your oven to 170°C / 325°F / GM 3.

Line an oven dish first with foil and then with greaseproof paper on the inside with enough margin to cover the fish once it has been placed in the dish.

Place the trout on the paper and put the sliced garlic inside the cavity in the trout's belly.

Arrange the sweet potatoes along each side of the fish.

Melt the butter and pour over the potatoes.

Place sprigs of rosemary in and around the fish and the sweet potatoes.

Season the cavity and sweet potatoes well.

Bring the sides of the greaseproof paper together, forming a seal around the fish.

Close the foil loosely around the top and seal.

Bake in the oven for 40 to 50 minutes, until the fish is tender.

Serve with Urban Caveman tartare sauce.

Fish pie

Ingredients:
Serves 6

- 700 g/1½ lb white fish, filleted and broken into large flakes
- 2 x 400 ml tins coconut cream
- 1 tbs kuzu
- 25 g/1 oz nutritional yeast flakes
- 6 cloves garlic, crushed
- Seasoning
- 1 portion mashed cauliflower (see page 268), swede or potato
- *Optional*: Urban Caveman breadcrumbs (see page 64)
- Ghee or butter to top
- Flatleaf parsley (to serve)

Pre-heat your oven to 170°C/325°F/GM 3.

Place the fish in a casserole dish.

Warm most of the coconut cream in a saucepan until nearly boiling.

Dissolve the kuzu in the remaining coconut cream.

Stir the kuzu into the almost boiling coconut cream together with the nutritional yeast flakes and garlic and stir until the sauce has thickened.

Season well and pour over the fish.

Top with mashed cauliflower and sprinkled breadcrumbs, if using, and dot with ghee or butter.

Bake in the oven for 35 to 45 minutes, until the fish is cooked and the top is golden.

Remove from the oven and sprinkle chopped parsley on top.

Serve with Urban Caveman ketchup and green vegetables.

Smoked haddock with coconut cream sauce

Ingredients:
Serves 4–6

- 700 g/1½ lb smoked haddock
- 1 bay leaf
- 275 ml/½ pt coconut milk, light
- Seasoning
- 50 g/2 oz ghee or butter
- 1 onion, finely chopped
- 1 dsp kuzu
- 1 egg, hard-boiled and chopped finely
- 3 tbs coconut cream

Pre-heat your oven to 180°C/350°F/GM 4.

Place the fish in a baking tin with the bay leaf and milk, and season well.

Dot with some of the butter or ghee and bake uncovered for about 20 minutes.

When the fish is cooked, remove it from the oven and keep warm.

Melt the remaining butter and sauté the onions without browning.

Pour the liquid in which the fish was cooked into the onions.

Dissolve the kuzu in a little water and stir into the liquid until thickened.

Cook for a few minutes before adding the chopped egg and coconut cream.

Serve the fish with the hot sauce on top.

Fish cakes

Ingredients:
Makes 4

- 450 g/1 lb white fish, flaked
- 1 tbs tomato purée or Urban Caveman tomato ketchup (see page 327)

- 1 tsp garlic powder
- 1 tsp onion powder
- Chopped fresh parsley
- 1 egg, beaten
- 2 dsp paprika
- 1 tbs coconut flour
- Seasoning
- Butter, ghee or coconut oil for frying
- Urban Caveman tartare sauce (see page 300), to serve
- Flatleaf parsley, chopped, to serve

Mix the fish, tomato purée, garlic powder, onion powder, parsley, egg, paprika and coconut flour together, season and form into balls, adding more coconut flour if needed.

Flatten into burger shapes.

Warm the oil in a large frying pan and fry the fish cakes for about 15 minutes, turning once.

Transfer to kitchen paper and serve with Urban Caveman tartare sauce and the chopped flatleaf parsley.

Side dishes

Vegetables

Asparagus with caraway seeds

Ingredients:
Serves 6
- 2 bunches asparagus, trimmed
- 2 tbs olive oil or ghee or butter
- 2 tbs caraway seeds, lightly toasted
- 2 spring onions, sliced
- Juice of 1 lemon
- Salt and black pepper

Pre-heat your oven to 200°C / 400°F / GM 6.

Steam the asparagus for about five to 10 minutes, depending on thickness of asparagus, until softened.

Toss the asparagus in olive oil in an ovenproof dish and bake for six to eight minutes, shaking them a few times during cooking.

Mix in the seeds and onions and return the asparagus to the oven for a further one to two minutes.

Pour freshly squeezed lemon juice over the asparagus and season before serving.

Broccoli bake

Ingredients:
Serves 6

- 1 large bunch broccoli
- 4 tbs butter or ghee, room temperature
- 4 eggs, lightly beaten
- 1 portion Urban Caveman coconut cream yoghurt
- 1 onion, small, finely diced
- Seasoning

Heat the oven to 180 C / 350 F / GM 4.

Cut the broccoli into florets and steam for a few minutes.

Transfer to a food processor and chop.

Add the butter, eggs, yoghurt and onion and whisk together using an electric stick blender. Add the seasoning.

Place in six ramekins and arrange in a pan of boiling water.

Bake in the oven for 20 minutes.

Loosen with a knife and turn upside down on to serving plates.

Brussels sprouts

Ingredients:

- Brussel sprouts – about 6 per person
- Butter or ghee for frying
- Seasoning
- *Optional*: Flaked almonds

Cut the ends off the brussels sprouts, and slice them lengthwise.

Steam for one minute.

Transfer to a pan with melted butter or ghee and sauté for a few minutes.

Season well.

Stir in some flaked almonds if using.

Red cabbage

This slow-cooker recipe is excellent in the cold months. A whole red cabbage can last a family for several days as a vegetable accompaniment. The caraway seeds help with digestion of the cabbage.

Ingredients:
- **1 red cabbage**
- **1 eating apple**
- **Sweetener**
- **225 ml/8fl oz water**
- **1 tsp caraway seeds**
- **A little lemon juice**

Set your slow cooker to High if cooking for three to four hours, or Low if cooking for six to eight hours.

Cut the cabbage into quarters and remove any tough outer leaves and the inner core.

Shred finely and then run through with cold water until the water runs clear.

Place in the slow cooker.

Peel, core and chop the apple and add to the slow cooker with all the other ingredients.

Cook for three to four hours on High or six to eight hours on Low.

German red cabbage

Ingredients:

- 2 red cabbages, finely shredded
- 480 ml/16 fl oz fermented apple cider vinegar
- 6 eating apples, sliced
- Few knobs of ghee or butter (could use coconut oil, but a buttery flavour is best)
- Seasoning
- Water if needed

Place all the ingredients in a large soup tureen and bring to the boil, stirring occasionally.

Simmer for three to four hours, adding a little water if necessary.

Provides an instant vegetable dish for those in a rush as it can be stored for several days in the fridge and warmed before serving.

Butternut squash with breadcrumbs

Ingredients:

Serves 6-8

- 3 butternut squashes
- 3 eggs, lightly beaten
- ¼ tsp nutmeg
- Seasoning
- 1 portion of Urban Caveman breadcrumbs (see page 64)
- 2 tbs ghee or butter

Pre-heat your oven to 180°C/350°F/GM 4.

Slice the squashes lengthwise and scoop out the seeds.

Place in an ovenproof dish with a little water in the bottom.

Bake for about one hour, until tender.

Once cooked, scoop out the flesh and process in a food processor, adding the eggs and nutmeg.

Season to taste.

Transfer the purée to an ovenproof dish.

Sprinkle breadcrumbs on top and pour melted butter over them.

Bake for about 25 minutes.

Mashed cauliflower

This is a great substitute for mashed potato.

Ingredients:
Serves 4–6 depending on size of cauliflower
- **1 cauliflower**
- **Seasoning**
- **Few knobs of butter or ghee**
- **Chopped fresh chives**

Steam the cauliflower until tender.

Drain and place in a bowl.

Season and add the butter.

Blend with an electric stick blender and stir in the chopped chives.

Cauliflower 'rice' 1

Cauliflower has a bitter taste when raw so it is necessary to cook it lightly, either by steaming as in this recipe, or by sautéing (see Cauliflower 'rice' 2). Serves four to six depending on size of cauliflower.

To make Paleo rice process raw cauliflower florets in a food processor until broken into rice-sized pieces. You may need to do this in more than one batch depending on the make of your food processor.

Lightly steam or boil the resulting 'grains'.

Cauliflower 'rice' 2

Ingredients:
Serves 4–6 depending on size of cauliflower
- **Florets of 1 cauliflower**
- **Approximately 110 g/4 oz butter or ghee (depends on size of cauliflower)**
- ***Optional:* 2–4 cloves garlic, crushed**
- **Seasoning**
- ***Optional:* chopped fresh herbs like parsley or basil depending on accompanying dish**

Process the florets in your food processor until broken into rice-size pieces.

Melt the butter or ghee and stir in the crushed garlic.

Toss the broken florets in the butter and garlic and sauté for about five minutes until the bitter taste has gone.

Season and add fresh herbs if using.

Cauliflower 'cheese'

Ingredients:
Serves 4–6
- 1 cauliflower
- 1 x 400 ml tin coconut cream
- 1 dsp kuzu
- 1 tsp onion powder
- 2 cloves garlic, crushed
- 2 beaten egg yolks
- 6 tbs nutritional yeast flakes
- Seasoning

Steam cauliflower and place florets in a bowl.

Warm three quarters of the coconut cream.

Mix kuzu in the remaining cream and add the onion powder and garlic.

Add the mixture to the warmed coconut cream and stir in the eggs.

Stir until thickened and add the nutritional yeast flakes.

Season and pour over the cauliflower.

Courgette 'pasta' with pesto sauce

Ingredients:
- 1–2 courgettes per person
- Olive oil or butter
- Urban Caveman pesto sauce (see page 304) – you could use the cheesy one (see page 303)
- Black pepper to taste
- Fresh basil leaves, chopped

Using a peeler, remove the skin and then cut the courgettes into wide but thin pasta-like strips

In a large frying pan, warm the olive oil or butter and then sauté the strips of courgette for two to three minutes to warm.

Stir in the pesto sauce and season well with black pepper, sprinkle with basil and serve.

Braised leeks

Ingredients:
Serves 4–6

- 6 medium-sized leeks, trimmed, washed and lightly steamed
- 425 ml/15 fl oz home-made beef stock
- ½ portion grated Urban Caveman cheddar

Place the leeks in an ovenproof dish.

Bring the stock to the boil and pour over the leeks.

Sprinkle the cheddar over the top and brown under the grill for a few minutes.

Leeks in cream sauce

Ingredients:
Serves 4–6

- Enough butter or ghee to coat the leeks
- Leeks, washed and then chopped into circles
- 2 cloves garlic, crushed or chopped
- 1 tbs kuzu
- 1 x 400 ml tin coconut cream or milk
- ¼ tsp nutmeg
- Seasoning

Melt the butter or ghee in a pan, then add the sliced leeks and garlic and sauté, stirring.

Dissolve the kuzu in one third of the coconut cream or milk.

Pour the rest of the milk into the leeks and bring to the boil.

Turn down the heat, cover and allow to simmer for about five minutes.

Then add the remaining milk and kuzu and stir until thickened.

Add nutmeg and seasoning to taste.

Oven-roasted vegetable medley

Ingredients:
Serves 6-8

- **Coconut oil to grease baking tray**
- **2 onions, quartered**
- **1 red pepper, cut into large chunks**
- **2 carrots, cut into large chunks**
- **1 parsnip, cut into large chunks**
- **1 butternut squash, cut into large squares**
- **6 tomatoes, cut into quarters**
- **2 stalks celery, cut into large chunks**
- **10 cloves garlic, crushed slightly with skins on**
- **4 sprigs fresh rosemary**
- **Enough olive oil to drizzle over the top of the vegetables**
- **Seasoning**

Heat your oven to 170°C/325°F/GM 3.

Place the coconut oil in a large baking tray and warm in the oven.

Arrange the vegetables in the warmed fat, tossing them to coat them in the oil.

Dribble a little olive oil over the top and season well.

Bake for about 45 minutes, turning once.

Baked sweet potatoes

Ingredients:

- **Olive oil, melted butter or ghee**
- **1 sweet potato per person**
- **Seasoning**

Pre-heat your oven to 180°C/350°F/GM 4.

Oil a biscuit baking tray and warm in the oven.

Slice the potatoes once lengthwise and then into chunks about ½ inch thick.

Arrange face down on the hot oil and season.

Bake for around 40 to 45 minutes, turning once, until golden.

Vegetable patties

Ingredients:
Serves 4 -6

- **Olive oil to oil baking tray**
- **40 g/1½ oz butter or ghee**
- **1–2 sweet potatoes per person, boiled and mashed – alternatively, you can use a mixture of carrots, parsnips or other root vegetables**
- **2 stalks celery, sliced and boiled for about half an hour until tender**
- **2 cloves garlic, crushed**
- **½-1 portion Urban Caveman coconut yoghurt (see page 39), or coconut cream**
- **Pinch nutmeg**
- **Seasoning**

Pre-heat your oven to 170°C/325°F/GM 3.

Coat an oven dish with olive oil, and place in the oven.

Mash the butter, sweet potatoes, celery and garlic together.

Add the yoghurt or cream to obtain the consistency of mashed potato.

Season to taste and stir in the nutmeg.

Form into balls and flatten down onto the oiled oven dish.

Bake for about 20 to 25 minutes, until browned on top.

Winter vegetable batons

Ingredients:
- **Carrots, cut into large batons**
- **Celery, cut into large batons**
- **Peppers, cut into large batons**
- **Cabbage, cut into large chunks**
- **Cauliflower florets, steamed for a few minutes, but still crunchy**
- **Radishes, sliced in half**
- **Fennel, sliced**

Ingredients for the sauce:
- **275 ml/½ pint coconut cream**
- **2–3 tsp garlic powder**
- **2 tsp anchovy paste**
- **3 tbs white wine vinegar**
- **150 ml/¼ pint olive oil**

Place the coconut cream, garlic powder and anchovy paste into a pan and bring the mixture to the boil, stirring.

Using an electric stick blender, whisk the sauce whilst *slowly* adding the vinegar and olive oil, as if making mayonnaise.

Serve hot with the vegetables.

Salads

Bacon and egg salad

Ingredients:
Serves 4
- Medium-sized bowl of watercress, rocket, salad leaves
- 2 eggs, hard-boiled and chopped
- 4 rashers bacon, grilled until crispy

Ingredients for the dressing:
- 2 tbs tamari or coconut soy-sauce substitute
- 3 tbs olive oil
- 3 tbs white wine vinegar
- 1 tsp lemon juice
- Seasoning
- Flatleaf parsley, chopped

Wash and completely dry the salad leaves.

Whisk the tamari, oil, vinegar and lemon juice together and the add seasoning.

Work the dressing into the salad leaves and garnish with the chopped eggs and crumbled bacon pieces.

Garnish with parsley.

Beetroot salad

Ingredients:
Serves 4-6

- Bunch fresh mint, chopped
- 8 spring onions, chopped
- 6 beetroots, cooked and diced
- 2 tbs balsamic vinegar
- 150 ml/¼ pt olive oil
- Seasoning

Place the chopped mint, onions and beetroot in a salad dish.

Blend the vinegar and olive oil, season and stir into the salad.

Beetroot salad with coriander

Beetroot is great for the liver and gall bladder.

Ingredients:
Serves 6-8

- 6–9 raw beetroots, grated, or cooked beetroots, diced
- 1 raw courgette, diced
- 1 washed carrot, sliced into strips using a peeler
- 5 tbs olive oil
- 150–275 ml/¼–½ pt Urban Caveman coconut yoghurt
- 1 tsp fresh dill, chopped
- 1 tsp fresh coriander, chopped
- 1 tsp coriander seeds, toasted and crushed
- Zest and juice of 1 lemon
- Seasoning
- Fresh coriander, to serve

Place the diced beetroot and courgette in a bowl.

Stir in ¾ of the carrot strips.

Mix the olive oil, yoghurt, herbs, lemon zest and juice and seasoning together to make the dressing and stir into the salad.

Add pepper.

Decorate with slithers of peeled carrot and fresh coriander leaves.

Coleslaw

Ingredients:
Serves 10

- 1 white cabbage, shredded
- 2 large carrots, grated
- 1 pepper, any colour except green which can be a bit bitter, thinly sliced
- 1 apple, grated or chopped
- Spring onions, sliced into strips
- Chopped fresh curly-leaf parsley
- Home-made coconut mayonnaise (see page 296)
- Black pepper

Special equipment:
This recipe requires a food processor to first of all make the mayonnaise and then to shred and slice the vegetables.

Mix all the vegetables together in a large salad bowl.

Stir in the mayonnaise, coating well.

Season with black pepper.

Cover with clingfilm and refrigerate until needed.

Green salad

Ingredients:
Serves 8

- 1 small lettuce
- Handful of rocket leaves
- ½ cucumber, diced
- 1 apple, diced
- 3 spring onions, sliced
- 2 stalks celery, sliced
- 1 green pepper, sliced
- 2 avocados, diced
- Parsley, chopped

Ingredients for the dressing:

- Approximately 110 ml/4fl oz olive oil
- 1 dsp balsamic vinegar
- 1 tsp anchovy paste
- 1 tsp Urban Caveman coconut mayonnaise (see page 296)
- Seasoning

Make the dressing by mixing the ingredients together in a food processor.

In a bowl mix the salad ingredients together and then stir the dressing into the salad.

'Rice' and vegetable salad

Ingredients:
Serves 6–8

- 2 packets konjac rice, or cauliflower rice (see page 268)
- 1 yellow and 1 red pepper, sliced
- ½ cucumber, diced
- 1 stalk celery, sliced

- 5 spring onions, sliced

Ingredients for the dressing:
- 2 cloves garlic, crushed
- 150–200 g/5–7 oz pine nuts, ground
- 1 dsp Urban Caveman mayonnaise (see page 296)
- 1 tsp mustard
- Olive oil
- Tamari or coconut soy-sauce substitute
- Dash maple syrup
- Seasoning

Make the dressing by mixing the ingredients together in a food processor.

In a bowl mix the salad ingredients together and then stir the dressing into the salad.

Olive and caper salad

Ingredients:
Serves 4-6
- 8–12 olives, stoned
- 1 small jar capers, drained
- 3 spring onions, chopped
- 6-8 cherry tomatoes, quartered
- 1 packet rocket leaves, washed

Ingredients for the dressing:
- 1 tsp lemon juice
- 1 tsp balsamic vinegar
- 1 tsp mustard
- 6 tbs olive oil, organic, first cold pressing
- 1 clove garlic, crushed
- Small bunch fresh parsley, chopped
- Seasoning

Make the dressing by mixing the ingredients together in a food processor.

In a bowl mix the salad ingredients together and then stir the dressing into the salad.

'Pasta' salad with Urban Caveman cheesy pesto

Ingredients:
Serves 4-6

- 3-4 packets konjac or kelp noodles, or strips of courgette lightly sautéed in virgin olive oil
- 1 portion Urban Caveman cheesy pesto (see page 303)
- Black pepper

Prepare the noodles as instructed on the packet.

Stir in the pesto and season generously with black pepper.

Potato salad

Ingredients:
Serves 6–8

- 900 g/2 lb small new potatoes or sweet potatoes
- 2 sprigs mint
- About 275 ml/½ pt vinaigrette dressing (see page 301)
- 3 tbs fresh mint, chopped
- 2 tbs fresh parsley, chopped
- 2 tbs chives, chopped
- 8 spring onions, finely chopped
- Salt and black pepper

Wash (don't scrape) the potatoes and place in a saucepan with the mint. Pour enough boiling water over them to almost cover them.

Simmer for about 10 minutes, until tender but firm.

Drain and place them in a salad bowl.

Dice them and pour on the vinaigrette dressing while they are still warm.

Once they have cooled, mix in the chopped herbs and spring onions.

Season to taste.

Red cabbage and coriander salad

Ingredients:
Serves 8

- 1 red cabbage, shredded
- 1 eating apple, grated with skin on
- 1 onion, finely chopped
- 2 stalks celery, chopped
- Fresh coriander leaves

Ingredients for the dressing:

- ¼ tsp coriander seeds, crushed
- 1 clove garlic, crushed
- ½ tsp Himalayan salt
- ½ tsp mustard powder
- Black pepper
- 2 tbs olive oil
- 2 tbs white wine vinegar
- 60 g/2½ oz Urban Caveman coconut yoghurt (see page 39)

Dry-fry the coriander seeds for about five to 10 minutes.

Mix the garlic, salt, mustard powder and pepper in a bowl and pour in the oil and vinegar. Stir thoroughly and then add the yoghurt and coriander, mixing well.

Shred the cabbage in a food processor and place in a salad bowl. Add the apple, onion and celery, stirring in well. Add fresh coriander.

Toss the dressing into the salad, adding a few coriander leaves as a garnish.

Salad niçoise

Ingredients:
Serves 6–8

- Fresh herbs (thyme, mint, chives)
- Garlic
- Approximately 275 ml/½ pt vinaigrette (see page 301)
- 1 lettuce, chopped
- 350 g/12 oz tomatoes, quartered
- Small cucumber, diced
- 4 spring onions, chopped
- 110 g/4 oz new potatoes or sweet potatoes, cooked, sliced
- 110 g/4 oz French or runner beans, cooked, cooled
- 2 eggs, hard-boiled and quartered
- 200 g/7 oz cooked fish (This salad is traditionally made with tuna, but tuna contains higher levels of mercury than most other fish, so I usually substitute haddock or wild salmon)
- 1 tin anchovy fillets, drained
- Black olives
- Bunch fresh parsley, chopped

Add the chopped herbs and garlic to the vinaigrette.

Place the lettuce in a salad bowl and sprinkle on some of the vinaigrette.

Add the tomatoes and cucumber and more dressing, together with the onions, slices of potatoes and beans.

Put the eggs on top with flakes of fish.

Decorate with lattice of anchovy and sprinkle on olives, parsley and the remainder of the dressing.

Salmon salad

Ingredients:
Serves 4

- 1 packet konjac rice or cauliflower rice (see page 268) made using 1 small cauliflower
- ½ cucumber, diced
- 1 tbs capers
- Couple of handfuls of samphire
- Parsley, chopped
- 1 tsp grated lemon zest
- ½ tsp balsamic vinegar
- Seasoning
- 1 wild salmon fillet, cooked and cooled

Ingredients for the dressing:
- 3 tbs olive oil
- 1 dsp white wine vinegar
- 1 tsp dried mustard powder
- Juice of ½ lemon

To serve:
- Lettuce leaves
- Lemon quarters
- Cayenne pepper

Drain and rinse the konjac and steep in boiling water to warm.

Mix the dressing ingredients together and pour over the drained konjac, while still warm. Then leave to cool.

Mix the salad ingredients (except the salmon) together in a bowl. Add the konjac.

Break the salmon into pieces and stir into the konjac salad.

Serve on a bed of lettuce decorated with lemon quarters, and sprinkle a small amount of cayenne on the top.

Tomato salad

Ingredients:
Serves 4-6
- **About 12 tomatoes on the vine (Capri are good)**
- **4 spring onions**
- **Seasoning**
- **Fresh basil leaves – lots**
- **110 ml/4 fl oz olive oil**
- **1 tbs tamari or coconut soy-sauce substitute**

Slice the tomatoes and onions and place them in a bowl with lots of black pepper and three quarters of the basil leaves, thinly sliced.

Place the remaining basil leaves, oil and tamari in a jug and whisk well using an electric stick blender.

Stir the dressing into the salad.

Yoghurt and sausage salad

Ingredients:

Serves 4-6

- 100 per cent meat sausages made by your butcher, grilled
- 1 lettuce, chopped
- 125 g/4½ oz mushrooms, grilled
- 2 avocados
- 4 spring onions, finely chopped

Ingredients for the dressing:

- Urban Caveman soured cream (see page 41)
- 2 cloves garlic, crushed or ½ tsp garlic powder
- 2 tbs Urban Caveman mayonnaise (see page 296)
- 1 tbs mustard powder
- 2 tbs olive oil
- 1 tbs white wine vinegar
- Seasoning

Combine the soured yoghurt with the garlic, mayonnaise and mustard powder.

Mix together the oil and vinegar and then gradually add to the soured yoghurt mixture. Season.

Slice the grilled sausages into chunks.

Arrange the lettuce in a salad bowl, wipe and slice the mushrooms and stir them into the lettuce.

Dice the avocado and add to the salad, together with the sausage chunks.

Add the dressing and sprinkle chopped spring onions over the top.

Waldorf salad

Ingredients:
Serves 4–6

- 2 tbs lemon juice
- 6 tbs Urban Caveman mayonnaise (see page 296)
- 250–350 g/9-12 oz walnuts, chopped into large pieces
- 2 stalks celery, sliced small
- 2 spring onions, chopped
- 2 eating apples, cored and diced
- Seasoning

Mix the lemon juice into the mayonnaise.

Combine the walnuts, celery, spring onions and apples.

Stir into the mayonnaise and season.

Winter coleslaw

Ingredients:
Serves 4–6

- Large red or white cabbage
- 1 small celeriac
- 3 large carrots
- Small bunch of radishes
- 1 eating apple
- 4 shallots, spring onions or red onions
- 2 stalks celery
- 1 pepper, any colour
- Flatleaf parsley
- Fresh basil leaves
- 1 clove garlic, crushed

- **Urban Caveman mayonnaise (see page 296)**
- **Black pepper**

Grate the cabbage, celeriac, carrots, radishes and apple in your food processor.
Finely chop the shallots, celery, pepper and parsley. Mix all in a large salad bowl.
Add fresh basil leaves and crushed garlic to the coconut mayonnaise.
Season generously with black pepper and work the mayonnaise into the salad.

Sauces and gravies

Hot sauces

Gravy to accompany a roast

Ingredients:
- Generous knob of goose fat, beef dripping, butter, ghee or coconut oil
- 1–2 onions, roughly chopped
- Selection of roughly diced root vegetables, such as one sweet potato, one parsnip, one carrot
- 2-3 stalks celery, in chunks
- 8-10 cloves garlic with skins on
- 570 ml/1 pint water or stock
- Seasoning

This method is based on vegetables that have been roasted under the joint. They should be added to the roasting dish one to one-and-a-half hours before the roast is due to be ready.

When the joint is cooked, remove it from the vegetable base and leave it to rest.

Place the roasting dish on the hob and add water – preferably the water in which you have cooked accompanying green vegetables.

Season to taste and purée.

Onion gravy

Ingredients:

- 2-3 onions, sliced into rings
- *Optional*: garlic, crushed
- Oil for frying – goose or bacon fat have a good flavour
- 1 tbs kuzu
- 570–725 ml/1–1¼ pt meat stock, depending on how thick you like the gravy
- Seasoning
- Tamari or coconut soy-sauce substitute

Fry the onions and garlic in the oil.

Dissolve the kuzu in a little cold water.

Add to the onions and garlic, stirring.

Add the stock, and continue stirring until the mixture thickens.

Season and flavour with the tamari or coconut soy-sauce substitute.

Mushroom gravy

As for onion gravy (see above) but fry some chopped mushrooms with the onions.

White sauce

Ingredients:
Makes 425 ml/¾ pt
- 1 dsp kuzu
- 1 x 400 ml tin coconut milk
- 1 dsp butter or ghee
- ¼ tsp nutmeg, grated
- 1 tsp mustard
- Seasoning

Stir the kuzu into one third of a tin of coconut milk.

Add the butter, nutmeg and mustard to the remaining milk in a saucepan and bring almost to the boil.

Pour over the kuzu mixture, stirring well.

Return to the pan and bring to a simmer, stirring constantly.

Season well.

Cheese sauce

Ingredients:
Makes 425 ml/¾ pt
- 1 x 400 ml tin coconut cream
- 2 cloves garlic, crushed
- Kuzu to thicken
- 1–2 tsp mustard
- 2 tbs nutritional yeast flakes
- 1 dsp onion powder
- Seasoning

Mix all the ingredients together and warm in a saucepan, stirring.

Season to taste.

Cold sauces and dressings

Hollandaise sauce

Ingredients:
- 2 tbs white wine vinegar
- 2 tbs coconut milk
- 4 egg yolks
- 200 g/7 oz ghee or butter, melted
- Pinch paprika
- 1 tsp mustard
- Juice of ½ lemon
- Seasoning – with white, not black, pepper

Bring the vinegar and coconut milk to the boil in a saucepan.

Simmer until the mixure is thick and has reduced by about a third.

Cool before whisking in the egg yolks.

Transfer the mixture to a glass bowl over a saucepan of simmering water.

Whisk until thick – this takes a few minutes.

Remove from the heat and gradually add the ghee, whisking as you do so. Add paprika and mustard.

Stir in the lemon juice and season to taste.

Urban Caveman paste

This can be added to hot soups, stocks etc for more flavour.

Ingredients:

- 1-2 bulbs garlic
- 2-inch piece fresh ginger
- 6 tbs extra virgin olive oil
- 1 tbs lemon juice

Mix all the ingredients in a food processor.

Store in a glass jar in the fridge.

This paste keeps for approximately 10 days.

Italian-style paste

To the basic paste add sun-dried tomatoes, fresh basil and fresh chillies, olive oil and lemon juice and blend in a food processor.

Mustard sauce

Ingredients:

- 6 tbs mustard seeds, roughly ground in a coffee grinder (but not powdered)
- 2 tbs mustard powder
- 2 tsp Himalayan salt
- 3 tbs apple cider vinegar
- 200 ml/⅓ pt water
- *Optional:* dash of sweetener of choice

Mix the seeds, mustard powder and salt together.

Place in a jar and add the vinegar and water.

Screw the lid on tightly and shake vigorously.

Refrigerate for 12 hours.

Will keep for several months in the fridge.

Tapenade

Tapenade is great served with fish or roasted vegetables.

Ingredients:
- 1 large tub pitted black olives
- 1 dsp anchovy paste
- 2 cloves garlic
- 2 tbs capers
- 5 basil leaves
- 1 tbs apple cider vinegar
- 2 tbs olive oil

Process all the ingredients together in a food processor and refrigerate.

Salsa

Ingredients:

- 2 onions, chopped
- ½ yellow pepper, chopped
- ½ green pepper, chopped
- ½ red pepper, chopped
- 2 tbs garlic cloves, crushed
- Coconut oil to cook
- 1 kg/2.2 lb tomatoes, peeled and chopped
- 110 ml/4 fl oz tomato juice
- 2 bay leaves
- 1 tsp dried basil
- 1 tsp dried oregano
- 1 tbs maple syrup
- Seasoning

Sauté the onions, peppers and garlic in the coconut oil.

Add all the other ingredients and bring to boil.

Simmer, uncovered, until thickened; then discard the bay leaves.

Store in an airtight container. Keeps for over a week in the fridge.

Serve with meat.

Coriander sauce

Use this coriander sauce as a dipping sauce for chicken that has been baked in ground cumin, paprika and seasoning.

Ingredients:

- 1 bunch fresh coriander
- 3 cloves garlic
- 40 g/1½ oz desiccated coconut

- 75 ml/3 fl oz fresh lemon juice
- 1 tsp Himalayan salt
- ½ tsp ground pepper
- ¼ tsp ground cumin
- 60 ml/2½ fl oz water

Purée all the ingredients in a blender.

Serve cold with hot, roast chicken.

Harissa

This is a spicy North African sauce which goes well with seafood. It can be added to seafood stews, or served as a dip. It will keep for three months in a jam jar in the fridge with a little olive oil poured on top.

Ingredients:
- 10 chillis, dried
- 3 cloves garlic
- ½ tsp Himalayan salt
- 2 tbs olive oil
- 1 tsp ground coriander
- 1 tsp ground caraway seed
- 1 tsp ground cumin

Soak the chillis in water for half an hour.

Remove the stems and seeds.

Blend the chillis, garlic, salt and olive oil in a food processor.

Add the remaining spices to form a paste.

Place in a glass jar with a tight-fitting lid.

Dollop olive oil over the top and screw lid on firmly.

Urban Caveman mayonnaise

Ingredients:

- **4 egg yolks**
- **425 ml/¾ pt olive oil**
- **4 tbs lemon juice**
- **Seasoning**
- **Pinch Cajun seasoning or paprika**
- **1 tbs wholegrain mustard**
- **200 ml/¹⁄₃ pint coconut oil, melted and left to cool**

Place the egg yolks, olive oil, lemon juice, seasoning, Cajun seasoning and mustard in a food processor and whizz until smooth.

Still processing, *slowly* dribble in the melted, cooled coconut oil, drop by drop to avoid curdling. It may also curdle if it is too warm.

Store in an airtight container. Keeps for at least two weeks in the fridge.

Horseradish sauce

Ingredients:

- **3 tbs dried horseradish powder**
- **1 tbs cider vinegar**
- **1 tsp mustard powder**
- **3 tbs Urban Caveman yoghurt (see page 39)**
- **3 tbs Urban Caveman mayonnaise (see page 299)**

Blend all the ingredients together and refrigerate in a glass jar. Keeps for about 2 weeks.

Thousand Island dressing 1

Ingredients:

- ½ portion Urban Caveman mayonnaise (see page 296)
- 2 tbs Urban Caveman tomato ketchup (see page 327)
- 1 jar capers

Mix all the ingredients together.

Store in an airtight jar in the fridge. Keeps for at least two weeks.

Thousand Island dressing 2

Ingredients:

- 1 portion Urban Caveman mayonnaise (see page 296)
- Small jar tomato purée
- A little ground chilli powder
- 1 small jar capers, drained
- Seasoning

Mix all the ingredients together and store in a covered container in the fridge.

Mint sauce

To accompany lamb

Ingredients:

- Large bunch mint leaves
- White wine vinegar
- A little water

Wash the mint leaves and place in a jug, adding about 2 dsp vinegar and a little water, depending on how thick or runny you want the sauce to be.

Whizz with an electric stick blender.

Place in a glass jar and refrigerate. Keeps for about two days but may discolour.

Creamy dressing for potato salad

Ingredients:
- **3 eggs, hard-boiled**
- **1 tbs cold water**
- **¼ tsp cayenne pepper**
- **¼ tsp Himalayan salt**
- **150 ml/¼ pt coconut cream**
- **4 tbs white wine vinegar**
- **Fresh chives, chopped**

Shell the eggs and place in a food processor.

Add the water and whizz to produce a smooth paste.

Add the cayenne and salt and process, *slowly* pouring in the coconut cream.

Then add the vinegar.

Cover and refrigerate to thicken.

Stir in the chopped chives before serving.

Italian dressing

Ingredients:
- **4 tbs olive oil**
- **4 tbs coconut oil**

- **4 tbs apple cider vinegar or lemon juice**
- **1 tsp tomato purée**
- **3 tbs water**
- **Oregano and basil**
- **Seasoning**

Put all the ingredients into a jar, cover and shake vigorously until well blended.

Let the dressing sit at room temperature for one hour.

Store in the fridge. Keeps for about two months.

Curried mayonnaise

This is excellent served hot with diced chicken.

Ingredients:
- **Curry powder**
- **1 portion Urban Caveman mayonnaise (see page 296)**
- **Coconut cream**
- **Fresh coriander, chopped, to serve**

Add the curry powder to the mayonnaise to taste.

Stir in the coconut cream to the desired consistency and warm in a saucepan. Add fresh coriander and serve.

Tartare sauce 1

Ingredients:

- 1 portion Urban Caveman mayonnaise (see page 296)
- 1 small jar capers, drained
- 2 eggs, hard-boiled, chopped
- 1 tsp mustard
- 1–2 tsp lemon juice
- 1–2 tsp white wine vinegar
- Chives or spring onions, finely chopped
- Seasoning

Mix all the ingredients together.

Season to taste.

Store in an airtight jar. Keeps for about two weeks.

Tartare sauce 2

Ingredients:

- 1 portion Urban Caveman mayonnaise (see page 296)
- 2 tbs capers
- 1 tsp fresh lemon juice
- Chives, chopped

Mix all the ingredients together.

Can be stored in a jar in the fridge for about two weeks.

Vinaigrette 1

Ingredients:

- 4 tbs virgin olive oil
- 4 tbs coconut oil
- 4 tbs balsamic vinegar
- 3 tbs water
- ½ tsp onion powder
- ½ tsp dill
- Seasoning to taste

Put all the ingredients into a jar, cover and shake vigorously until well blended.

Let it sit at room temperature for one hour.

Store in an airtight jar in the fridge. Keeps for a few weeks but needs to be left at room temperature before using.

Vinaigrette 2

Ingredients:

- 1 tsp Himalayan salt
- 1 clove garlic
- 1 tsp mustard powder
- 1 tbs balsamic vinegar
- Black pepper
- 6 tbs olive oil

Grind the salt and garlic in a pestle and mortar until they form a smooth paste.

Add the mustard powder, vinegar and pepper and mix until the salt dissolves.

Finally, add the olive oil and shake in a screw-top jar.

Vinaigrette 3

Ingredients:

- 1 clove garlic, crushed
- 1 tsp mustard powder or ready-made mustard
- 1 tsp Himalayan salt
- Lashings of black pepper (this can *make* a vinaigrette!)
- 6 tbs olive oil
- 1 tbs balsamic vinegar

Put all the ingredients in a jug and whizz to a creamy consistency with a stick blender. Store in a screw-top jar in the fridge.

Tomato vinaigrette

As for any of the above vinaigrettes, but add some fresh tomatoes.

Maple syrup vinaigrette

As for any of the above vinaigrettes, but add 1 dsp maple syrup.

Caesar dressing

Ingredients:

- 300 ml/½ pt olive oil
- 250 g/9 oz pine nuts, ground in a coffee grinder
- 1–2 cloves garlic, crushed

- Fresh basil leaves (lots!)
- 2 tbs coconut oil, melted
- Juice of 1 lemon
- 1 tsp Urban Caveman mayonnaise (see page 296)
- 1 tsp anchovy paste
- Black pepper

Combine all the ingredients in a food processor.

Store in an airtight container in the fridge. Will last for about a week.

Cheesy pesto

Ingredients:
- 2 tbs coconut oil
- 2 tbs nutritional yeast flakes
- 1 tsp onion powder
- 150 ml/¼ pt olive oil
- 125 g/4½ oz pine nuts, ground in a coffee grinder
- 1–2 cloves garlic, crushed
- 2-3 tbs fresh basil leaves, chopped
- Juice of 1 lemon
- 1 tsp Urban Caveman mayonnaise (see page 296)
- 1 tsp anchovy paste
- Ground black pepper

Melt the coconut oil in a saucepan with the nutritional yeast flakes and onion powder, stirring until a creamy consistency is formed.

Add to your food processor and blend with the other ingredients.

Store in an airtight jar in the fridge. Will last for about two weeks.

Green pesto

Ingredients:

- Large bunch fresh basil leaves
- 250 g/9 oz pine nuts, ground in a coffee grinder
- 110 ml/4 fl oz olive oil
- 3 cloves garlic
- 1 tsp lemon juice
- Seasoning
- *Optional:* ½ tsp anchovy paste

Place all the ingredients in a food processor and blend well.

Store in an airtight jar in the fridge. Keeps for about two weeks.

Tomato pesto

Ingredients:

- 1 small packet sun-dried tomatoes
- 300 ml/½ pt olive oil
- 2 cloves garlic, chopped
- Bunch fresh basil leaves, to taste
- 110 g/4 oz pine nuts, ground
- 1 tbs tomato purée
- Seasoning

Place all the ingredients in a food processor and whizz up.

This pesto is great stirred into konjac noodles or courgette spaghetti to make a salad.

Store in an airtight jar in the fridge. Keeps for about two weeks.

Barbecue sauce

Ingredients:

Makes enough to marinate 4 large steaks

- 1 tbs olive oil
- 1 dsp lemon juice
- 1 tbs tamari or coconut soy-sauce substitute
- 1 tbs balsamic vinegar
- 2 cloves garlic
- 1 tsp mustard
- 1 dsp tomato purée
- Seasoning

Blend all the ingredients together with an electric stick blender and place over the meat that is to be barbecued, as a marinade, for at least two hours.

The sauce can be frozen.

Spicy chilli barbecue marinade

Ingredients:

Makes enough to marinate 4–6 pieces of meat

- 200 ml/⅓ pint olive oil
- Juice and zest of 1 lemon
- 1 tsp ground cumin
- ½ tsp ground tumeric
- ¼ tsp ground cinnamon
- 1 tsp ground coriander
- 1 red chilli, de-seeded and finely chopped
- 2 cloves garlic, crushed
- 2 tbs fresh coriander
- Seasoning

Blend all the ingredients together with an electric stick blender.

This marinade is great for chicken and lamb. Marinate the meat for a minimum of two hours, in the fridge.

Italian barbecue marinade

Great for chicken, will marinate 1 whole chicken or 4 breasts.

Ingredients:

- 1 tsp fennel seeds
- 2 cloves garlic
- 2 tsp dried oregano
- Black pepper, coarsely ground
- Zest and juice of 1 lemon
- 2 tbs olive oil

Crush the fennel seeds in a pestle and mortar.

Blend all the ingredients together using an electric stick blender.

Spread on the meat and marinate for at least two hours, in the fridge.

Desserts

Apple-cake pudding

Ingredients:
Serves 6

- 450 g/1 lb cooking apples or other fruit
- Sweetener of choice
- 3 tbs melted ghee, butter or coconut oil or a mixture
- 3 eggs
- ½ tsp Himalayan salt
- 1 tsp vanilla extract
- 40 g/1¼ oz coconut flour, sifted
- ½ tsp gluten-free baking powder

Pre-heat your oven to 180°C/350°F/GM 4.

Stew half the fruit in a saucepan with the sweetener and approximately 1 tbs water, until soft, and then arrange in the bottom of a casserole dish.

In a food processor, cream the fat, eggs, sweetener to taste, salt and vanilla extract and add about 1 tbs water.

Combine the coconut flour with the baking powder and whisk into the egg mix. Spread the mixture over the top of the fruit.

Bake for 20 to 30 minutes.

Serve hot with coconut cream, or coconut milk custard (see page 312).

Apple pie

Ingredients:
Serves 6-8

- 6 cooking apples, peeled, cored and sliced
- Sweetener of choice
- 1 tbs ground cinnamon
- 1 dsp allspice
- 1 tsp nutmeg, grated
- *Optional:* sultanas
- 1 double pie crust (see page 175) – bottom layer baked for 10 minutes on 190°C/375°F/GM 5
- 1 egg, beaten, for glazing

Cook the apples in a little water.

Add the sweetener, cinnamon, allspice and nutmeg, and sultanas if using, cover and cook for about 10 minutes, until the apples have softened and the mixture thickens.

Spoon the mixture into a pie dish lined with the partially cooked pastry base.

Cover with the pastry topping, sealing with water.

Glaze with beaten egg.

Using a fork, make indentations around the edge of the pie.

Pierce holes in the top to let steam out.

Bake at 200°C/400°F/GM 6 for 15 minutes or until golden.

Serve with Urban Caveman vanilla ice cream (see page 44), custard (page 312) or coconut yoghurt (page 39).

Apple crumble

Ingredients:
Serves 6–8
- 450 g/1 lb cooking apples, roughly chopped and cored
- Pinch cinnamon
- Sweetener of choice

Ingredients for the topping:
- 200 g/7oz butter or coconut oil, cold from fridge
- 300 g/11 oz coconut flour
- 50 g/2 oz ground almonds
- Sweetener of choice
- 200 g/7 oz flaked almonds

Pre-heat your oven to 150ºC/300ºF/GM 2.

Place the apples in large saucepan with a little water, pinch of cinnamon and the sweetener.

Simmer for about 10 minutes, until they have softened.

Cut the butter into cubes and 'rub in' in the food processor with the flour, ground almonds and sweetener. Don't overdo it – try to keep a rough texture.

Mix in the flaked almonds.

Transfer the cooked apple mixture to an ovenproof dish and top with the crumble.

Bake for about 20 minutes to half an hour – until the top is starting to turn golden.

Eat either hot or cold with Urban Caveman coconut yoghurt (page 39), coconut custard (page 312) or ice cream (page 44).

Bread and butter pudding

Ingredients:
Serves 6–8

- Butter or ghee for spreading on the bread
- ½ loaf fruit tea bread, sliced (see page 73)
- 2 eggs and one egg yolk
- 1 tsp vanilla extract or seeds from 1 vanilla pod
- ¼ tsp allspice
- *Optional:* Sweetener of choice
- 1 tsp ground nutmeg plus extra to sprinkle on top
- 1 x 400 ml tin coconut cream
- *Optional:* Maple sugar, Palmyra Jaggery or xylitol to sprinkle on top.

Pre-heat your oven to 200°C/400°F/GM 6.

Spread the butter on slices of the bread and place in an ovenproof dish.

Whisk the eggs, vanilla, allspice, sweetener, and nutmeg into the coconut cream.

Pour over the bread.

Sprinkle the maple sugar, Palmyra Jaggery or xylitol on top and sprinkle on more nutmeg.

Place in the oven and bake for about 25 to 35 minutes until brown.

Delicious hot or cold.

Cheesecake using coconut yoghurt

You may prefer to use a thermometer for this recipe.

Ingredients for the filling:
Serves 8–10

- 3 strips gelatine, unsulphured
- 1 x 400 ml tin coconut cream
- ½ x 400 ml tin coconut milk
- Juice and zest of 1 lemon
- Sweetener of choice
- 1 tsp vanilla extract or seeds from 1 vanilla pod
- 3 eggs
- 1 coconut milk yoghurt or 1 portion Urban Caveman cream cheese

Ingredients for the base:
- Crumbed Urban Caveman butter biscuits (see page 92) – enough to line your flan dish
- Coconut oil, butter or ghee

Pre-heat your oven to 150°C/300°F/GM 2 while you make the base.

Place the biscuits in a food processor and lightly process until crumbed.

Add a little coconut oil, butter or ghee and process further.

Oil a flan dish and transfer the biscuit crumbs to it, flattening them down. Bake for about 10 minutes.

Meanwhile, soak the gelatine strips in cold water for about five minutes. Squeeze out and discard any excess water.

Add the softened gelatine to the other filling ingredients, except the yoghurt, and warm in a saucepan, stirring continuously.

Allow it to simmer for a few minutes to cook the eggs, continuing to stir. It will thicken slightly. You may find a wire whisk more efficient than a wooden spoon.

Allow it to cool down to 40°C (just warm) and then stir in the yoghurt or cream cheese.

Pour over the base and refrigerate overnight. Once cooled you may wish to top with fruit of your choice.

Coconut crème brulée

This is for special occasions only as it is very sweet.

Ingredients:
Serves 6–8 depending on size of ramekins
- **1 large egg plus 3 large egg yolks**
- **1 tsp vanilla extract or the seeds from 1 vanilla pod**
- **1 x 400 ml tin coconut cream**
- **Sweetener of choice**
- **Maple sugar, Palmyra Jaggery or xylitol to sprinkle on top**

Pre-heat the oven to 180°C/350°F/GM 4.

Whisk the whole egg, egg yolks and vanilla together.

Heat the cream and sweetener. Gradually whisk the hot cream into the egg mixture to make a custard.

Divide the custard into the ramekins and top with the sweetener of choice.

Set the ramekins in a roasting pan, adding enough hot water to come halfway up the sides of the dishes. Cover the whole pan with Roastcosy or foil but make sure it doesn't come into contact with the food.

Bake the custards in centre of oven for 35 to 55 minutes until set. They should be firm in the centre but wobbly.

Chill the custards, leaving them uncovered until cold – at least five hours. (They can be made in advance and refrigerated overnight.)

Alternatively you could caramelise with either a blowtorch or under the grill for a couple of minutes.

Custard

Ingredients:
- **1 dsp arrowroot or kuzu**
- **2 egg yolks, beaten**
- **1 x 400 ml tin coconut cream**

- **1 tsp vanilla extract or the seeds from 1 vanilla pod**
- ***Optional:* sweetener of choice**

Stir the arrowroot or kuzu, beaten egg yolks, one quarter of the coconut cream and vanilla together, forming a paste.

Heat the remaining coconut cream.

Just before the coconut cream boils, add the paste and stir until the mixture thickens, sweetening to taste.

Can be served hot or cold.

Frozen mixed berry soufflés

Ingredients:

Serves 6-8 depending on size of ramekins

- **350 g/12 oz mixed, fresh berries (strawberries, raspberries, blueberries etc) plus extra for garnish**
- **Sweetener of choice**
- **2 egg whites**
- **1 strip of gelatine, unsulphured**
- **1 x 400 ml tin coconut cream or milk**

Wash the berries and purée them in a food processor with half the sweetener.

Whisk the egg whites until they start to form peaks. Then add the remaining sweetener and whisk until light and fluffy and peaked.

Soak the gelatine strip in cold water for five minutes and then squeeze out and discard any excess water.

Whisk the coconut milk to ensure there are no lumps.

Place the softened gelatine in a small saucepan. Heat gently, stirring all the time until dissolved and then stir into the coconut cream or milk.

Pour the berry purée into a large bowl and stir in the coconut cream or milk with the gelatine. Then using a metal spoon, fold the egg-white mixture in.

Transfer the mixture into the ramekins and freeze for about four or five hours, covering with either foil or greaseproof paper, making sure that this does not come into contact with the soufflés.

Remove from the freezer about 20 minutes before serving and place a raspberry or strawberry in the middle of each.

Fruit jelly

Jellies can be made from any seasonal fresh fruit.

Ingredients:
- **Gelatine strips, unsulphured – 1 strip per 100 g fruit**
- **Fresh fruit of choice (strawberries, raspberries, etc)**
- **Sweetener of choice**

Soak the gelatine in cold water for five minutes.

Squeeze out any excess water, and warm the softened gelatine in a pan, stirring.

Wash the fruit and place it in a bowl.

Add the gelatine and sweetener.

Whisk well using an electric stick blender and transfer to a jelly mould.

Refrigerate until set.

Delicious with Urban Caveman coconut yoghurt.

Lime or lemon mousse

Ingredients:
Serves 6–8 depending on the size of the ramekins
- **Zest and juice of 1 lime or lemon**

- **1 x 400 ml tin coconut cream**
- **Sweetener of choice**
- **3 strips gelatine, unsulphured**
- **1 x 400 ml tin mangoes**

Add the lime or lemon zest and juice to the coconut cream.

Sweeten and whisk until smooth.

Soak the gelatine in a little cold water and steep for five minutes. Squeeze out and discard any excess water.

Warm the coconut cream mixture in a pan and stir in the softened gelatine.

Pour into ramekins and chill until set.

To serve, purée the mangoes and pour over the top.

Pannacotta

This is a really indulgent Italian dish that is usually made with double cream. The Urban Caveman alternative is made from coconut cream and it tastes just as good!

Ingredients:
Serves 6-8 depending on size of ramekins
- **1–2 strips of gelatine, unsulphured**
- **1 x 400 ml tin coconut cream**
- **1 dsp kuzu or arrowroot**
- **Yolks of 2 eggs**
- **Sweetener of choice**
- **2 tsp pure vanilla extract or the seeds from 2 vanilla pods**
- **1 dsp sunflower or egg lecithin powder (not soya)**

Soak the gelatine in a little cold water and steep for five minutes. Squeeze out and discard any excess water.

Add a small amount of coconut cream to a jug and stir in the kuzu or arrowroot until dissolved.

Whisk in the egg yolks, sweetener, vanilla and gelatine.

Meanwhile, gently heat the remainder of the coconut cream and lecithin in a saucepan until just boiling.

Remove from the heat and stir into the egg yolk mixture.

Return to the heat and stir until thickened.

Place in the ramekins and chill in the fridge.

Plum crumble

Ingredients:

Serves 8-10
- 800–1000 g/1¾–2.2 lb plums, cut in half and stones removed
- 110 g/4 oz butter, cold and cut into squares
- 150 g/5 oz coconut flour
- Sweetener of choice
- 125 g/4½ oz nuts, e.g. pecans, almonds, hazels, macadamia, roughly ground

Pre-heat your oven to 180°C/350°F/GM 4.

Place the plums, skin-side down, in an ovenproof dish.

Rub the butter into the flour to form a crumb texture. Stir in the sweetener and the nuts.

Sprinkle over the plums and bake for 25 minutes.

Serve with coconut cream, custard (see page 312) or ice cream (see page 44).

Rice pudding with hot cherry sauce

This is an Urban Caveman equivalent to the rice pudding served in Germany and Scandinavia at Christmas.

Ingredients:
Serves 6–8 depending on size of ramekins
- **2–3 packets konjac rice**
- **Sweetener of choice**
- **1 tsp vanilla extract or seeds from 1 vanilla pod**
- **1½ x 400 ml tins coconut cream**
- **Large bag of fresh cherries**
- **1 dsp kuzu**

Rinse and drain the konjac rice as directed and place in a serving dish.

Mix the sweetener and vanilla into the coconut cream and stir into the rice. Place the mixture in the fridge to chill.

Stone the cherries and place them in a saucepan with a little water and sweetener, into which you have stirred enough kuzu to thicken the mixture. Bring to the boil and simmer, stirring occasionally, for 15 minutes, until glazed and thickened.

Serve the cold rice pudding in the ramekins and spoon the hot cherry sauce on top.

Aromatic 'rice' pudding

Ingredients:
Serves 6

- 4 packets konjac rice
- Seeds from 10-12 cardamom pods, crushed in a pestle and mortar
- Seeds from 1 vanilla pod
- 1 cinnamon stick, broken into three
- 1 tsp nutmeg
- 4 egg yolks
- Sweetener
- Ghee, goat's butter or coconut oil, to taste – makes it creamy
- 1 dsp rosewater
- 2 x 400 ml tins coconut cream

Rinse and drain the rice and pat dry.

Using a heavy-bottomed pan, warm the cardamom, vanilla, cinnamon and half the nutmeg together.

Whisk the egg yolks, sweetener, fat, rosewater and coconut cream together and add to the spices.

Bring to boiling point, stirring until thickened into a custard.

Mix the rice into the pan. Remove the cinnamon stick.

Transfer to a serving dish and dot the top with the remaining nutmeg.

Serve either hot or cold.

Strawberry flan

Ingredients:
Serves 8-10

- Single-crust sweet pastry (see page 174)
- 3 strips gelatine, unsulphured

- 1 x 400 ml tin coconut cream
- 2 egg yolks
- *Optional:* sweetener of choice
- 1 tsp vanilla extract or the seeds from 1 vanilla pod
- Fresh strawberries

Make the pastry and line a flan dish with it. Bake at 180°C/350°F/GM 4 for 15 minutes.

Meanwhile, make the custard.

Soak the gelatine in a little cold water for five minutes, until softened.

Squeeze out any excess water.

Place the coconut cream in a small saucepan and whisk in the egg yolks, sweetener, if using, and vanilla.

Stir in the gelatine.

Heat gently, stirring. Simmer and stir until thickened.

Cool slightly and pour over the baked pastry case.

Refrigerate until set.

Decorate with fresh strawberries before serving.

Strawberry mousse

Ingredients:
Serves 4

- 3 strips gelatine, unsulphured
- Punnet fresh, organic strawberries (non-organic strawberries are best avoided as they are one of the most heavily sprayed crops)
- *Optional:* 2 egg whites, beaten

Soak the gelatine in a little water for five minutes.

Squeeze out and discard any excess water, then warm in a pan, stirring. Whisk the gelatine into the strawberries until frothy and chill in four ramekins.

Optional: for a creamier texture, the whites of two beaten eggs could be added after whisking.

In addition to being eaten as a mousse, this dish can be frozen and eaten as a sorbet.

'Tapioca' pudding

Ingredients:

- **2 packets konjac rice**
- **2 eggs, beaten**
- **2 x 400 ml tins coconut cream**
- **1 tsp vanilla extract or seeds from 1 vanilla pod**
- **Sweetener of choice**
- **Nutmeg to taste**

Rinse the rice well and leave to drain for a few minutes; then transfer to a dish.

Stir the eggs into the coconut cream and add the vanilla, sweetener and nutmeg.

Bring to the boil, stirring continuously.

Once thickened, stir into the noodles.

Sprinkle a little more nutmeg on top.

Delicious hot or cold.

Mango and tapioca pudding

Ingredients:
Serves 6-8
- 1 ripe mango
- 1 x 400 ml tin coconut cream
- 1 strip gelatine, unsulphured
- 3 packets konjac rice
- *Optional*: Cardamom powder

Chop the mango and whizz in the food processor.

Pour in the coconut cream.

Soak the gelatine strips in a little cold water for five minutes. Squeeze out and discard the excess water.

Warm the coconut cream mixture and stir in the softened gelatine.

Wash the konjac rice under the cold tap and leave for a few minutes to drain the water.

Transfer the rice to a bowl and stir in the mango mixture.

Pour into individual ramekins and sprinkle cardamom on the top if using.

Chill in the fridge.

Pickles and chutneys

Traditionally developed to preserve vegetables through the cold winter months, chutneys (which tend to be sweeter) and pickles can make the plainest meal interesting. Commercially produced products contain sugar as a preservative, so it is good to make your own. Why not try a 'Paleo Ploughman's', combining Urban Caveman bread, pickles and Urban Caveman hard cheese – great for a picnic with some cold meats.

Autumn relish

Ingredients:
Makes 6–8 jars
- 700 g/1½ lb cooking apples, peeled, cored and chopped
- 2 large onions, diced
- 1-2 red chillies, de-seeded and chopped
- 225 g/8 oz firm but ripe pears, peeled, cored and chopped
- 1 red pepper, de-seeded and chopped
- 2-3 cloves of garlic, peeled and crushed
- Sweetener of choice
- 225 g/8 oz dried apricots, chopped
- 1 tsp ground ginger
- 1 tsp ground allspice
- Juice of 1 lemon
- *Optional*: Fresh sprigs herbs, to garnish

Special equipment:
- 6-8 jam jars, washed, with lids
- Waxed paper
- Slow cooker

Set the slow cooker to high.

Place all the ingredients in a saucepan and heat, stirring until the sweetener has dissolved.

Transfer to the slow cooker, cover and cook for six to eight hours, stirring occasionally.

Sterilise the jam jars by putting them in a cold oven with their lids off. Then, heat the oven to 150°C/300°F/GM 2 and leave the jars and lids in the oven for 20 minutes. Finally, turn the oven off, leaving the jars inside to cool.

Stir the relish mixture well, place into the sterilised, glass jars and cover each with a waxed disc, waxed side down.

Once cold, screw the lids on.

Use within three months.

Classic pickle

Ingredients:
Makes 6–8 jars
- 2 kg/4½ lb mixed, chopped vegetables: carrots, cauliflower, cucumber, courgette, peppers
- 450 g/1 lb onions, finely chopped
- 450 g/1 lb eating apples, cored and diced
- 2 green chillies, de-seeded and chopped
- 250 g/9 oz dates, chopped
- 110 g/4 oz dried mixed vine fruit
- 2 tbs onion powder
- 2 tbs garlic powder
- Juice of 2 lemons
- 350 g/12 oz tomato purée
- 1 tbs Himalayan salt
- 3 tbs maple syrup
- Sweetener of choice
- 275 ml/10 fl oz apple cider vinegar

Special equipment:

- 6-8 jam jars, washed, with lids
- Waxed paper
- Large preserving (Maslin) pan or tureen

Sterilise the jam jars by putting them in a cold oven with their lids off. Then heat the oven to 160°C/300°F/GM 2 and leave the jars and lids in the oven for 20 minutes. Finally, turn the oven off, leaving the jars inside to cool.

Place all the ingredients in a large Maslin pan or tureen.

Bring the mixture to the boil, then simmer gently for about three hours, stirring occasionally.

It will be ready when you can drag a spoon through it and it doesn't leave a gap that fills with vinegar.

Pour the hot chutney into the sterilised jars.

Cover each with a disc of waxed paper, waxed side down. Once cooled, screw the lids on.

Don't eat for at least a month.

Unopened it will last for a year. Once opened, store in the fridge.

Plum chutney

Ingredients:
Makes 6–8 jars

- 2 kg/4½ lb tomatoes, finely chopped
- 450 g/1 lb onions, finely chopped
- 350 g/12 oz eating apples, cored and diced
- 20 plums, stoned and diced
- 2 green chillies, de-seeded and chopped
- 200 g/7 oz dried mixed vine fruit.
- 1 tbs Himalayan salt
- 2 tbs maple syrup

- Sweetener of choice
- 6 cloves garlic, crushed
- 275ml/ ½ pt apple cider vinegar
- Small piece ginger
- 2 cinnamon sticks
- 10 cloves garlic

Special equipment:
- 6-8 jam jars, washed, with lids
- Waxed paper
- Muslin square/tea ball
- Large preserving (Maslin) pan or tureen

Sterilise the jam jars by putting them in a cold oven with their lids off. Then heat the oven to 160°C/300°F/GM 2 and leave the jars and lids in the oven for 20 minutes. Finally, turn the oven off, leaving the jars and lids inside to cool.

Place all the ingredients except the ginger, cinnamon and garlic in a large Maslin pan or tureen.

Wrap the ginger, cinnamon and garlic cloves in a muslin square or tea ball and hang over the edge of the tureen into the mixture – you may need to attach some string.

Bring to the boil, then simmer gently for about three hours, stirring occasionally.

It will be ready when you can drag a spoon through it and this doesn't leave a gap that fills with vinegar.

Pour the hot chutney into the sterilised jars.

Cover each with a disc of waxed paper, waxed side down. Once cooled, screw the lids on.

Don't eat for at least a month.

Unopened it will last for a year. Once opened store in the fridge.

Green tomato chutney

Ingredients:
Makes about 8–10 jars

- 500 g/1 lb 2 oz small onions, finely chopped
- 2.5 kg/5½ lb green tomatoes, finely chopped
- 1 tbs Himalayan salt
- 250 g/9 oz raisins, seedless
- 250 g/9 oz sultanas
- 40 g/1½ oz fresh root ginger
- 570 ml/1 pint apple cider vinegar
- 1 tsp to 1 dsp sweetener of choice
- 12 cloves, whole
- 4 red chillies

Special equipment:
- 6-8 jam jars, washed with lids
- Waxed paper
- Muslin square
- Large preserving (Maslin) pan or tureen

Sterilise the jam jars by putting them in a cold oven with their lids off. Then heat the oven to 160°C/300°F/GM 2 and leave the jars and lids in the oven for 20 minutes. Finally, turn the oven off, leaving the jars and lids inside to cool.

Place the chopped onions and tomatoes in a bowl and stir in the salt.

Leave for one hour.

Place the onion and tomato mix in the Maslin pan with the dried fruits.

Lightly crush the ginger and chillies and place in a muslin square with the cloves.

Tie securely and add to the pan.

Pour in the vinegar.

Stir in the sweetener.

Bring to the boil, stirring.

Reduce to a simmer and leave to cook for three to four hours, stirring occasionally and pressing the muslin so that the flavours are released.

Once ready pour the hot chutney into the sterilised jars. Cover each with a disc of waxed paper, waxed side down. Once cooled, screw the lids on.

Store in a cool place and eat after at least one month, but preferably after three.

Tomato ketchup

Ketchup was traditionally made by fermenting but this recipe does not rely upon fermentation.

Ingredients:

- 200 g/7 oz tomato purée
- 2 tbs apple cider vinegar
- 1 tbs balsamic vinegar
- ½ tsp mustard powder
- 110 ml/4 fl oz cold water
- ¼ tsp ground cinnamon
- Pinch allspice
- 1 clove garlic, crushed
- 1 bay leaf
- A little seasoning (not too much or it will interfere with the flavours)
- *Optional*: sweetener of choice
-

Mix all the ingredients together in a saucepan.

Bring to the boil, stirring.

Leave uncovered to simmer for about 25 minutes, until it starts to thicken.

Remove the bay leaf and allow to cool.

Store in a glass bottle in the fridge.

Resources

Suppliers of specialist cookware and ingredients

www.green-pan.co.uk
Supplies non-toxic cookware with ceramic coating. Available from John Lewis and Amazon.

www.roastcosy.co.uk
Alternative to aluminium foil for roasting meat.

www.coconutty.co.uk
Supplies coconut products.

www.myprotein.com
For whey protein.

www.pinksun.co.uk
For whey protein also from goats and sheep.

www.healthmonthly.co.uk
Supplies Luo Han Guo and stevia.

www.therealfoodcompany.org.uk
Supplies organic, unsulphured gelatine from grass-fed pigs plus many foods including raw dairy.

www.red23.co.uk
Supplies a variety of health foods, including whey protein and fermented and coconut products.

www.seventhwaveuk.com

Supplies health products including Green Pastures X-Factor Gold Vitamin-rich butter oil.

www.greenpasturefarms.co.uk

Online supplier of grass-fed, organic produce.

www.naturalfoodfinder.co.uk

Sources local producers.

www.trealyfarm.com

Natural charcuterie.

www.consciousfood.co.uk

Supplies Palmyra Jaggery and other health foods.

Alternative health information

www.westonprice.org

www.21stcenturypaleo.com

www.mercola.com

www.naturalnews.com

www.wddty.com

www.greenhealthwatch.com

References

1   Cordain L (2012). The truth about saturated fats. In: *The Paleo Answer*. USA: John Wiley & Sons. Page 18.

2   Groves B (2008). *Trick and Treat*. London: Hammersmith Books. Page 241.

3. Mosley M (22.11.2012). www.bbc.co.uk – Horizon *'Eat, Fast and Live Longer'*.

Index

German-sausage stew, 240

ghee, 16

ginger biscuits, 95

glucomannon, 24

gluten, 58

    substitutes, 23, 58

gluten-free setting on bread-maker, 62

goji berry fairy cakes, 84

goulash (pork), 242

grain-free bread (basic recipe), 64–65

grain-free breakfast nutmeal, 144–145

grape and cream cheese pancakes, 130–131

gravies, 23

    chicken with stuffing and gravy, 212–213

    mushroom, 289

    onion *see* onion gravy

    roast beef with Yorkshire pudding and gravy, 234–235

    for roasts, 288

    see also sauces

Greek avgolemeno chicken soup, 158

Greek-style lamb kebabs, 189

Greek-style marinated lamb cutlets, 188

green pesto, 304

green salad, 278

green salsa (salsa verde), Sicilian-style barbecued salmon or trout with salsa verde, 255

green tomato chutney, 326–327

griddle pan, cast-iron, 13

grilled lamb chops with damson glaze, 192–193

Groves, Barry, 5

guar gum, 32

haddock, smoked, with coconut cream sauce, 262

ham

    ham and cheese breakfast pancakes, 126

    ham and rocket salad, 165

    ham pizza, 181–182

    ham soup, 161

hamburger (beefburger), 220

harissa, 295

herbs

    barbecued lamb kebabs with yoghurt and herb sauce, 243–244

    carrot and herb bread, 70

    herby yoghurt waffles, 106–107

herrings, Scandinavian soused, 259–260

high-fructose corn syrup (HFCS), 26, 27

Himalayan salt, 20

Hollandaise sauce, 291

honey, 28

hors d'oeuvres, 165–173

horseradish powder, 25

horseradish sauce, 296

legumes, 26

lemon

barbecued sea bass in dill and, 256

chicken in lemon sauce, 210–211

fried chicken with coconut cream and, 205

lemon biscuits, 96

lemon fairy cakes, 86–87

lemon mousse, 314–315

lemon pancakes with trout, 123–124

lemon waffles, 115

sweet waffles with cherry sauce and lemon yoghurt, 113

lime mousse, 314–315

liquid added to bread, 60–61

liver paté

chicken or calf, 170

Urban Caveman, pancakes filled with, 121–122

luo han guo (monkfruit), 29, 31, 60, 174, 328

macaroons, 105

mackerel, smoked

kedgeree, 143–144

paté, 169

mango and tapioca pudding, 321

mango sorbet, 48–49

maple syrup, 27, 31, 60

vinaigrette, 302

margarines, 14

margherita pizza, 182–183

marinade

barbecued sliced lamb, 191

Greek-style lamb kebabs, 189

Greek-style marinated lamb cutlets, 188

Scandinavian soused herrings, 259

spicy chilli barbecue, 305–306

maslin pan, 13

mayonnaise, 20–21

curried, 299

egg, 166

Urban Caveman, 296

measurements

bread-making, 61

conversion tables, viii–ix

measuring spoons, 13

meat

dishes, 188–252

jerky, 248–252

minced *see* minced...

soups, 156–161

stocks, 147–149

see also bacon; beef; chicken; lamb; pork; sausage

meat loaf, 229, 229

tomato, 229–230

meatballs, 220–221